JERRY
AND THE
JOKER
ADVENTURES AND COMIC ART
BY JERRY ROBINSON

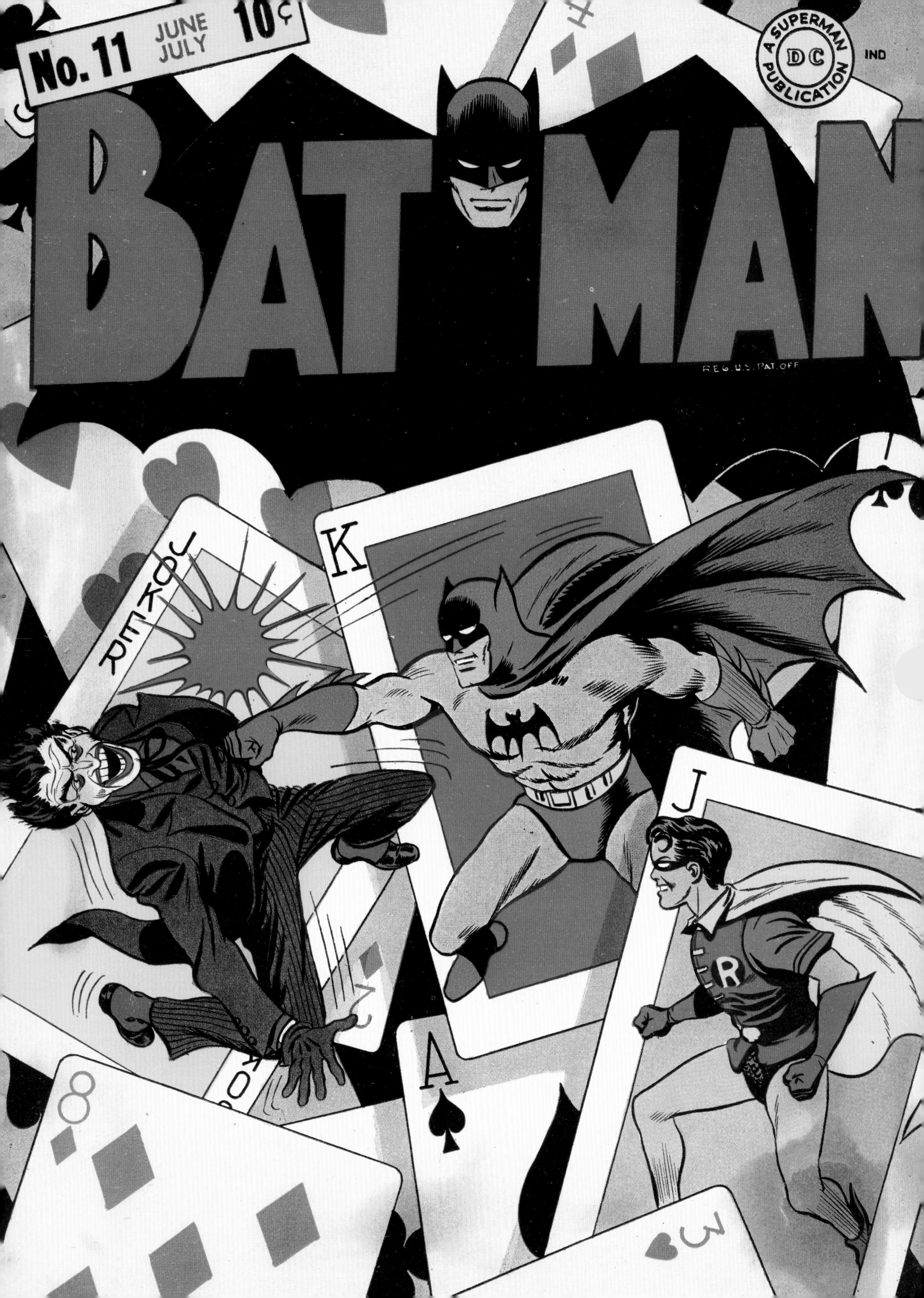

No. 11
JUNE JULY
10¢
A SUPERMAN DC PUBLICATION
IND
BATMAN
REG. U.S. PAT. OFF.
JOKER
K
J
A
8
3

JERRY
AND THE
JOKER
ADVENTURES AND COMIC ART
BY JERRY ROBINSON

WITH NOTES BY
JENS ROBINSON

DARK HORSE BOOKS

Publisher
MIKE RICHARDSON

Editors
JENS ROBINSON,
DANIEL CHABON &
HANNAH MEANS-SHANNON

Assistant Editor
CARDNER CLARK

Designer
DAVID NESTELLE &
PATRICK SATTERFIELD

Digital Art Technician
ADAM PRUETT

Jerry and the Joker: Adventures and Comic Art

Published by Dark Horse Books
A division of Dark Horse Comics, Inc.
10956 SE Main Street
Milwaukie, OR 97222

DarkHorse.com

To find a comics shop in your area, call the Comic Shop Locator Service toll-free at (888) 266-4226.
International Licensing: (503) 905-2377

First edition: August 2017
ISBN 978-1-50670-225-4
10 9 8 7 6 5 4 3 2 1
Printed in China

Library of Congress Cataloging-in-Publication Data

Names: Robinson, Jerry, 1922-2011, author. | Robinson, Jens.
Title: Jerry and the Joker : adventures and comic art / by Jerry Robinson ; with additional notes by Jens Robinson.
Description: First edition. | Milwaukie : Dark Horse Books, 2017.
Identifiers: LCCN 2016042156 | ISBN 9781506702254
Subjects: LCSH: Robinson, Jerry, 1922-2011. | Artists--United States--Biography. | Comic books, strips, etc.--United States--History and criticism.
Classification: LCC NC1429.R635 A2 2017 | DDC 741.5/9092 [B] --dc23
LC record available at https://lccn.loc.gov/2016042156

CONTENTS

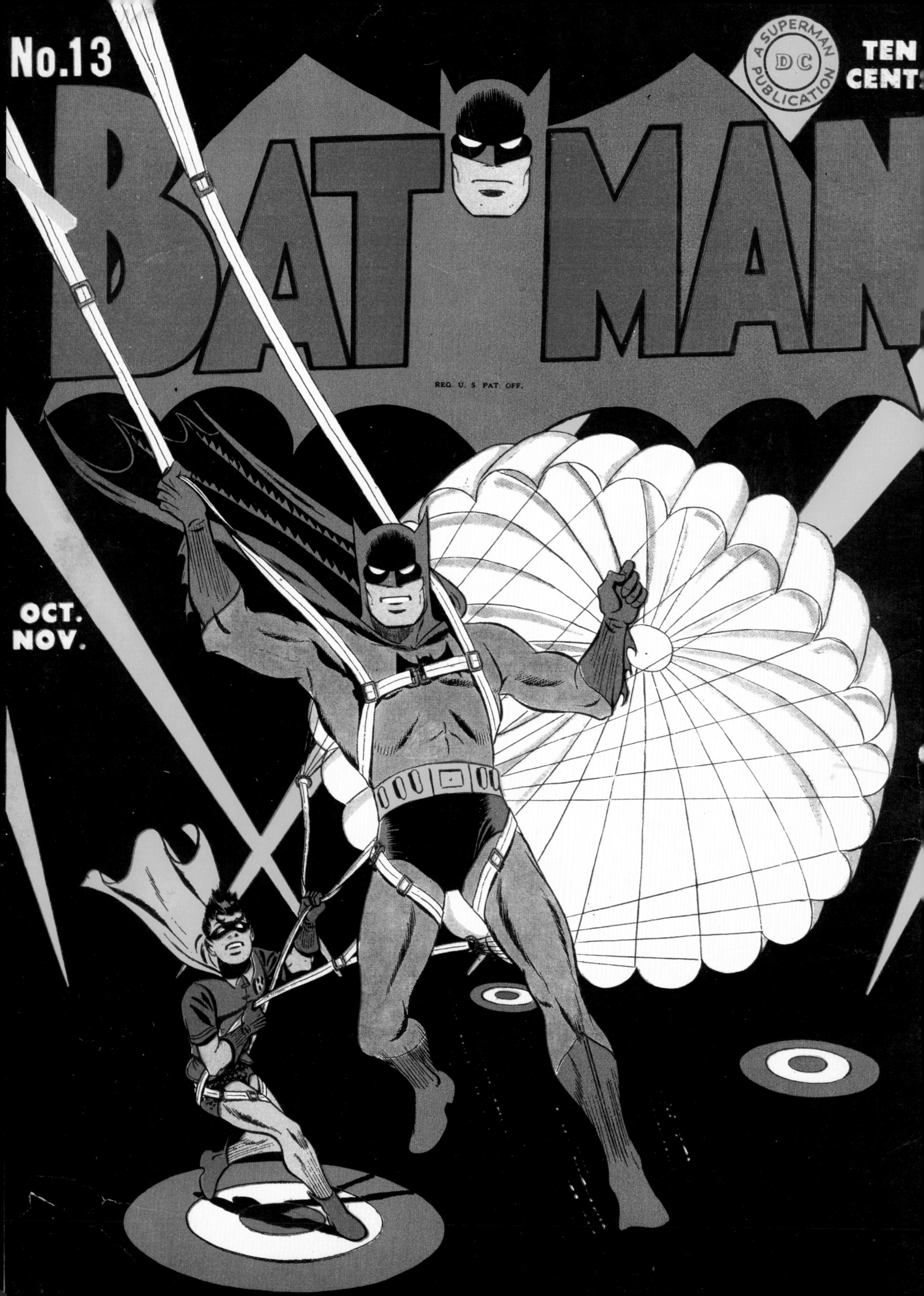

No.13
A SUPERMAN DC PUBLICATION
TEN CENTS
BATMAN
REG. U. S. PAT. OFF.
OCT. NOV.

CHAPTER 1:
HOW TO START OUT SELLING ICE CREAM AND END UP DRAWING *BATMAN*

The summer of 1939 was hot and humid. A proud recent graduate of Trenton Central High, I set out to conquer the world—but doing what, I knew not. So I got a job selling ice cream, pedaling a bicycle hauling a freezer cart to help pay for my first year of college. I couldn't possibly have imagined it then, but that job, that scorching summer, and a serendipitous meeting at a tennis court would lead to my drawing *Batman* and thus would set my entire life's course.

I had been torn as to what I wanted to do. My older sister gave up a photography career when she married. My three big brothers (all significantly older) were professionals—a dentist, a surgeon chiropodist, and a lawyer. I was impatient to get started with my life. My parents were finally recovering from the depths of the Depression, in which they had lost everything in the crash of 1929, including their business and our home. They'd managed to put my brothers through college with the help of scholarships. Each brother in turn took a year off from college to work to help the next brother. So I had a high bar to live up to.

Deciding what path to take was difficult. Having ruled out the traditional professions, I was left with my love of reading and writing. I had been an editor on the *Spectator*, my high-school paper, for which I did reporting, humorous pieces, and occasional cartoons. I loved the short story form and avidly read everything from Twain, O. Henry, and Poe to Chekhov, Dostoyevsky, and de Maupassant.

A career in art or cartooning had not occurred to me. I never took an art course because they did not give enough college credit. So I decided to be a writer. My school adviser recommended applying to Penn, Columbia, and Syracuse, because they were the best schools for journalism. Happily, I was accepted to all three. Never having visited any of the colleges or even set foot in New York City or Syracuse, I was torn as to where to go. I settled on Syracuse, probably because I envisioned it as more of a college town, like nearby Princeton.

At that time, I did have one unusual encounter with a cartoonist. On a story for the *Spectator*, I drove to Princeton, which was only about fifteen miles away, to interview George Washington. For the anniversary of our first leader's inauguration, his trip by horse and carriage from Mount Vernon to New York City was being reenacted, duplicating every stop

Left
COLOR COVER OF
***BATMAN* NO. 13**
October – November 1942, pencils, inks, and colors by Jerry Robinson.

he made on the way. Dressed in the attire of our forefathers' day, from the buckled shoes to the powdered wig, a tall, imposing figure met me at the venerable Nassau Inn, the same inn our Founding Father had visited 150 years before. It was an exciting moment for me—the first time I dined with a president-to-be and, as I was to learn, my first meal with a cartoonist as well.

Unable to tell a lie, George admitted that his alter ego was Denys Wortman, the cartoonist creator of *Metropolitan Movies*, a syndicated panel then appearing daily in the *New York World-Telegram*. He looked just like our first president and might even have fooled Martha. In the years to come, I had the pleasure of following Wortman's feature. He was a superb artist who captured the gritty New York street life in his cartoons. Although I never met him again, I was pleased thirty years later to include his work in my book on the history of comic strips in America, *The Comics: An Illustrated History of Comic Strip Art*.

> WHEN HE REPEATED THAT HE NEEDED SOMEONE TO ASSIST HIM ON *BATMAN* AND I COULD MAKE AS MUCH AS TWENTY-FIVE DOLLARS A WEEK, THE COMIC BOOK LOOKED MUCH BETTER!

I was offered a job after graduation doing drawings using the chalk plate process of my cartoons for the school paper. I assumed it was the cheapest way to make an engraving of a cartoon for reproduction. It was an exasperating procedure that involved drawing the cartoon on the chalk surface and then using a sharp tool much like a dental probe to scrape the chalk down to the metal plate for every line that was to be reproduced. Often large pieces of chalk would break off when lines intersected. Liquid chalk would then be used to fill in the gaps, and all the work had to be redone after it dried. The plate would be mailed off to the company in Philadelphia to make the engraving. The only problem was that this job involved engraving chalk plates that I never wanted to see again. It was very strange to me. I couldn't imagine anybody needing or wanting a chalk plate engraving. I don't think I ever replied to the offer, and I never regretted missing out on a career in chalk plates.

As the ice-cream company's new hire, I was given the least desirable area in which to sell popsicles from a bicycle—the western residential suburb of Trenton, sparsely populated and hilly. I had to pedal the whole day to sell my quota—at 1¼ cents commission per popsicle. For a big sale, an ice-cream brick, I would receive a whopping 5 cents commission. After about two months, I was down to ninety-eight pounds. My mother thought I wouldn't survive the first semester at college. She persuaded me to take $25 from my hard-earned savings and go to the mountains to fatten up. The Catskill resorts were famous for their ample meals—just the place for me to gain some weight!

I probably decided on the President Hotel because of its tennis courts—tennis was my lifelong passion—and perhaps because of one David Daniel Kaminsky. Kaminsky, a.k.a. Danny Kaye, the "King of the Catskills," was performing at the President and only a couple of years from launching his Broadway career. The Catskill Mountains summer resorts were popular for their lavish food and top entertainment set against a backdrop of shimmering mountain lakes. As soon as I arrived by bus and checked in, I couldn't wait to change clothes, grab my racket, and head for the courts. If it weren't for tennis, I might actually have gained a pound or two.

I started playing tennis at about four years old, when I was about as tall as a racket. I had sorely missed playing that summer due to my ice-cream venture. Tennis was a family tradition—all my brothers played a top game. One was city champion, and my three nephews were state champions. In fact, I had once reached the semifinals of the city boys' tournament, only to be beaten badly by the winner, Eddie Moylan. Eddie was a terrific player with a superb backhand who was to rise to become a top-ten-rated player in the United States. I did have a few moments of tennis glory, however, as a two-time winner of the Lee Falk Annual Invitational Tournament on Cape Cod. Lee was a dear friend and, as all comics fans know, the creator of *Mandrake the Magician* and *The Phantom*.

That first day at the resort, I wore a painter's jacket festooned with my cartoons that I put on during warm-up. This was a fad we copied from the college kids at nearby Princeton. The jacket was white linen with a lot of pockets. I was watching a match when I felt a tap on my shoulder, and someone asked, "Who did the drawings?"

Without turning around, I said meekly, "I did." I was worried I'd be arrested, because I couldn't remember what I had drawn on the back of the jacket.

The voice said, "They're pretty good." He introduced himself as Bob Kane, the creator of Batman, and said that the character's first appearance (in *Detective Comics* #27) had just been published. He didn't play tennis and, as fate would have it, was just passing by at the moment I arrived. He promptly showed me a copy. I had never seen a comic book before. I wasn't very impressed.

The Batman character reminded me of the Shadow, whom I had seen in pulp magazines. I had grown up with the comics in the newspapers and loved them. I would get both the Sunday *Philadelphia Record* and the *Philadelphia Inquirer* when I could. They had terrific comics sections, including all the great strips of the time: glorious full pages in color of *Prince Valiant, Flash Gordon, Terry and the Pirates* . . . The Batman art appeared crude by comparison. The *Record* also had a new comics insert of several features, the first being *The Spirit* by Will Eisner, which was impressive. I later met Will, one of the great creators the genre ever produced, in New York, and we became lifelong friends. Interestingly, Eisner and Kane were classmates at DeWitt Clinton High School in the Bronx.

Humor comics also enthralled me. I appreciated their styles—*Mutt and Jeff, Bringing Up Father, Skippy*, and so many others. In fact, when I was sent to a boys' summer camp at age eight or ten, I begged my parents to bring me the latest of the collections of famous humor strips that were being published at the time (now known by collectors as the Cupples and Leon series). I still have some of them—after over eighty years. One, a Rube Goldberg collection, was signed for me decades later by Rube himself.

Back to my first encounter with Bob Kane. He was then about twenty-four, which was quite mature to me at seventeen, but we seemed to establish a rapport. He was about five foot ten, slim, with a dark complexion and sleek black hair—fairly good looking. He was very personable. He talked about his success at DC Comics, as well as with women. He painted a glamorous picture of an artist's life in New York meant to impress a naive kid from the sticks, which it did.

When I told Bob I was going to Syracuse University in the fall, he said, "Oh, it's too bad—if you came to New York, you could work on my comic book." I'd never read a comic book before, but when he repeated that he needed someone to assist him on Batman stories and I could make as much as twenty-five dollars a week, the comic book looked much better!

I made an instant decision. I ran to a phone booth and contacted Columbia to see if my application was still good. Luckily it was, so I told them I was enrolling and then called Syracuse and told them I wasn't coming. I called my parents and said I had a job in New York, I was switching to Columbia, and I was going to the city straight from the mountains.

I didn't know how to get to New York City. The desk clerk explained that the only way was complicated and involved a change of buses. Suddenly he had a thought. "Mr. Peerce is driving to New York shortly. Why don't you ask him? He might give you a ride." It was Jan Peerce, the celebrated tenor, who had given a concert at the hotel that weekend.

I shyly approached the great man. "I'm trying to get to New York . . . I'm starting classes at Columbia," I sputtered.

"Sure, kid," he said as his enormous, chauffeured limousine pulled up the driveway. "Hop in!" I quickly hopped in, along with my battered suitcase and tennis racket, before he changed his mind. In retrospect it seems like a script for a Frank Capra movie. The fact that he was a Columbia graduate (as I learned on the way) didn't hurt. He plied me with stories of his experiences on the concert tour, none of which I recall. My mind was on the future. New York! Columbia! And Batman! It was too overwhelming to think about at once. I don't think I uttered more than a few words during the several-hour trip.

That's how I made my grand entrance to New York. I asked to be let out of the limo somewhere in the Bronx to fend for myself in the big city. Actually, my survival skills were not needed right away, as I was dropped off at my aunt Mae and uncle Arthur's comfortable apartment!

Right
COLOR COVER OF BATMAN NO. 10
April – May 1942, pencils, inks, and colors by Fred Ray and Jerry Robinson.

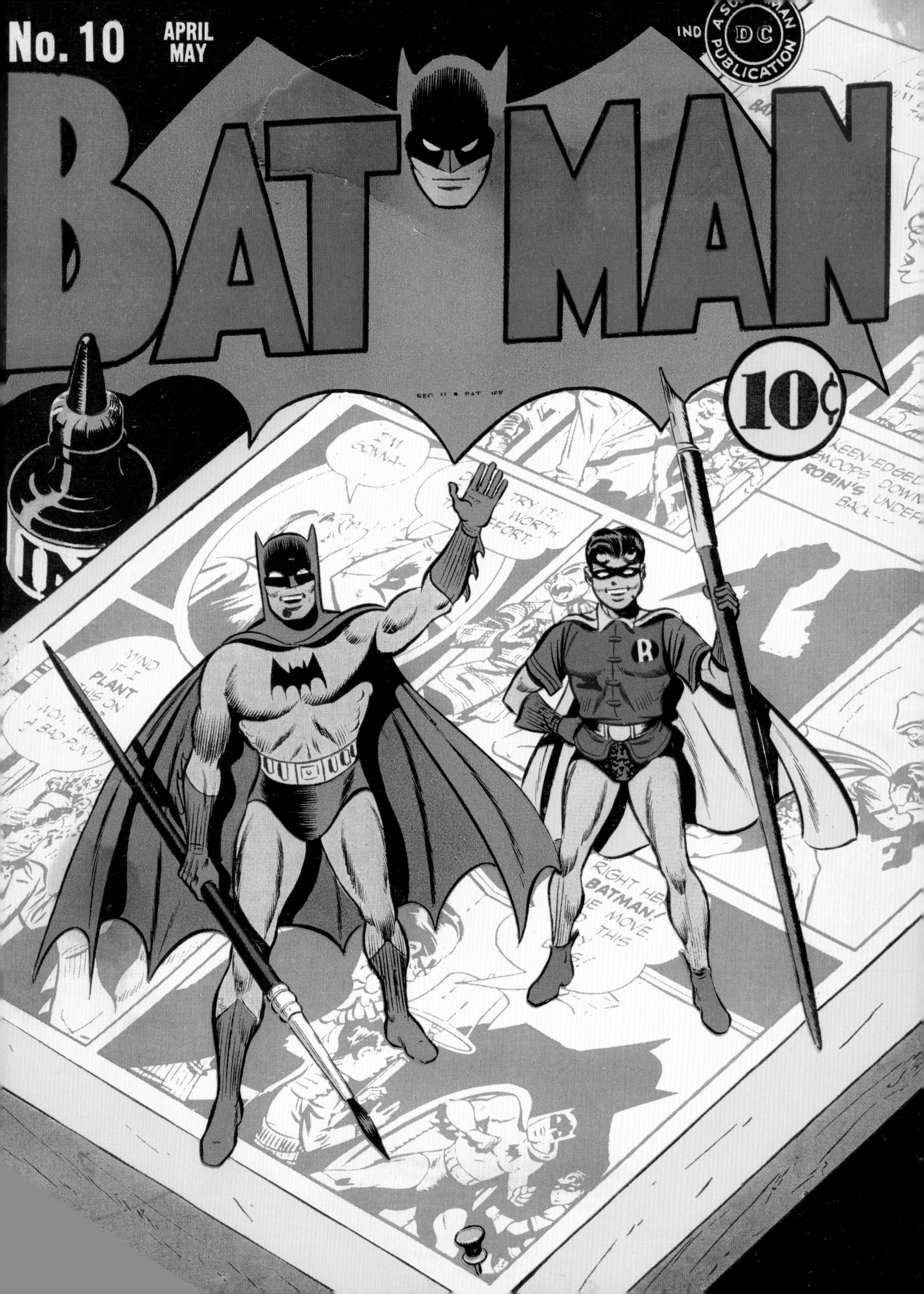

No. 10
APRIL
MAY
IND
DC
PUBLICATION
BATMAN
10¢
I'M GONNA--
MIND IF I PLANT THIS ON

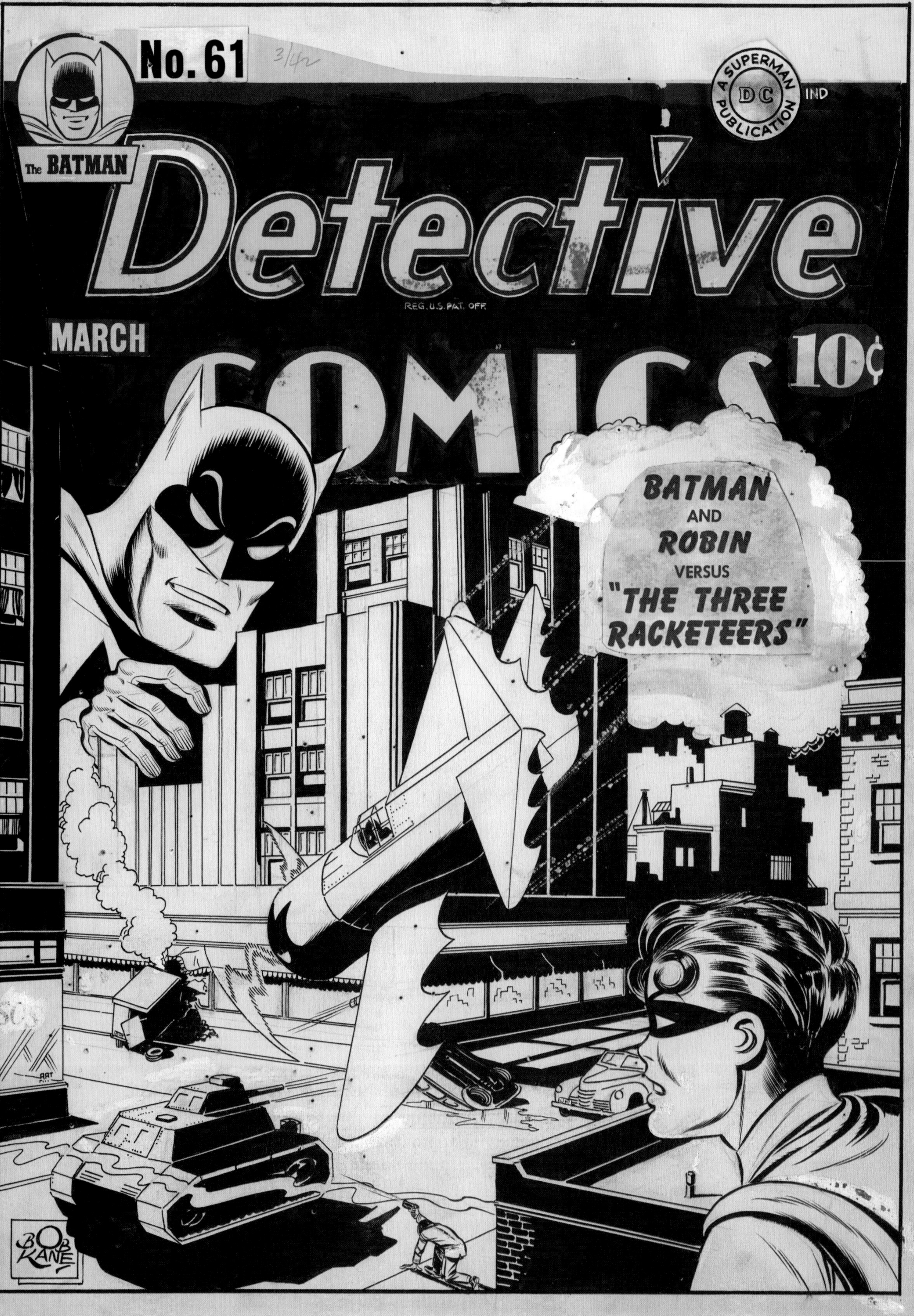

No. 61
3/42
A SUPERMAN DC PUBLICATION
IND
The BATMAN
Detective
REG. U.S. PAT. OFF.
MARCH
COMICS
10¢
BATMAN AND ROBIN VERSUS "THE THREE RACKETEERS"
BOB KANE

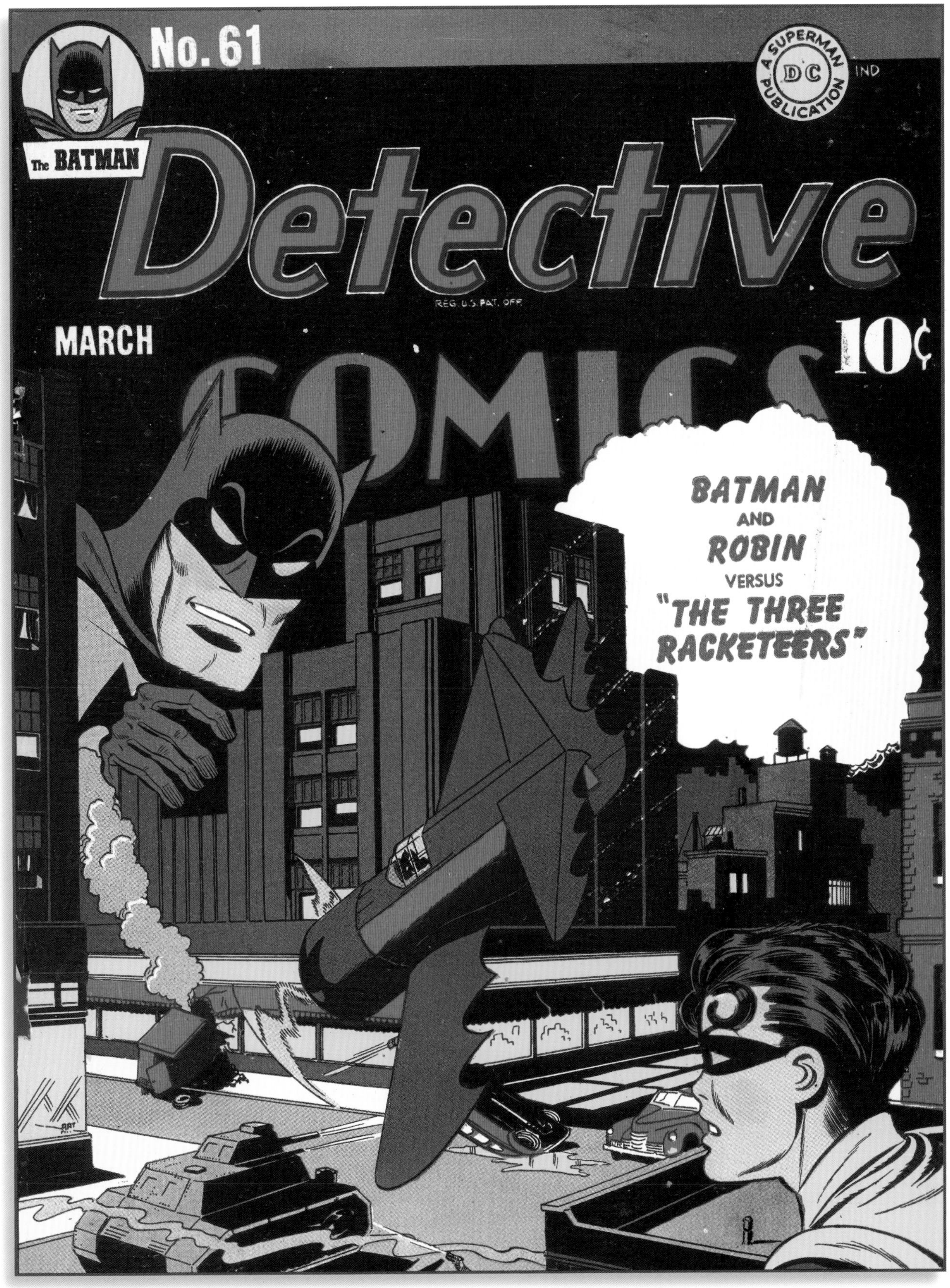

No. 61
The BATMAN
A SUPERMAN DC PUBLICATION
IND
Detective
REG. U.S. PAT. OFF.
MARCH
10¢
COMICS
BATMAN AND ROBIN VERSUS "THE THREE RACKETEERS"

Left
ORIGINAL ART TO COVER OF *DETECTIVE COMICS* NO. 61
March 1942, pencils by Bob Kane and Jerry Robinson, inks by Jerry Robinson.

Above
COLOR COVER OF *DETECTIVE COMICS* NO. 61
March 1942, pencils by Bob Kane and Jerry Robinson, inks by Jerry Robinson.

Validity - degree to which it measures what it is supposed to measure
Test-retest method
intelligence - measure of present ability which tries to predict future ability
I.Q. measure of rate of development

Jerry Robinson

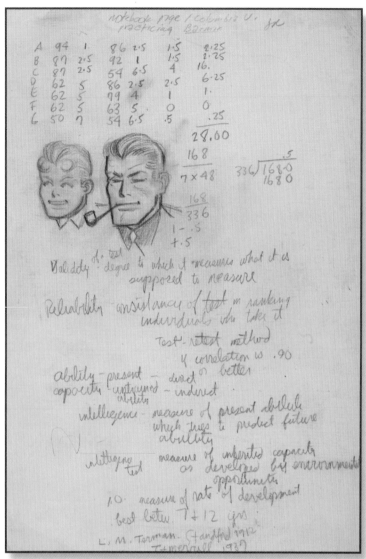

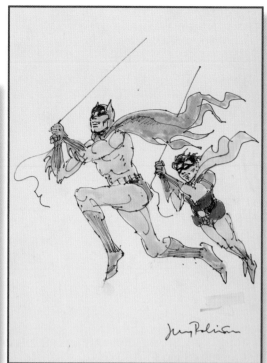

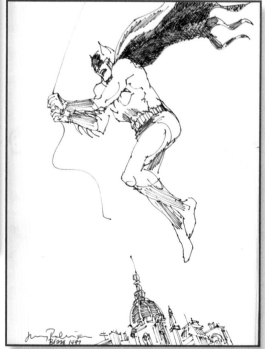

Left
COLUMBIA UNIVERSITY CLASSROOM NOTES WITH SKETCHES OF DICK GRAYSON AND BRUCE WAYNE
1940, by Jerry Robinson.

Top right
COLOR SKETCH OF BATMAN AND ROBIN SWINGING ON ROPES
By Jerry Robinson.

Bottom right
SKETCH OF BATMAN SWINGING ABOVE BELO HORIZONTE
Brazil, 1997, by Jerry Robinson.

Right page
PERSONAL CHRISTMAS CARD
1941, by Jerry Robinson.

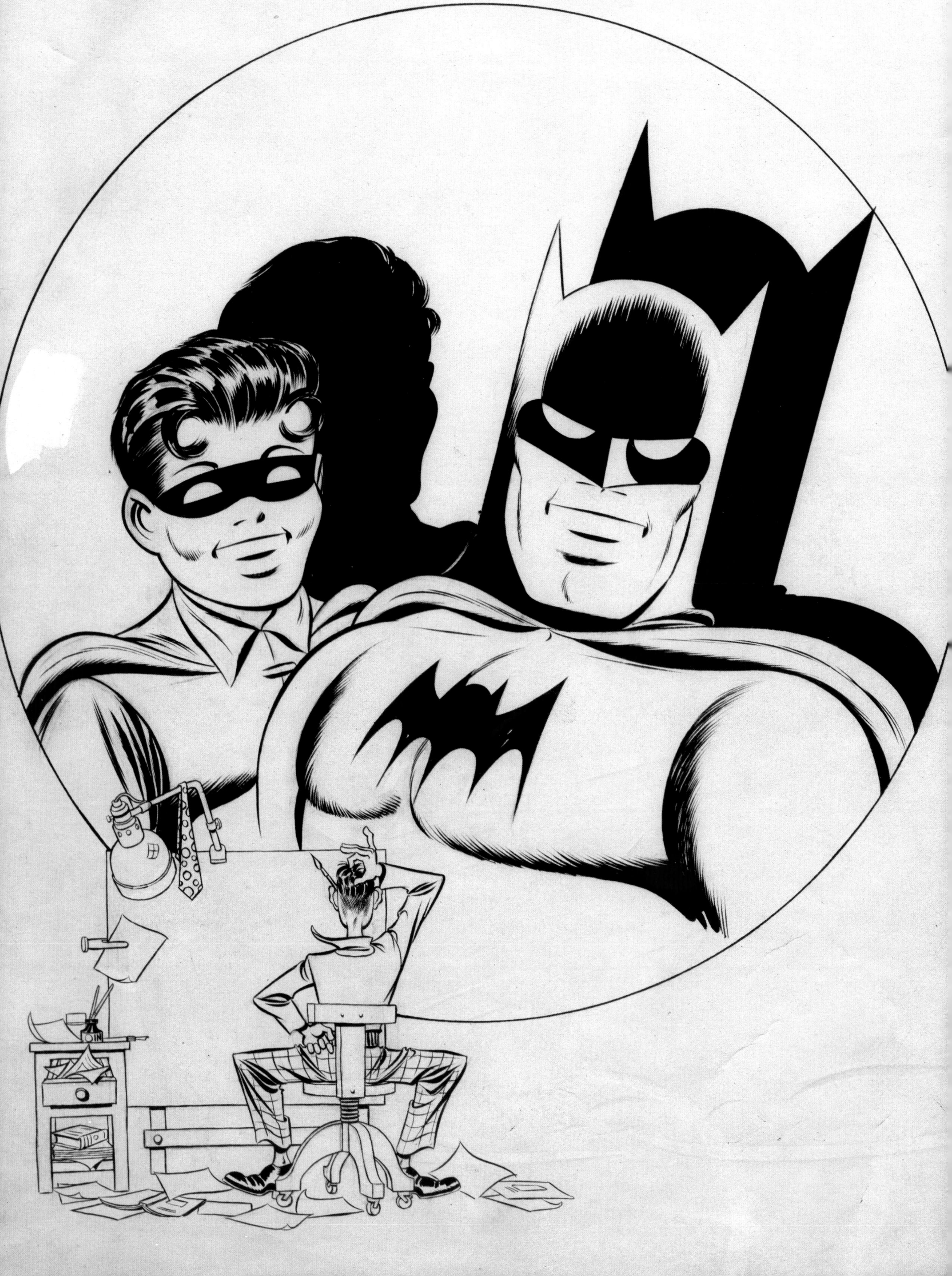

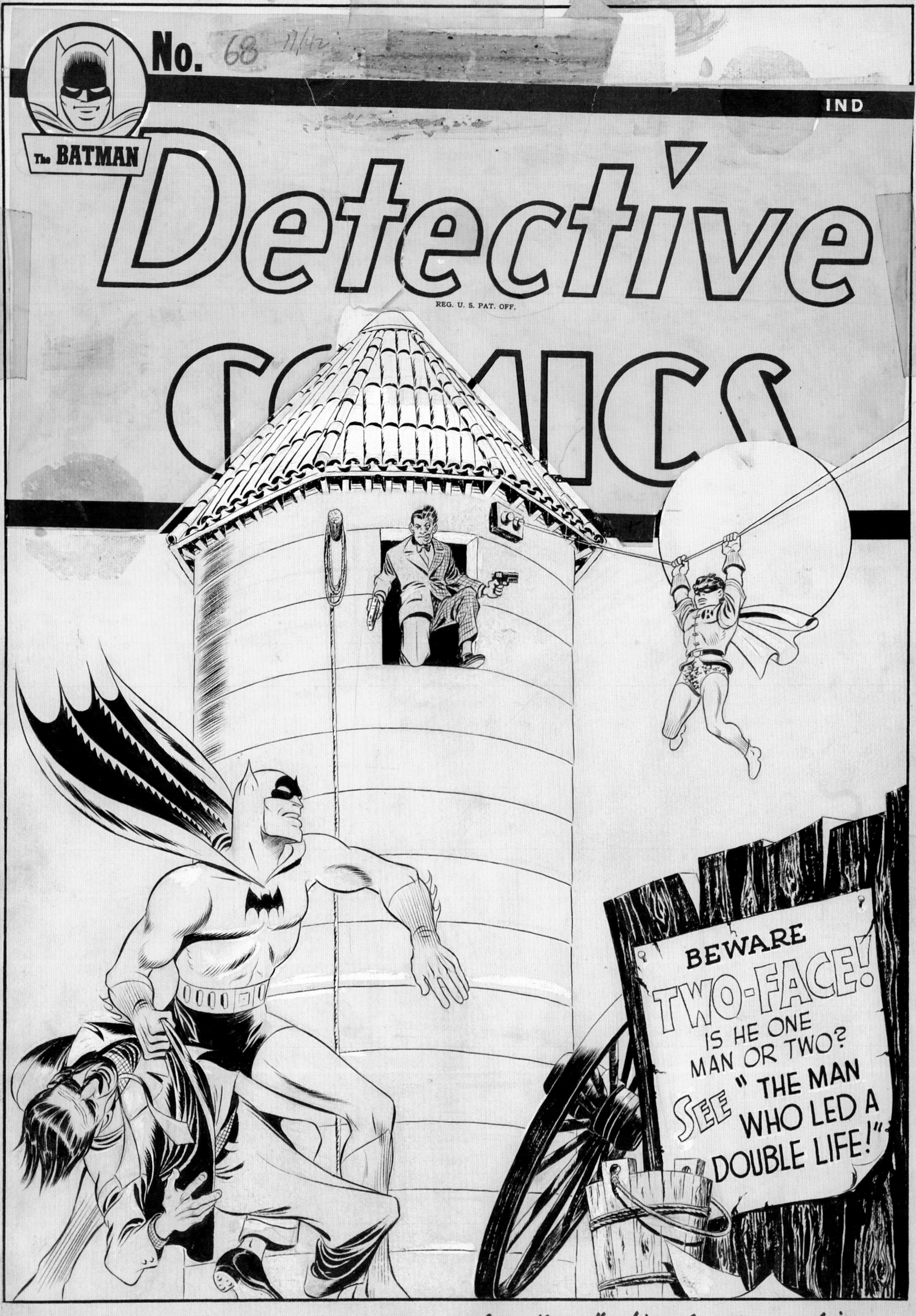
The BATMAN
No. 68 11/42
IND
Detective
REG. U. S. PAT. OFF.
COMICS
BEWARE
TWO-FACE!
IS HE ONE MAN OR TWO?
SEE "THE MAN WHO LED A DOUBLE LIFE!"

from the collection of jerry robinson

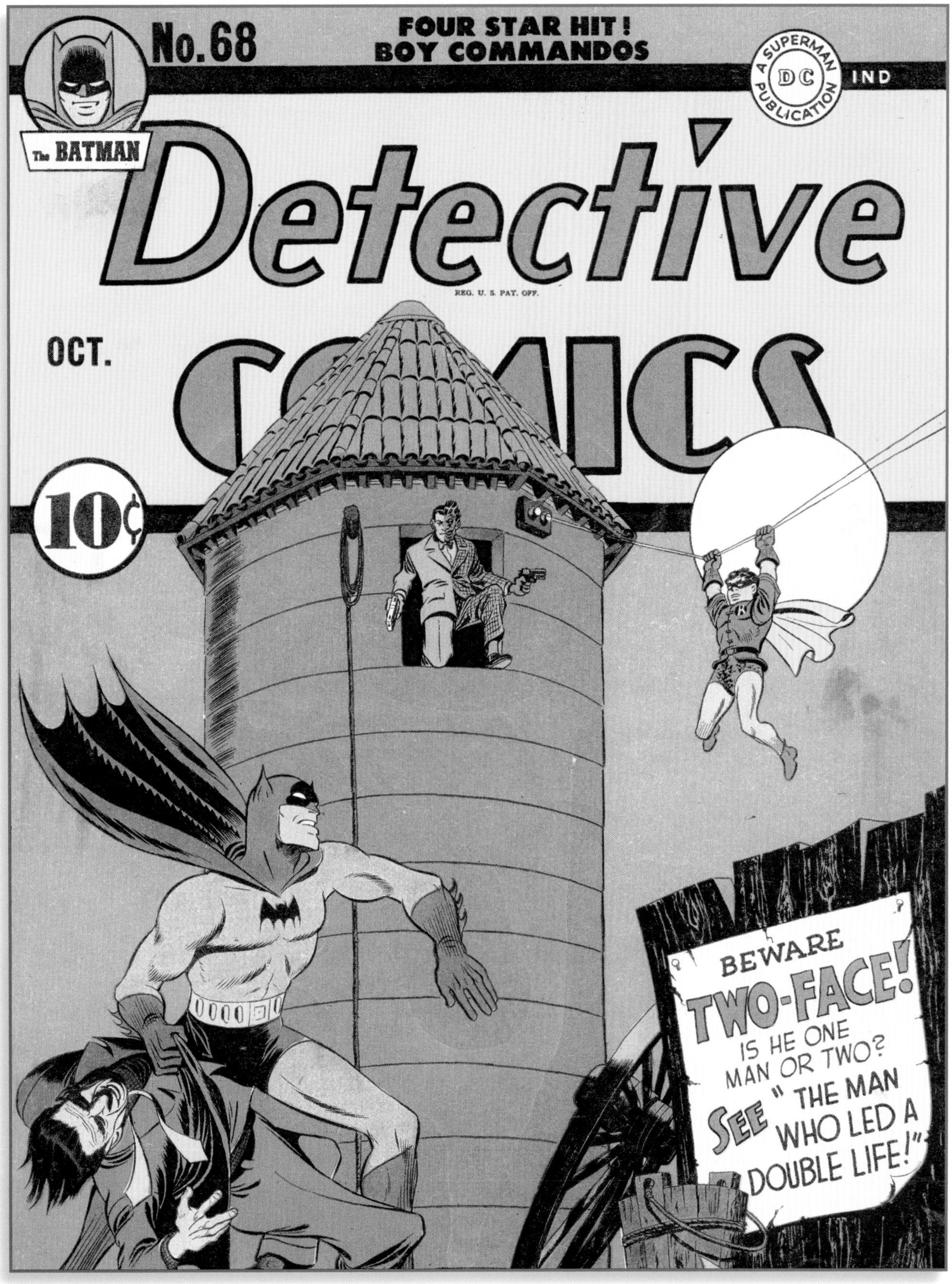
No.68
FOUR STAR HIT!
BOY COMMANDOS
A SUPERMAN DC PUBLICATION
IND
The BATMAN
Detective
REG. U. S. PAT. OFF.
OCT.
COMICS
10¢
BEWARE
TWO-FACE!
IS HE ONE
MAN OR TWO?
SEE "THE MAN
WHO LED A
DOUBLE LIFE!"

Left
ORIGINAL ART TO COVER OF *DETECTIVE COMICS* NO. 68
October 1942, pencils and inks by Jerry Robinson.

Above
COLOR COVER OF *DETECTIVE COMICS* NO. 68
October 1942, pencils, inks, and colors by Jerry Robinson.

#68

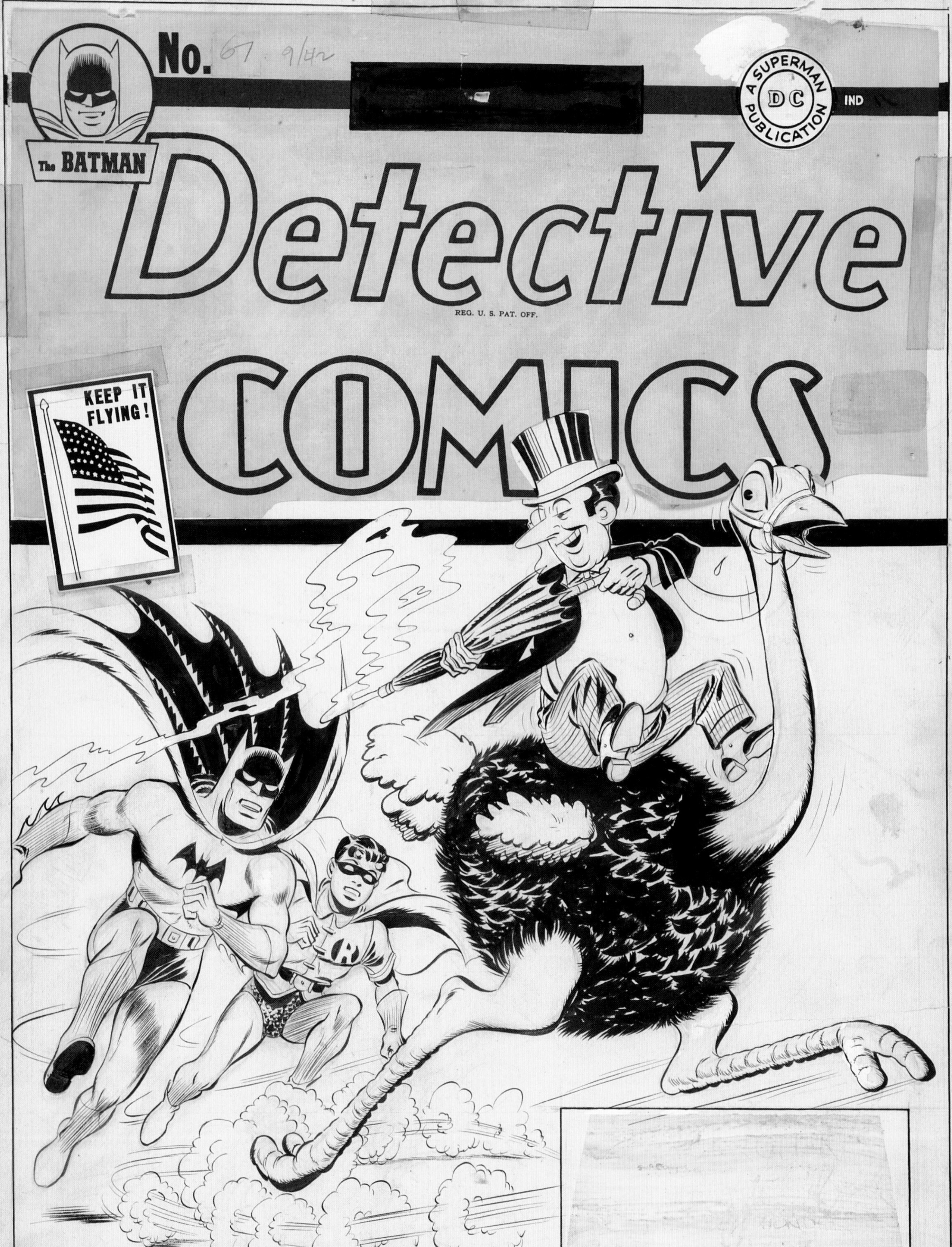

No. 67 9/42
The BATMAN
A SUPERMAN DC PUBLICATION
IND
Detective
REG. U. S. PAT. OFF.
COMICS
KEEP IT FLYING!

from the collection of
Jerry Robin

#67

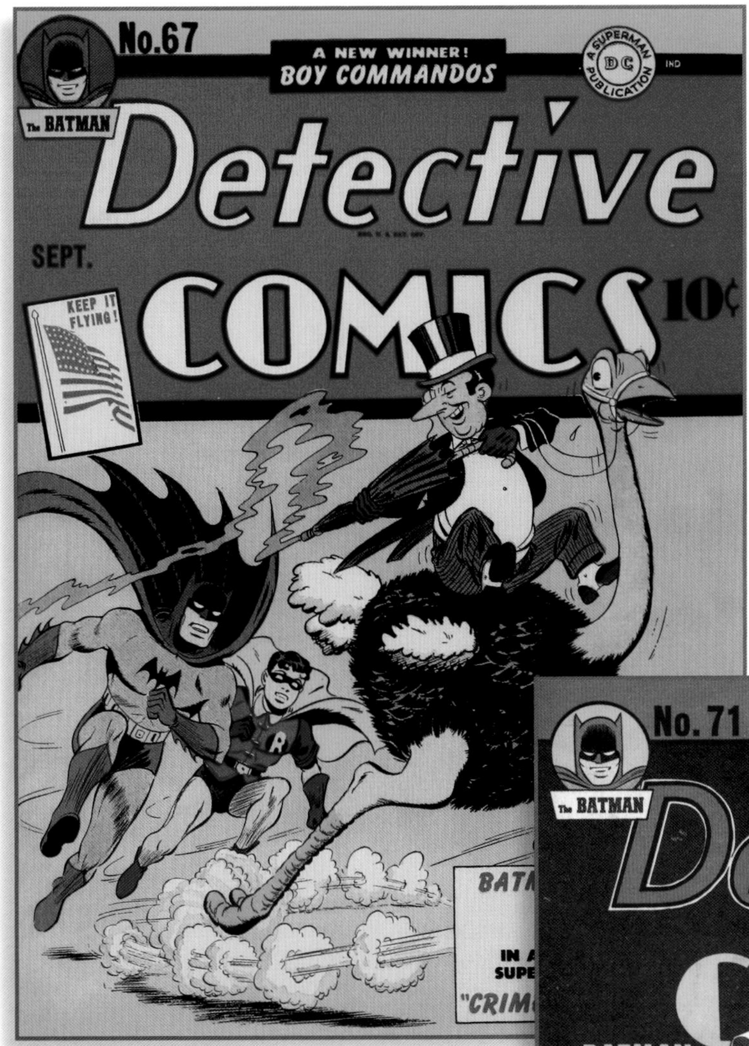
No.67
A NEW WINNER!
BOY COMMANDOS
A SUPERMAN DC PUBLICATION
IND
The BATMAN
Detective
SEPT.
COMICS
10¢
KEEP IT FLYING!

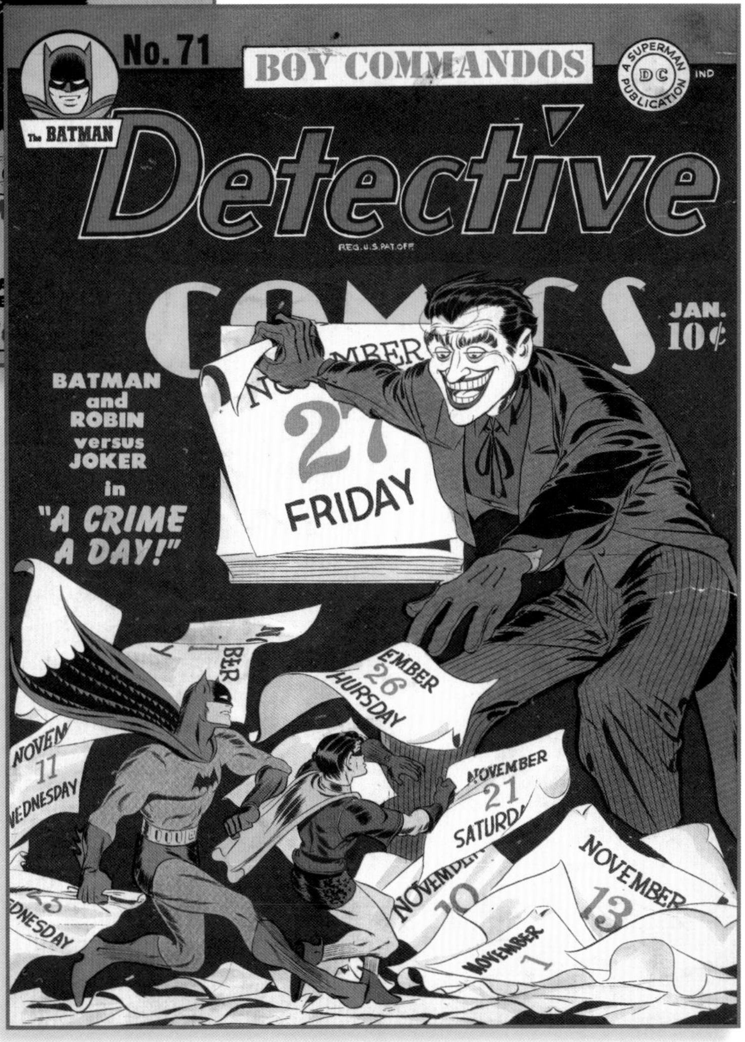
No. 71
BOY COMMANDOS
A SUPERMAN DC PUBLICATION
IND
The BATMAN
Detective
REG. U.S. PAT. OFF
JAN.
10¢
BATMAN and ROBIN versus JOKER in "A CRIME A DAY!"
27
FRIDAY
NOVEMBER
21
NOVEMBER
13

Left
ORIGINAL ART TO COVER OF *DETECTIVE COMICS* NO. 67
September 1942, pencils and inks by Jerry Robinson.

Top
COLOR COVER OF *DETECTIVE COMICS* NO. 67
September 1942, pencils, inks, and colors by Jerry Robinson.

Bottom
COLOR COVER OF *DETECTIVE COMICS* NO. 71
January 1943, pencils, inks, and colors by Jerry Robinson.

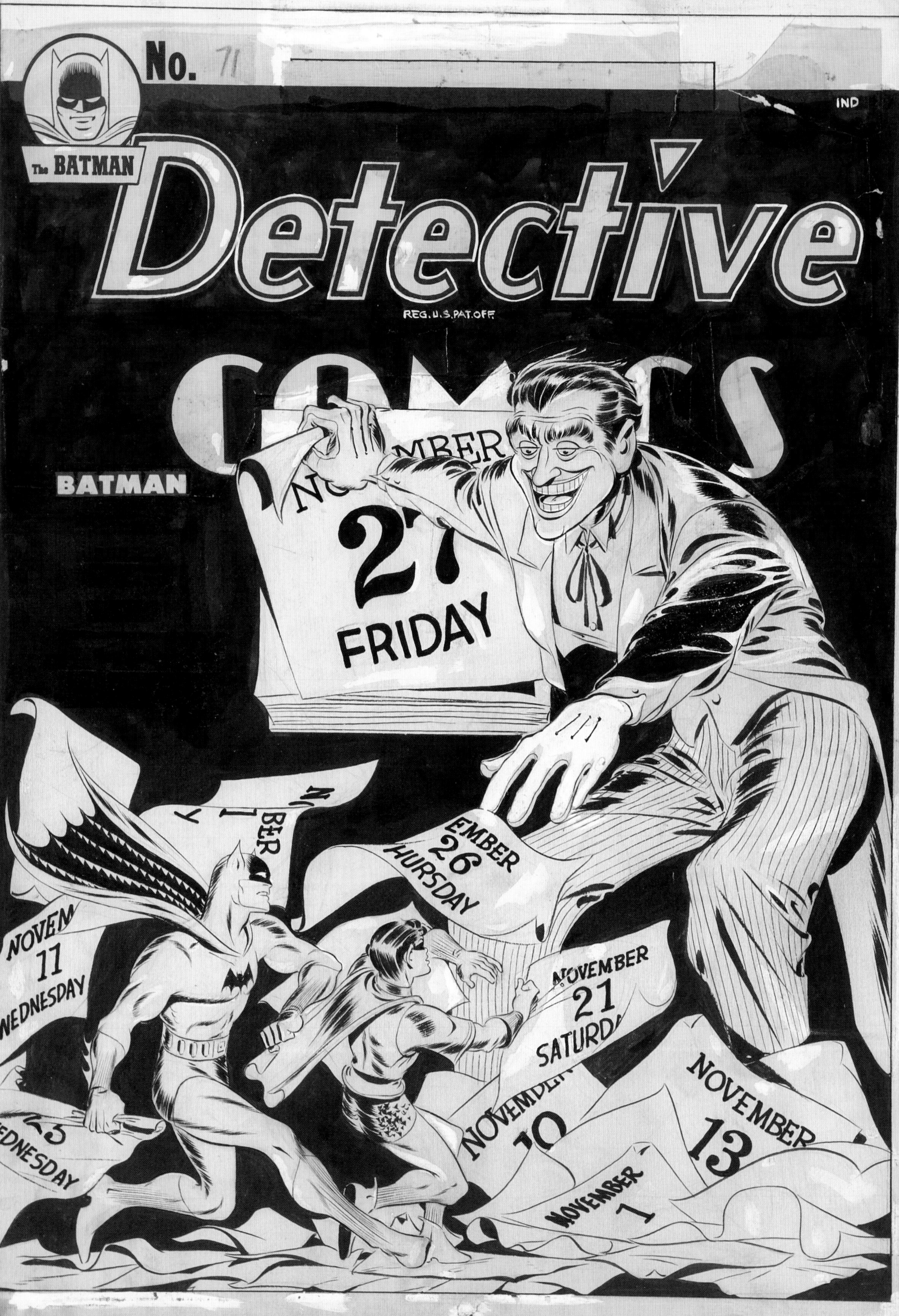

No. 71
IND
The BATMAN
Detective
REG. U.S. PAT. OFF.
BATMAN
27
FRIDAY
EMBER
26
HURSDAY
NOVEM
11
WEDNESDAY
NOVEMBER
21
SATURDA
NOVEMBER
10
NOVEMBER
13
NOVEMBER
1
WEDNESDAY

CHAPTER 2: THE BIRTH OF THE JOKER

In 1939, as a seventeen-year-old journalism student at Columbia University, I joined the team of Bob Kane and co-creator Bill Finger on their new Batman series, started just two months before in *Detective Comics*. With his popularity growing, Batman was given his own book the following year. The need for four more stories for the new *Batman* quarterly, in addition to a monthly story for *Detective Comics*, was a challenge for the team, especially Bill, the writer. Bill's dynamic and innovative scripts were the best in the fledgling comics genre. He was a craftsman, but he was not prolific. As an aspiring writer myself, I eagerly volunteered to pen one of the four new stories required for the new quarterly.

Bob and Bill took me up on the offer. They were aware of my creative-writing courses, had read some of my short stories, and knew of my career ambitions in journalism. What began as a job to pay for college turned into an incredibly exciting opportunity to write and draw a Batman story! This was going to be great—I'd get paid for writing a comics story that I'd also turn in for credit in my creative-writing class!

The 1930s was the era of the gangster—Dillinger, Capone, Machine Gun Kelly, Pretty Boy Floyd, Bonnie and Clyde. Hijackers, embezzlers, and bank robbers (and occasionally a mad scientist) were the models for most of the villains in the comics. I knew from my studies of literature that the greatest heroes had memorable antagonists—from David's Goliath to Sherlock Holmes's Moriarty. In keeping with *Batman's* grounded-in-reality concept, the ultimate worthy adversary should have no superpowers. But I wanted a distinctive and nuanced villain who would be a true test for Batman. Some argued that an overly striking villain would detract from the hero, but I disagreed. Heroes can be dull because they must always be good. With their essential flaws, villains are more interesting. The more formidable the foe, the stronger the hero.

That night I couldn't wait to get back from my class at Columbia to the room I rented from my aunt. It was just off the Grand Concourse in the Bronx, a few blocks from Bob's place. With a breadboard balanced on my lap against a table, I set out to dream up a story with a villain worthy of Batman. My writings in high school and at Columbia had been short stories of satire and humor. I knew from reading the classics that memorable characters often have an internal contradiction—such as a deadly villain with a sense of humor. "That's it!" I shouted to myself in a eureka moment. I had the name: *the Joker*! I immediately thought of playing cards. It was around two in the morning. I frantically searched my room for a deck of cards—there was always one around. Bridge was a family tradition—my brother Maury was a champion contract bridge player with many masterpoints. My mother was also a fine player, and I dabbled. Luckily, I found a deck with the classic jester image I wanted. I was incredibly excited. I drew the first concept sketch based loosely on the joker card. I kept the card figure's white face and red lips. I wanted him to be not just clever, dangerous, and mysterious, but also

Left
ORIGINAL ART TO COVER OF *DETECTIVE COMICS* NO. 71
January 1943, pencils and inks by Jerry Robinson.

uniquely bizarre with an added dimension of humor. I wanted a villain who was unpredictable and therefore frightening. And, naturally, his calling card would be the joker playing card.

Edgar Allan Poe was a great literary influence of mine growing up. When I was about ten or twelve, I was given a wonderful birthday present that I always kept in my library—a book of Poe's complete stories, with illustrations in color and black and white by the English artist Harry Clarke. Clarke's art captured all the fascination of the gothic horror tales. I read the Poe book over and over with those beautiful yet strange drawings. The figures were elongated, elegant, and mysterious. Channeling Aubrey Beardsley, the drawings were decorative and detailed with muted colors; you could pore over them and see something new each time. The atmosphere and characters created by Poe and Clarke fired my imagination in such stories as "The Murders in the Rue Morgue," "The Masque of the Red Death," "The Raven," and "The Tell-Tale Heart."

> **WITH THE GENIUS OF BILL FINGER'S FINISHED SCRIPT AND ART BY BOB AND MYSELF, THE JOKER TURNED OUT TO BE THE FIRST SUPERVILLAIN IN THE COMIC BOOKS.**

I envisioned the Joker in that same tradition. Physically, I made the Joker elongated, elegant, and mysterious with a frightening edge. This inspiration also showed up in my subsequent opportunities to develop the Joker's look—such as the surreal, oversized evildoer on the cover of *Detective Comics* #71.

I spent the rest of the night visualizing the Joker and writing a profile to round out his persona and purpose for the story. In the morning when I briefed Bob and Bill, they were as excited about the new character as I was. They liked him too much, in fact: they persuaded me to let Bill write the finished script. As it was my very first script, it would have taken me too long, they argued. The deadline was short, and I still had classes at Columbia, so I reluctantly agreed. I worked with Bill, however, to flesh out the concept. It was scheduled to be the lead story in *Batman* #1, published in spring 1940. With the genius of Bill Finger's finished script and art by Bob and me, the Joker turned out to be the first supervillain in the comic books, and thereafter it was de rigueur for every superhero to have such a foil.

It was Bill who first noticed the striking resemblance between the Joker and the actor Conrad Veidt in *The Man Who Laughs* by the German director Paul Leni. Neither Bob nor I had seen or even heard of the movie. Bill often sought out New York's auteur and art films and was soon to introduce me to the world of great foreign films. A day or two later, Bill brought in a magazine clipping of Veidt from the film. The resemblance was uncanny. I also once read that the giant image of a clown painted on the side of an attraction at Coney Island was reputed to be the inspiration for the Joker. Subsequently, at various comic cons and cartoon festivals where fans with Batman and Joker makeup and costumes flourish, it became apparent to me that virtually anyone, short or tall, with white makeup, ruby-red lips, and a wide grin, is . . . *voilà!* . . . the Joker!

The only artwork from that night to survive through the years is the first concept sketch of the Joker's head. I have never thought about letting go of that drawing. It was loaned to an exhibition of rare, original comic art I curated, *The Superhero: The Golden Age of Comic Books, 1938–1950*, which opened at the Breman Museum in Atlanta in 2006 and went on to tour the United States.

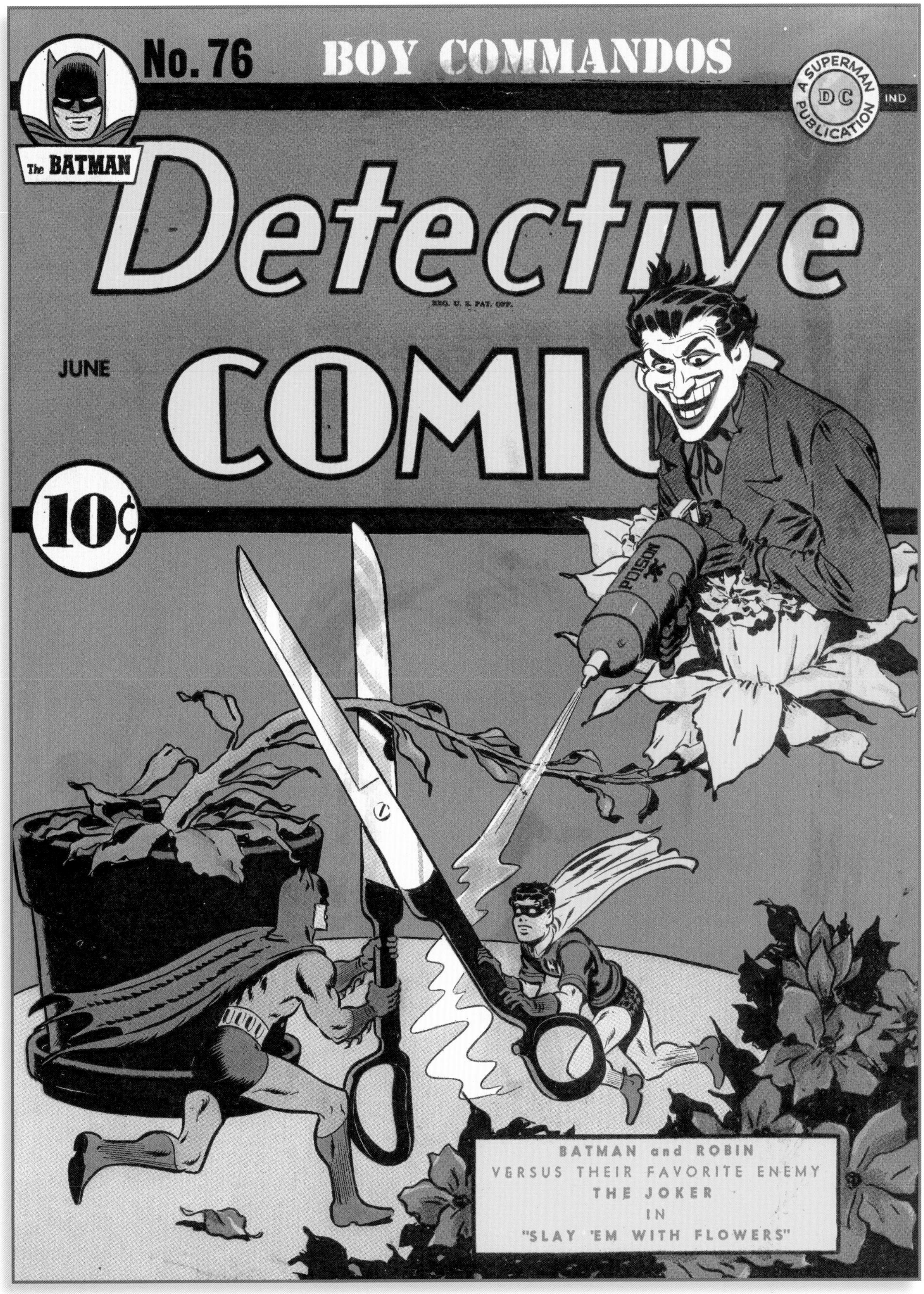
No. 76
BOY COMMANDOS
The BATMAN
A SUPERMAN DC PUBLICATION
IND
Detective
REG. U. S. PAT. OFF.
JUNE
COMICS
10¢
POISON
BATMAN and ROBIN
VERSUS THEIR FAVORITE ENEMY
THE JOKER
IN
"SLAY 'EM WITH FLOWERS"

Left
ORIGINAL ART TO SPLASH PAGE OF "SLAY 'EM WITH FLOWERS" FROM *DETECTIVE COMICS* NO. 76
June 1943, pencils and inks by Jerry Robinson.

Above
COLOR COVER OF *DETECTIVE COMICS* NO. 76
June 1943, pencils, inks, and colors by Jerry Robinson.

Following Pages
ORIGINAL ART PAGES 2-11 OF "SLAY 'EM WITH FLOWERS" FROM *DETECTIVE COMICS* NO. 76
June 1943, pencils and inks by Jerry Robinson.

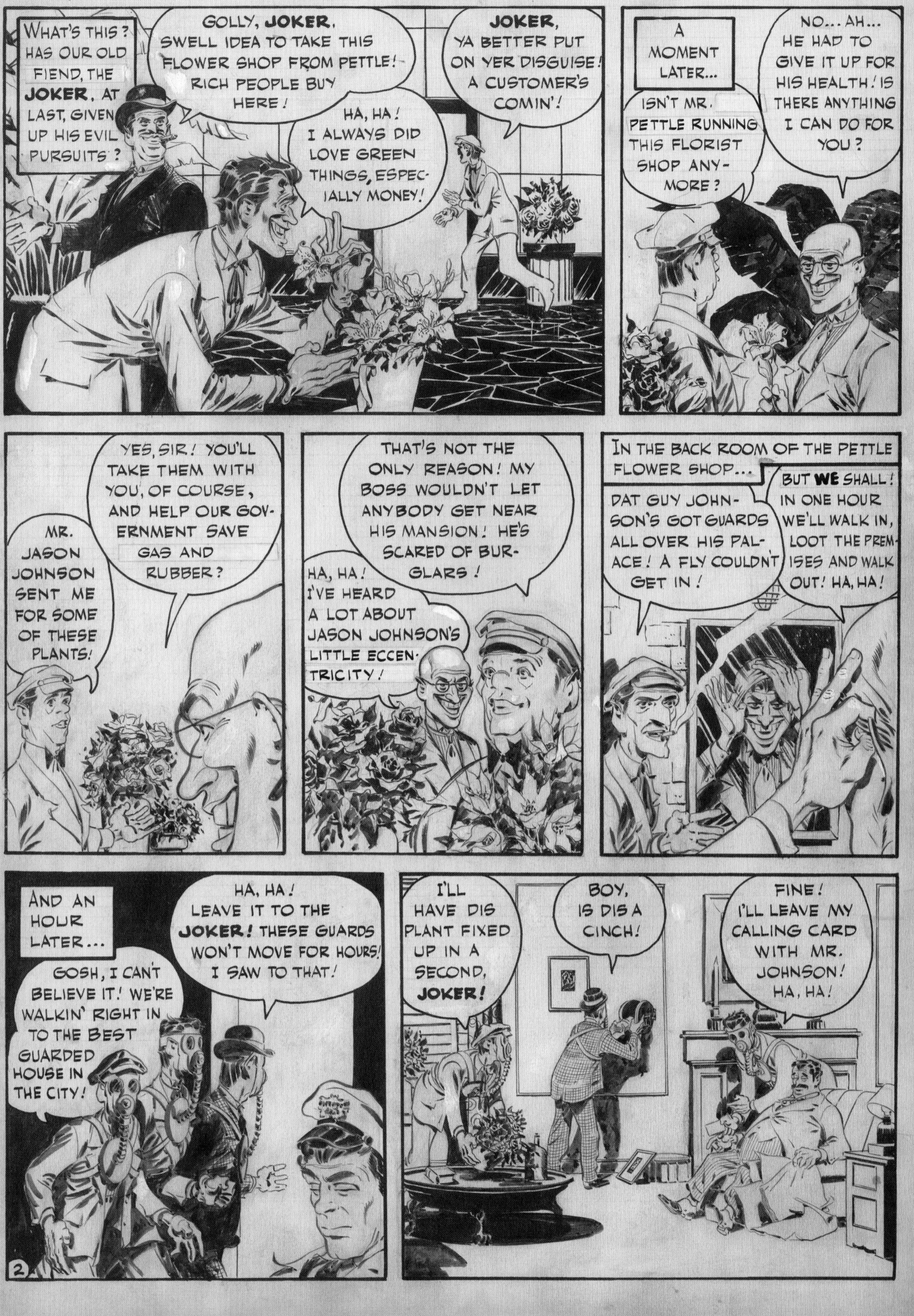
WHAT'S THIS? HAS OUR OLD FIEND, THE JOKER, AT LAST, GIVEN UP HIS EVIL PURSUITS?
GOLLY, JOKER, SWELL IDEA TO TAKE THIS FLOWER SHOP FROM PETTLE! RICH PEOPLE BUY HERE!
HA, HA! I ALWAYS DID LOVE GREEN THINGS, ESPECIALLY MONEY!
JOKER, YA BETTER PUT ON YER DISGUISE! A CUSTOMER'S COMIN'!
A MOMENT LATER...
ISN'T MR. PETTLE RUNNING THIS FLORIST SHOP ANYMORE?
NO... AH... HE HAD TO GIVE IT UP FOR HIS HEALTH! IS THERE ANYTHING I CAN DO FOR YOU?
MR. JASON JOHNSON SENT ME FOR SOME OF THESE PLANTS!
YES, SIR! YOU'LL TAKE THEM WITH YOU, OF COURSE, AND HELP OUR GOVERNMENT SAVE GAS AND RUBBER?
THAT'S NOT THE ONLY REASON! MY BOSS WOULDN'T LET ANYBODY GET NEAR HIS MANSION! HE'S SCARED OF BURGLARS!
HA, HA! I'VE HEARD A LOT ABOUT JASON JOHNSON'S LITTLE ECCENTRICITY!
IN THE BACK ROOM OF THE PETTLE FLOWER SHOP...
DAT GUY JOHNSON'S GOT GUARDS ALL OVER HIS PALACE! A FLY COULDN'T GET IN!
BUT WE SHALL! IN ONE HOUR WE'LL WALK IN, LOOT THE PREMISES AND WALK OUT! HA, HA!
AND AN HOUR LATER...
GOSH, I CAN'T BELIEVE IT! WE'RE WALKIN' RIGHT IN TO THE BEST GUARDED HOUSE IN THE CITY!
HA, HA! LEAVE IT TO THE JOKER! THESE GUARDS WON'T MOVE FOR HOURS! I SAW TO THAT!
2
I'LL HAVE DIS PLANT FIXED UP IN A SECOND, JOKER!
BOY, IS DIS A CINCH!
FINE! I'LL LEAVE MY CALLING CARD WITH MR. JOHNSON! HA, HA!

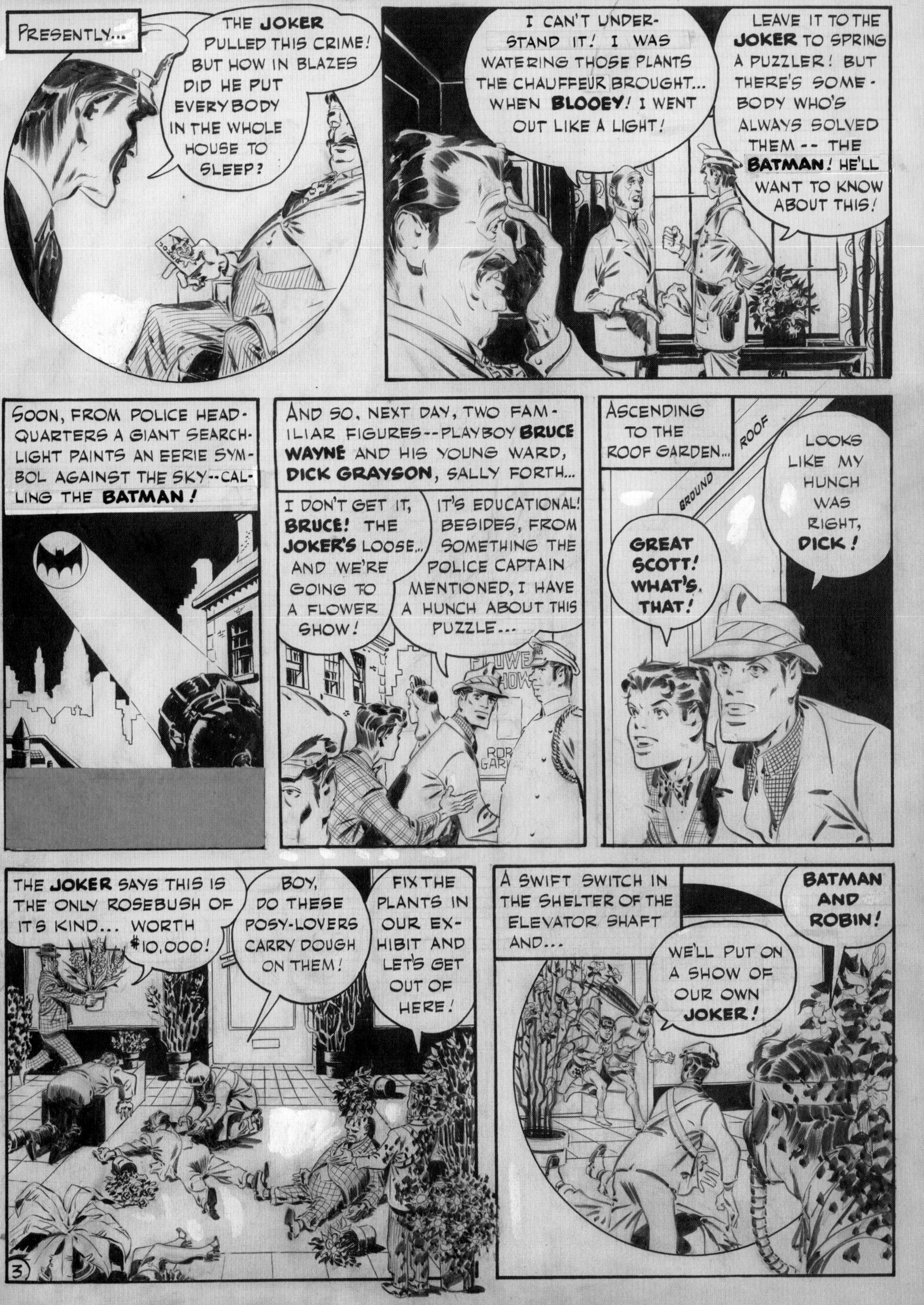
PRESENTLY...
THE JOKER PULLED THIS CRIME! BUT HOW IN BLAZES DID HE PUT EVERYBODY IN THE WHOLE HOUSE TO SLEEP?
I CAN'T UNDERSTAND IT! I WAS WATERING THOSE PLANTS THE CHAUFFEUR BROUGHT... WHEN BLOOEY! I WENT OUT LIKE A LIGHT!
LEAVE IT TO THE JOKER TO SPRING A PUZZLER! BUT THERE'S SOMEBODY WHO'S ALWAYS SOLVED THEM -- THE BATMAN! HE'LL WANT TO KNOW ABOUT THIS!
SOON, FROM POLICE HEADQUARTERS A GIANT SEARCHLIGHT PAINTS AN EERIE SYMBOL AGAINST THE SKY--CALLING THE BATMAN!
AND SO, NEXT DAY, TWO FAMILIAR FIGURES--PLAYBOY BRUCE WAYNE AND HIS YOUNG WARD, DICK GRAYSON, SALLY FORTH...
I DON'T GET IT, BRUCE! THE JOKER'S LOOSE... AND WE'RE GOING TO A FLOWER SHOW!
IT'S EDUCATIONAL! BESIDES, FROM SOMETHING THE POLICE CAPTAIN MENTIONED, I HAVE A HUNCH ABOUT THIS PUZZLE...
ASCENDING TO THE ROOF GARDEN...
ROOF
GROUND
LOOKS LIKE MY HUNCH WAS RIGHT, DICK!
GREAT SCOTT! WHAT'S THAT!
THE JOKER SAYS THIS IS THE ONLY ROSEBUSH OF ITS KIND... WORTH $10,000!
BOY, DO THESE POSY-LOVERS CARRY DOUGH ON THEM!
FIX THE PLANTS IN OUR EXHIBIT AND LET'S GET OUT OF HERE!
A SWIFT SWITCH IN THE SHELTER OF THE ELEVATOR SHAFT AND...
BATMAN AND ROBIN!
WE'LL PUT ON A SHOW OF OUR OWN JOKER!
3

(4) DET JUNE 84 '43 #76

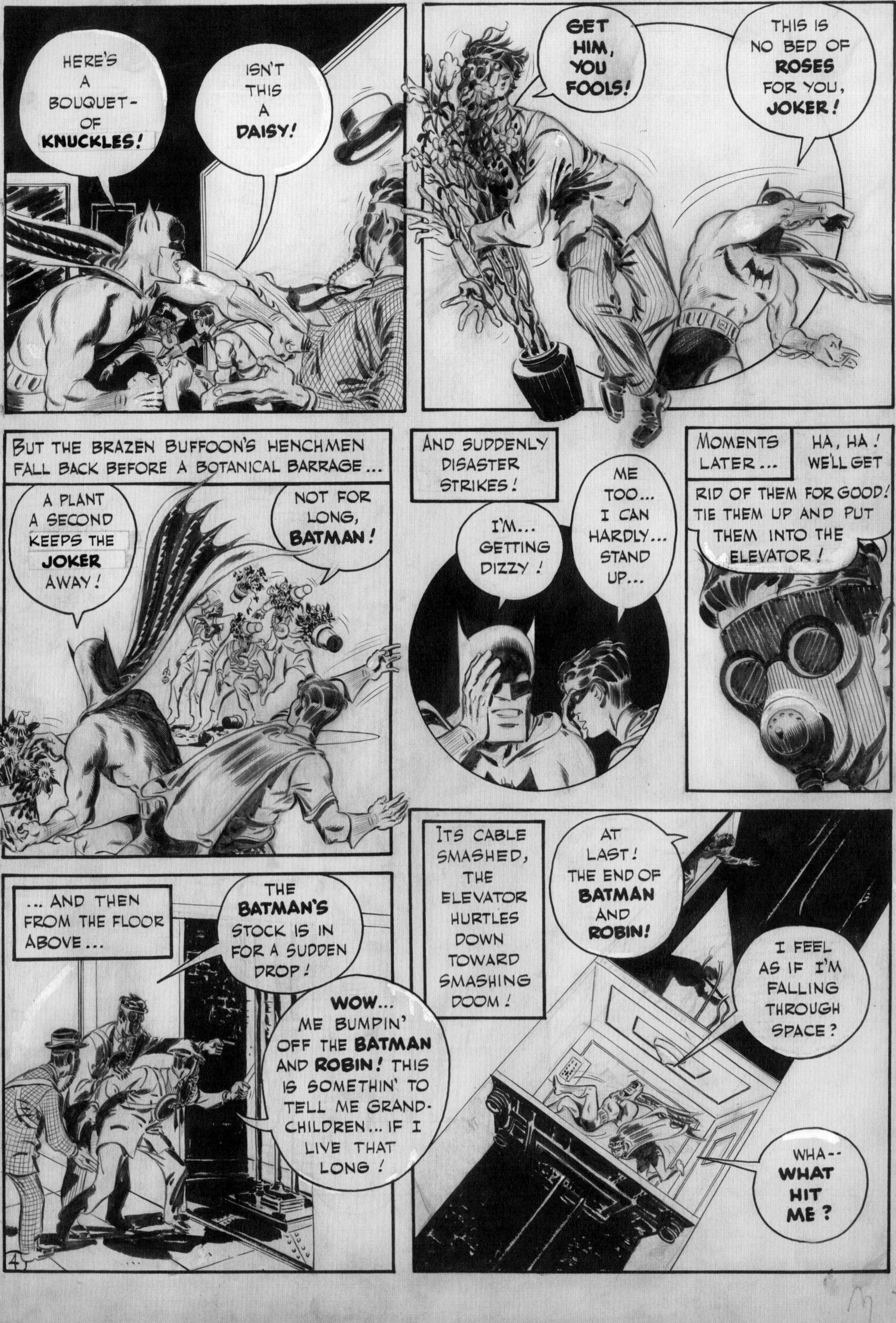

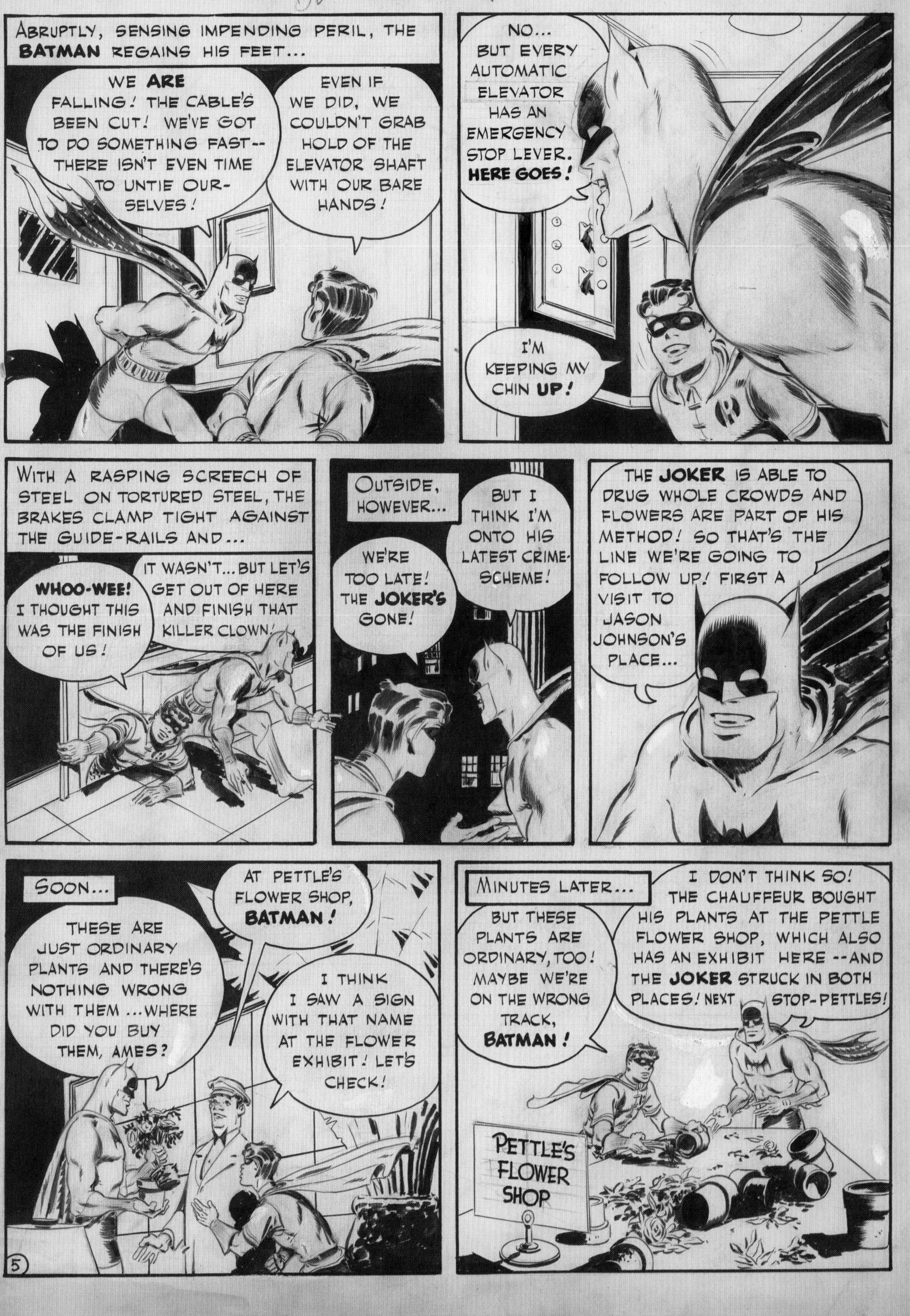
ABRUPTLY, SENSING IMPENDING PERIL, THE BATMAN REGAINS HIS FEET...
WE ARE FALLING! THE CABLE'S BEEN CUT! WE'VE GOT TO DO SOMETHING FAST-- THERE ISN'T EVEN TIME TO UNTIE OURSELVES!
EVEN IF WE DID, WE COULDN'T GRAB HOLD OF THE ELEVATOR SHAFT WITH OUR BARE HANDS!
NO... BUT EVERY AUTOMATIC ELEVATOR HAS AN EMERGENCY STOP LEVER. HERE GOES!
I'M KEEPING MY CHIN UP!
WITH A RASPING SCREECH OF STEEL ON TORTURED STEEL, THE BRAKES CLAMP TIGHT AGAINST THE GUIDE-RAILS AND...
WHOO-WEE! I THOUGHT THIS WAS THE FINISH OF US!
IT WASN'T... BUT LET'S GET OUT OF HERE AND FINISH THAT KILLER CLOWN!
OUTSIDE, HOWEVER...
WE'RE TOO LATE! THE JOKER'S GONE!
BUT I THINK I'M ONTO HIS LATEST CRIME-SCHEME!
THE JOKER IS ABLE TO DRUG WHOLE CROWDS AND FLOWERS ARE PART OF HIS METHOD! SO THAT'S THE LINE WE'RE GOING TO FOLLOW UP! FIRST A VISIT TO JASON JOHNSON'S PLACE...
SOON...
THESE ARE JUST ORDINARY PLANTS AND THERE'S NOTHING WRONG WITH THEM ...WHERE DID YOU BUY THEM, AMES?
AT PETTLE'S FLOWER SHOP, BATMAN!
I THINK I SAW A SIGN WITH THAT NAME AT THE FLOWER EXHIBIT! LET'S CHECK!
5
MINUTES LATER...
BUT THESE PLANTS ARE ORDINARY, TOO! MAYBE WE'RE ON THE WRONG TRACK, BATMAN!
I DON'T THINK SO! THE CHAUFFEUR BOUGHT HIS PLANTS AT THE PETTLE FLOWER SHOP, WHICH ALSO HAS AN EXHIBIT HERE --AND THE JOKER STRUCK IN BOTH PLACES! NEXT STOP-PETTLES!
PETTLE'S FLOWER SHOP

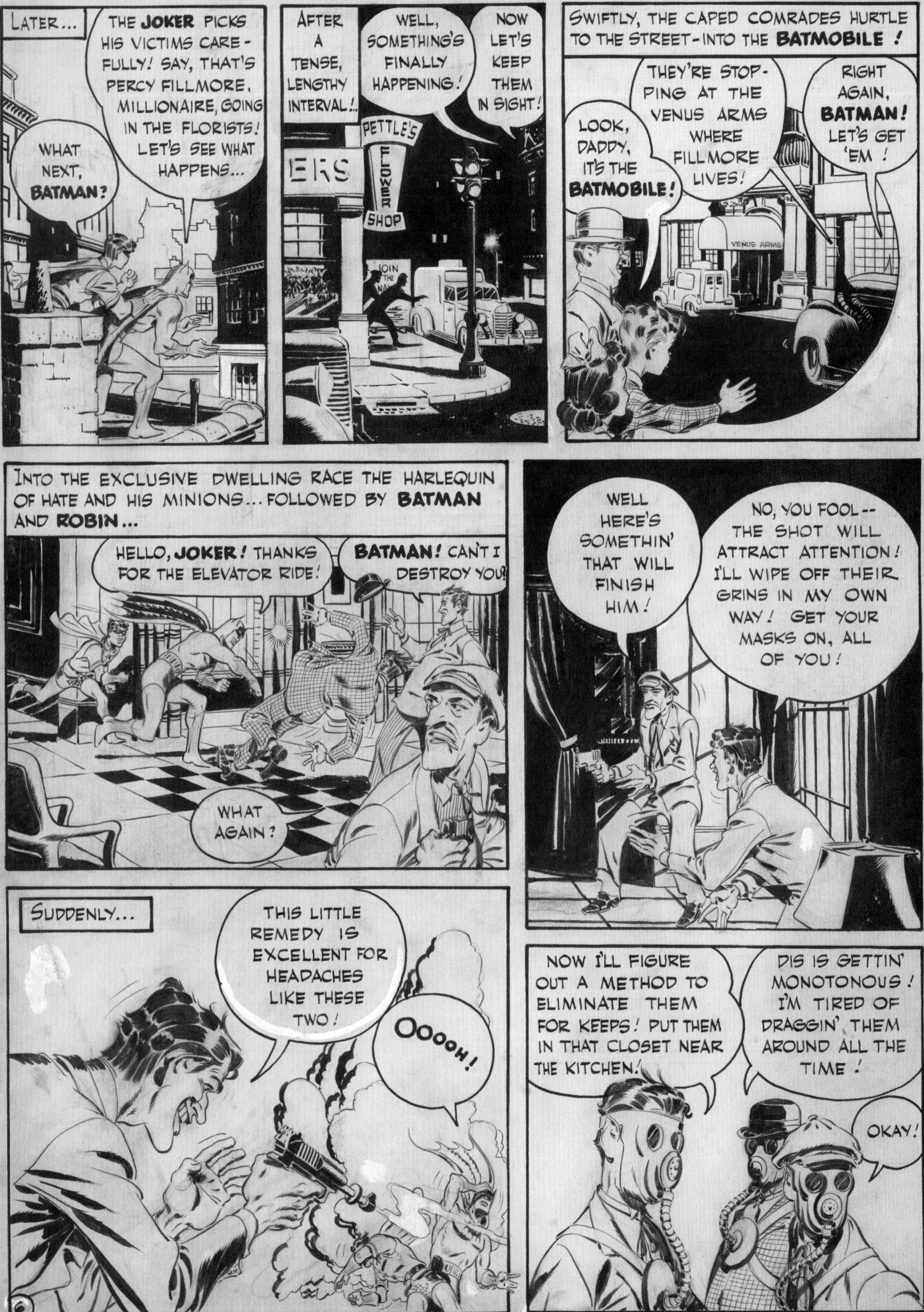

LATER...
THE JOKER PICKS HIS VICTIMS CAREFULLY! SAY, THAT'S PERCY FILLMORE, MILLIONAIRE, GOING IN THE FLORISTS! LET'S SEE WHAT HAPPENS...
WHAT NEXT, BATMAN?
AFTER A TENSE, LENGTHY INTERVAL!...
WELL, SOMETHING'S FINALLY HAPPENING!
NOW LET'S KEEP THEM IN SIGHT!
ERS
PETTLE'S FLOWER SHOP
JOIN THE NA
SWIFTLY, THE CAPED COMRADES HURTLE TO THE STREET-INTO THE BATMOBILE!
LOOK, DADDY, IT'S THE BATMOBILE!
THEY'RE STOPPING AT THE VENUS ARMS WHERE FILLMORE LIVES!
RIGHT AGAIN, BATMAN! LET'S GET 'EM!
VENUS ARMS
INTO THE EXCLUSIVE DWELLING RACE THE HARLEQUIN OF HATE AND HIS MINIONS... FOLLOWED BY BATMAN AND ROBIN...
HELLO, JOKER! THANKS FOR THE ELEVATOR RIDE!
BATMAN! CAN'T I DESTROY YOU?
WHAT AGAIN?
WELL HERE'S SOMETHIN' THAT WILL FINISH HIM!
NO, YOU FOOL-- THE SHOT WILL ATTRACT ATTENTION! I'LL WIPE OFF THEIR GRINS IN MY OWN WAY! GET YOUR MASKS ON, ALL OF YOU!
SUDDENLY...
THIS LITTLE REMEDY IS EXCELLENT FOR HEADACHES LIKE THESE TWO!
OOOOH!
NOW I'LL FIGURE OUT A METHOD TO ELIMINATE THEM FOR KEEPS! PUT THEM IN THAT CLOSET NEAR THE KITCHEN!
DIS IS GETTIN' MONOTONOUS! I'M TIRED OF DRAGGIN' THEM AROUND ALL THE TIME!
OKAY!
6

INSIDE FILLMORE'S APARTMENT...

WONDER HOW LONG THEY'LL STAY QUIET IN HERE, JOKER?

A LITTLE GAS WILL KEEP THEM QUIET FOREVER... AND I'LL PLAY A DEATH MARCH! HA, HA!

THIS DOUGH IS MUSIC TO ME!

NICE OF FILLMORE TO SAVE SCRAP RUBBER... THIS OLD HOSE WILL JUNK THE BATMAN AND HIS BRAT WONDER! IT'S CONNECTED TO THE KITCHEN RANGE! TURN ON THE GAS!

OKAY, JOKER! LET'S GET GOIN'!

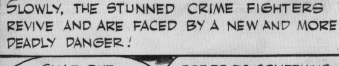

SLOWLY, THE STUNNED CRIME FIGHTERS REVIVE AND ARE FACED BY A NEW AND MORE DEADLY DANGER!

SNAP OUT OF IT, B-BATMAN! TH-THE P-PLACE IS BEING FILLED WITH G-GAS! WE-WE'LL BE S-SUFFOCATED!

GOT TO DO SOMETHING RIGHT AWAY...'NOTHER FEW MINUTES MIGHT BE TOO LATE!

N-NO USE! WE'RE T-TOO WEAK!

CAN'T GIVE UP... GOT TO GET OUT OF HERE! MY BRAIN IS FILLED WITH FUMES! ...CAN'T THINK... BUT I'VE GOT TO!

THEN, A SOLUTION, STARTLING IN ITS SIMPLICITY, SEEPS THROUGH BATMAN'S TORPID MIND!

PULL OUT THE PINS AND THE DOOR HINGES COME APART! THEN THE LOCK'S THE ONLY THING HOLDING UP THE DOOR...

W-WE'RE F-FINISHED, IF THIS D-DOESN'T WORK!

BUT IT DOES WORK! A FEEBLE PUSH AND THE DOOR COLLAPSES! AND THEN...

THE JOKER WAS TOO FAST THIS TIME! HE SPILLED SOIL AROUND THE POT! THAT'S PROOF THESE THINGS ARE PART OF HIS SCHEME!

FILLMORE'S OKAY NOW! LET'S BARGE IN AND CLEAN UP THE FLOWER SHOP!

NO, BECAUSE, IF I KNOW THE JOKER, HE'S GOT THE LOOT HIDDEN AT SOME OTHER HIDEOUT! WE'VE GOT TO LEARN WHERE...WE'LL OFFER OURSELVES AS BAIT TO FIND OUT!

7

DET JUNE '43 P 8 #76

PRESENTLY, AT THE PETTLE FLOWER SHOP, TWO BITTER FOES IN DISGUISE FACE EACH OTHER ACROSS A COUNTER!
TOO BAD MR. PETTLE HAD TO GIVE UP THE SHOP! I'VE DEALT WITH HIM FOR YEARS!
YES, IT'S A PITY, MR. WAYNE! BUT HE HAD NO CHOICE!
WISH WE COULD WADE RIGHT IN WITHOUT FENCING AROUND LIKE THIS!
I WANT A FEW OF THESE PLANTS! I'LL TAKE THEM WITH ME!
CERTAINLY, MR. WAYNE! HA, HA! WE'VE BEEN VERY SUCCESSFUL WITH THEM! I'LL HAVE TO ORDER A LOT MORE!
WHEN THE CUSTOMERS DEPART...
BRUCE WAYNE, DA SOCIETY PLAYBOY! WHAT A HOUSE HE'S GOT TO KNOCK OVER! WE'LL GRAB US A FORTUNE!
RIGHT! THIS WILL BE THE EASIEST AND MOST PROFITABLE HAUL OF ALL! HA, HA, HA!
PERHAPS, JOKER - AND PERHAPS NOT! FOR THE MOMENT THE INTENDED VICTIMS REACH HOME...
CAN'T TAKE ANY CHANCES WITH ONE OF THE JOKER'S CUNNING INVENTIONS! IT'S SAFER TO FLUOROSCOPE IT FIRST!
WOW! YOU WERE RIGHT, BRUCE! THERE IS SOMETHING AT THE BOTTOM OF THAT POT!
VERY CLEVER! THE JOKER MERELY SETS THIS CLOCKWORK! THEN, AT THE APPOINTED TIME, A CLOUD OF CHLOROFORM IS RELEASED THROUGH THE HOLLOW STEMS OF THE PLANT DRUGGING HIS VICTIMS!
AND AFTER EACH ROBBERY, THE JOKER JUST TAKES THESE THINGS OUT AND FILLS THE POTS WITH SOIL! WHAT ARE YOU DOING? HE'LL GET SUSPICIOUS IF THEY'RE GONE!
I'M JUST EMPTYING THE CHLOFORM IN THE OPEN AIR AND LEAVING EVERYTHING ELSE INTACT! HE'LL BE HERE SOON! RING FOR ALFRED!
8
SWIFTLY BRUCE INSTRUCTS HIS BUTLER, ALFRED, THE ONLY PERSON IN THE WORLD WHO KNOWS THE TRUE IDENTITIES OF BATMAN AND ROBIN...
BUT THE JOKER! WHY DON'T WE OFFER RESISTANCE? MY PUGILISTIC INSTINCTS ARE AROUSED!
NEVER MIND THE FISTICUFFS, ALFRED! DON'T MAKE A SINGLE MOVE WHEN THE GANG COMES IN! OUR PLAN WOULD BE RUINED... AND THE JOKER WOULD CERTAINLY KILL US!

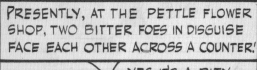

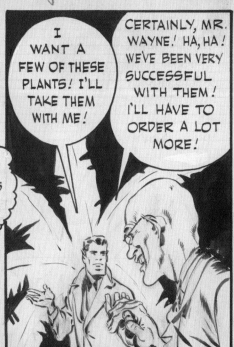

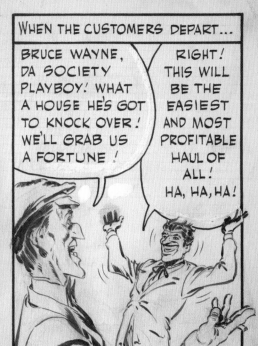

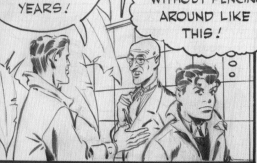

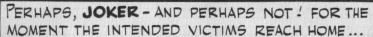

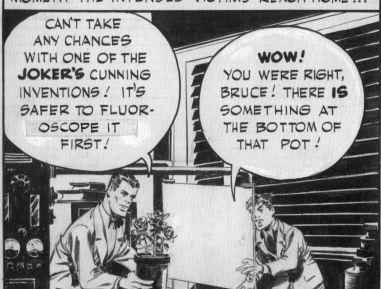

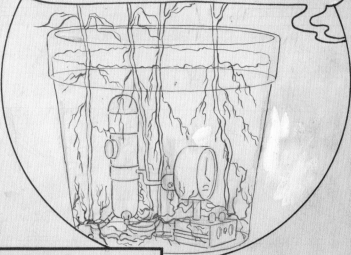

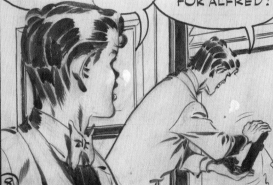

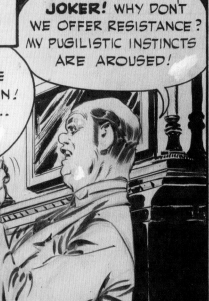

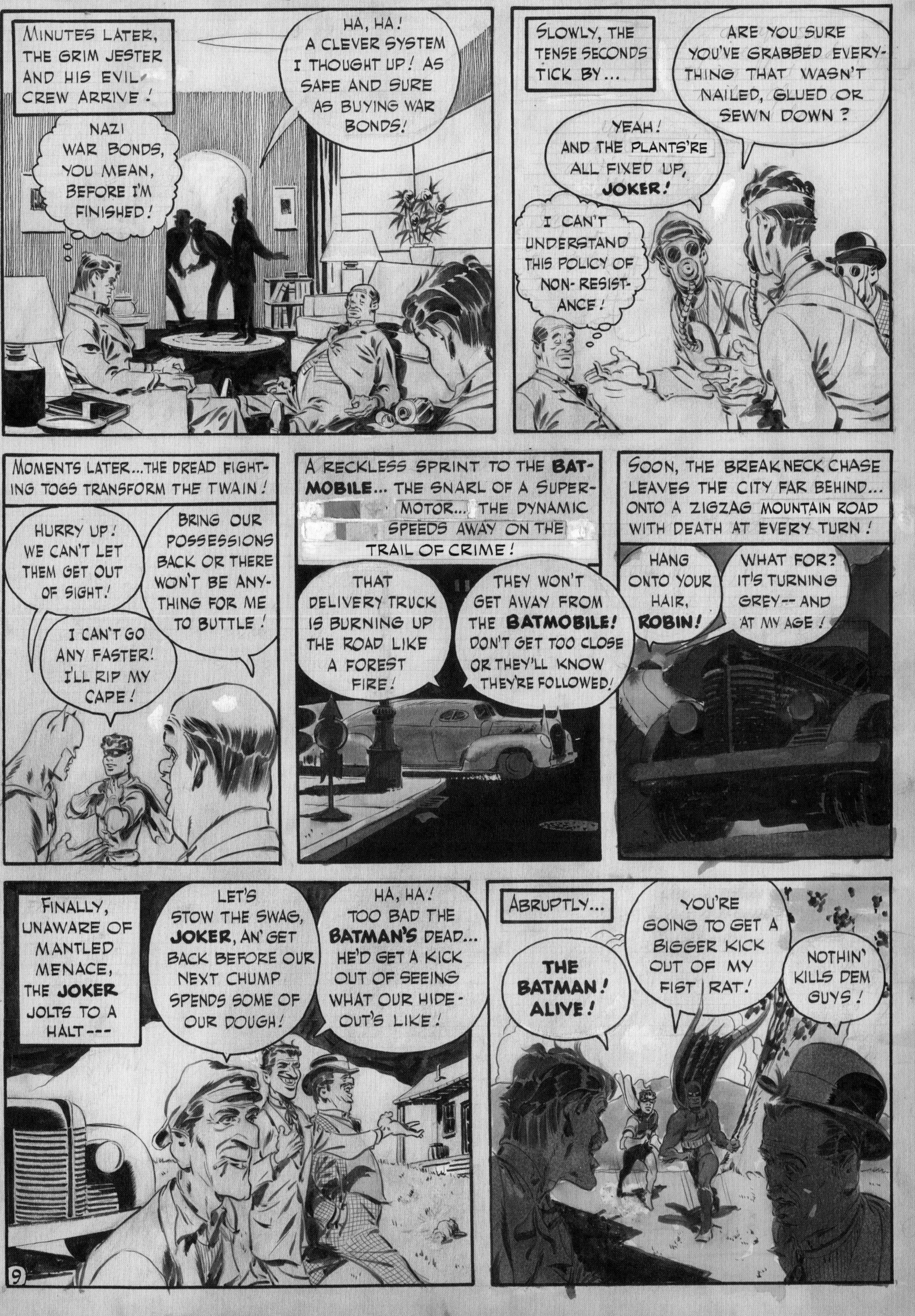

MINUTES LATER, THE GRIM JESTER AND HIS EVIL CREW ARRIVE!
HA, HA! A CLEVER SYSTEM I THOUGHT UP! AS SAFE AND SURE AS BUYING WAR BONDS!
NAZI WAR BONDS, YOU MEAN, BEFORE I'M FINISHED!
SLOWLY, THE TENSE SECONDS TICK BY...
ARE YOU SURE YOU'VE GRABBED EVERYTHING THAT WASN'T NAILED, GLUED OR SEWN DOWN?
YEAH! AND THE PLANTS'RE ALL FIXED UP, JOKER!
I CAN'T UNDERSTAND THIS POLICY OF NON-RESISTANCE!
MOMENTS LATER...THE DREAD FIGHTING TOGS TRANSFORM THE TWAIN!
HURRY UP! WE CAN'T LET THEM GET OUT OF SIGHT!
BRING OUR POSSESSIONS BACK OR THERE WON'T BE ANYTHING FOR ME TO BUTTLE!
I CAN'T GO ANY FASTER! I'LL RIP MY CAPE!
A RECKLESS SPRINT TO THE BATMOBILE... THE SNARL OF A SUPER- MOTOR... THE DYNAMIC SPEEDS AWAY ON THE TRAIL OF CRIME!
THAT DELIVERY TRUCK IS BURNING UP THE ROAD LIKE A FOREST FIRE!
THEY WON'T GET AWAY FROM THE BATMOBILE! DON'T GET TOO CLOSE OR THEY'LL KNOW THEY'RE FOLLOWED!
SOON, THE BREAKNECK CHASE LEAVES THE CITY FAR BEHIND... ONTO A ZIGZAG MOUNTAIN ROAD WITH DEATH AT EVERY TURN!
HANG ONTO YOUR HAIR, ROBIN!
WHAT FOR? IT'S TURNING GREY-- AND AT MY AGE!
FINALLY, UNAWARE OF MANTLED MENACE, THE JOKER JOLTS TO A HALT---
LET'S STOW THE SWAG, JOKER, AN' GET BACK BEFORE OUR NEXT CHUMP SPENDS SOME OF OUR DOUGH!
HA, HA! TOO BAD THE BATMAN'S DEAD... HE'D GET A KICK OUT OF SEEING WHAT OUR HIDE-OUT'S LIKE!
9
ABRUPTLY...
THE BATMAN! ALIVE!
YOU'RE GOING TO GET A BIGGER KICK OUT OF MY FIST RAT!
NOTHIN' KILLS DEM GUYS!

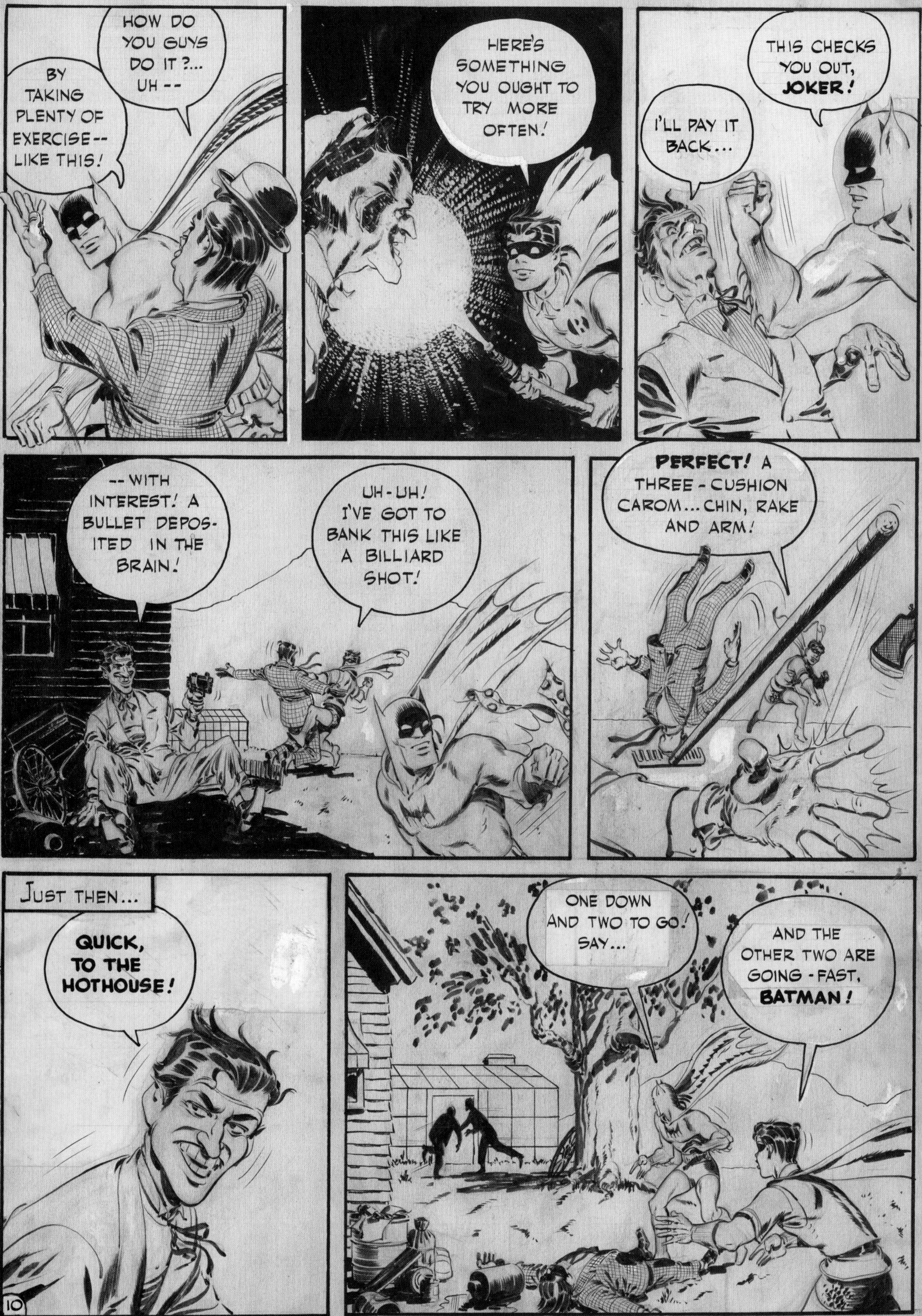
HOW DO YOU GUYS DO IT ?... UH --
BY TAKING PLENTY OF EXERCISE -- LIKE THIS!
HERE'S SOMETHING YOU OUGHT TO TRY MORE OFTEN!
THIS CHECKS YOU OUT, JOKER!
I'LL PAY IT BACK...
-- WITH INTEREST! A BULLET DEPOSITED IN THE BRAIN!
UH - UH! I'VE GOT TO BANK THIS LIKE A BILLIARD SHOT!
PERFECT! A THREE - CUSHION CAROM... CHIN, RAKE AND ARM!
JUST THEN...
QUICK, TO THE HOTHOUSE!
ONE DOWN AND TWO TO GO! SAY...
AND THE OTHER TWO ARE GOING - FAST, BATMAN!

JUNE DET. '43 #76

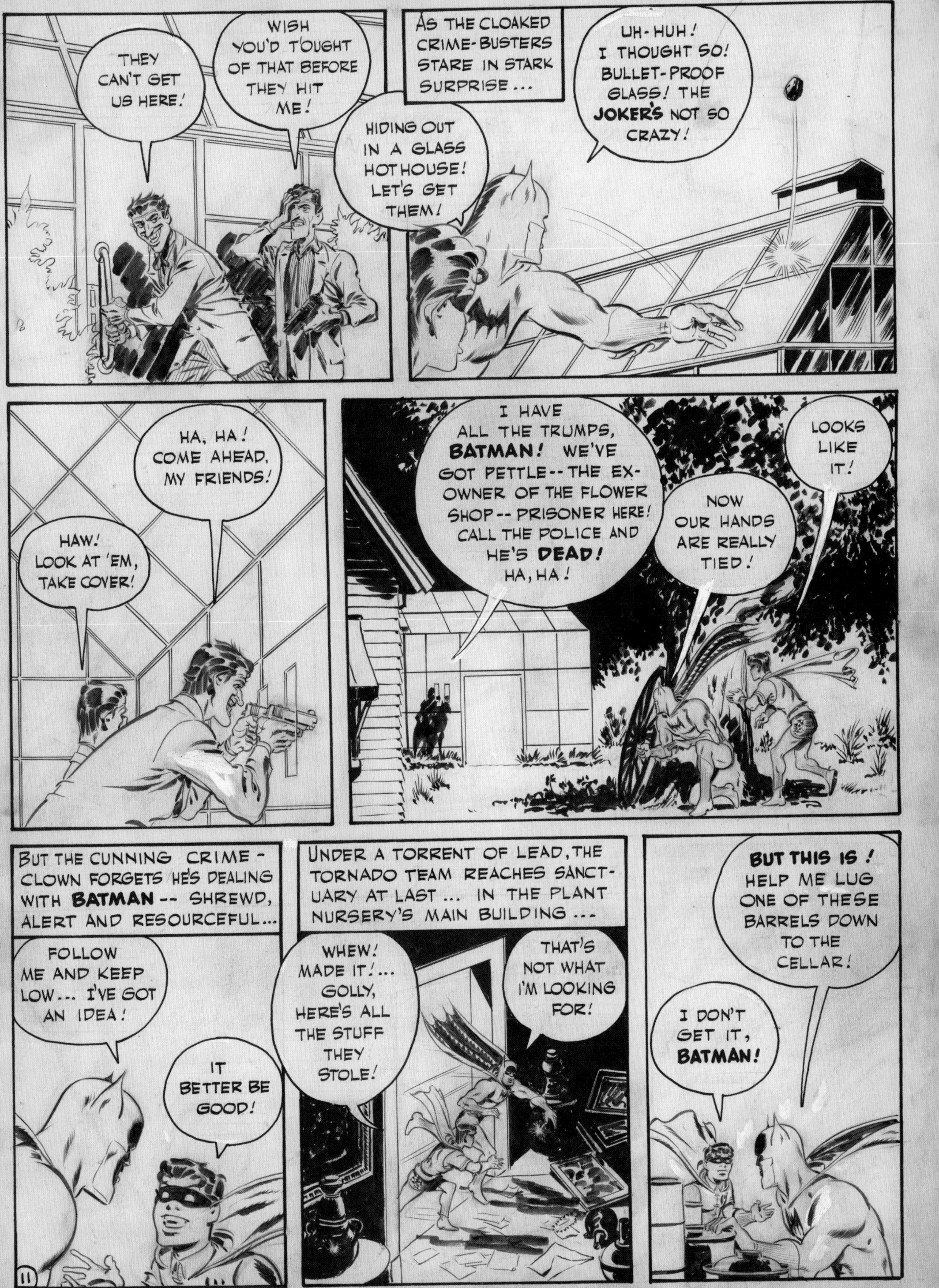

THEY CAN'T GET US HERE!
WISH YOU'D T'OUGHT OF THAT BEFORE THEY HIT ME!
AS THE CLOAKED CRIME-BUSTERS STARE IN STARK SURPRISE...
HIDING OUT IN A GLASS HOTHOUSE! LET'S GET THEM!
UH-HUH! I THOUGHT SO! BULLET-PROOF GLASS! THE JOKER'S NOT SO CRAZY!
HA, HA! COME AHEAD, MY FRIENDS!
HAW! LOOK AT 'EM, TAKE COVER!
I HAVE ALL THE TRUMPS, BATMAN! WE'VE GOT PETTLE -- THE EX-OWNER OF THE FLOWER SHOP -- PRISONER HERE! CALL THE POLICE AND HE'S DEAD! HA, HA!
NOW OUR HANDS ARE REALLY TIED!
LOOKS LIKE IT!
BUT THE CUNNING CRIME-CLOWN FORGETS HE'S DEALING WITH BATMAN -- SHREWD, ALERT AND RESOURCEFUL...
FOLLOW ME AND KEEP LOW... I'VE GOT AN IDEA!
IT BETTER BE GOOD!
UNDER A TORRENT OF LEAD, THE TORNADO TEAM REACHES SANCTUARY AT LAST... IN THE PLANT NURSERY'S MAIN BUILDING...
WHEW! MADE IT!... GOLLY, HERE'S ALL THE STUFF THEY STOLE!
THAT'S NOT WHAT I'M LOOKING FOR!
BUT THIS IS! HELP ME LUG ONE OF THESE BARRELS DOWN TO THE CELLAR!
I DON'T GET IT, BATMAN!
11

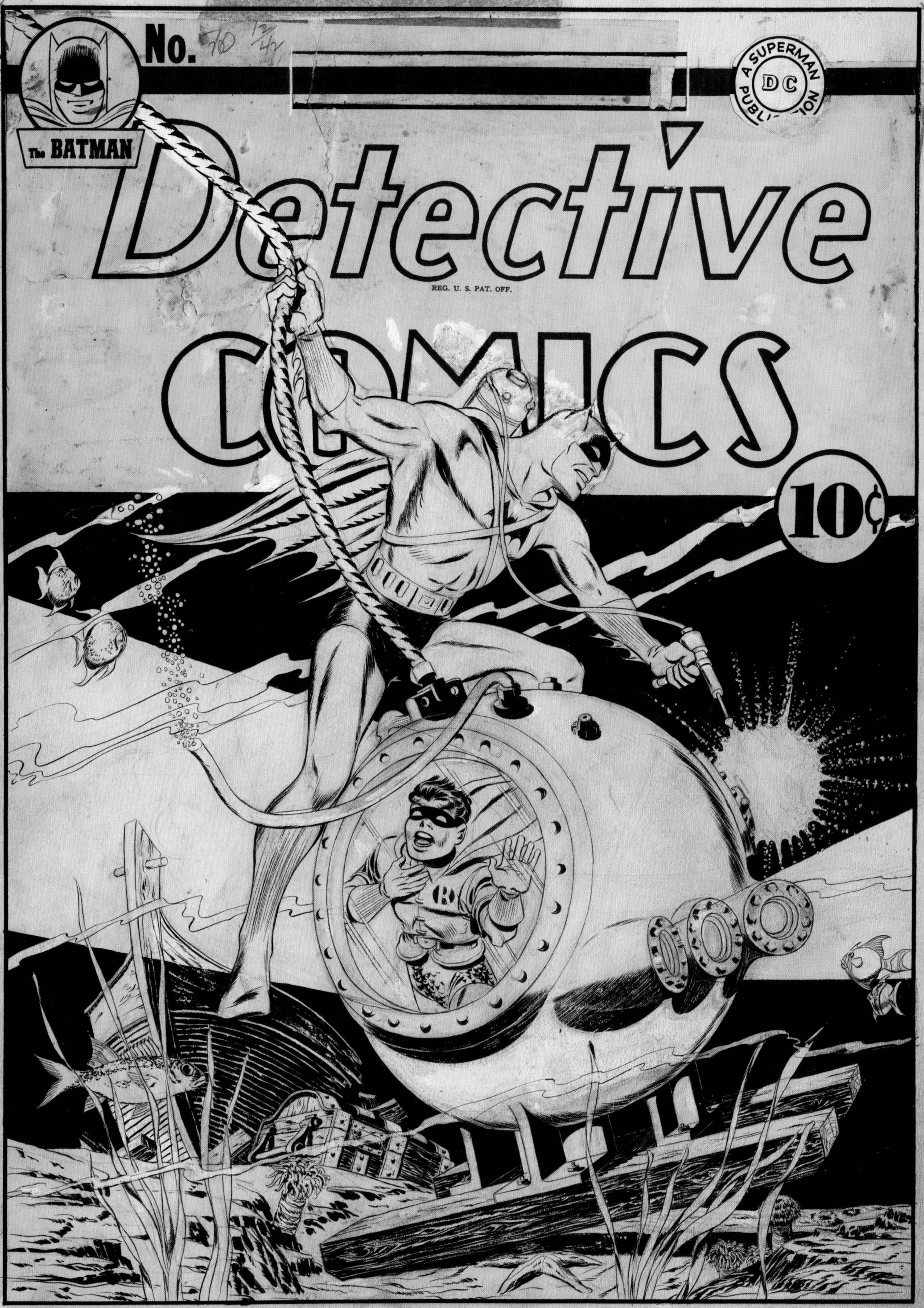
No. 70 12/42
The BATMAN
A SUPERMAN PUBLICATION
DC
Detective
REG. U. S. PAT. OFF.
COMICS
10¢

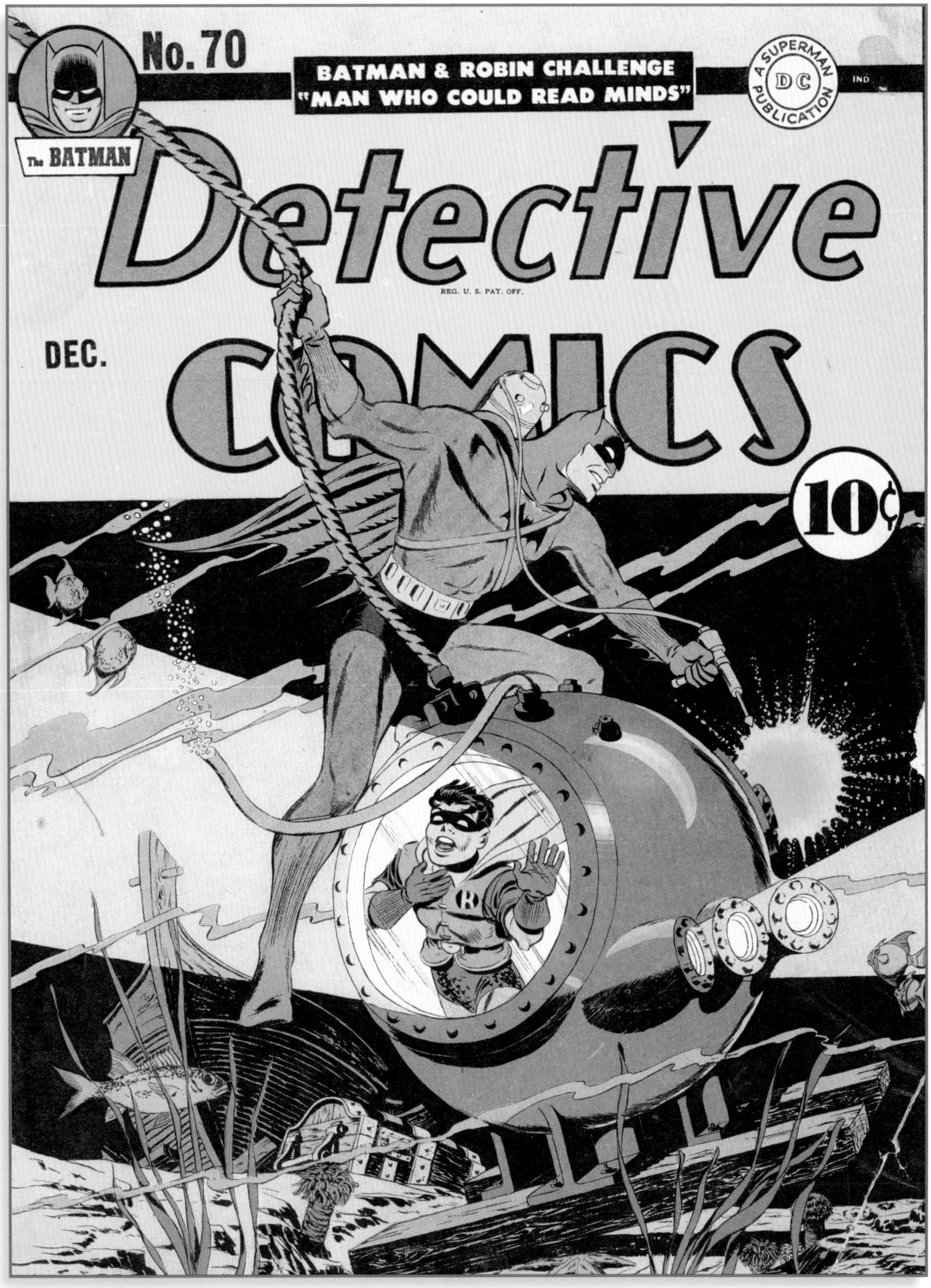
No. 70
BATMAN & ROBIN CHALLENGE
"MAN WHO COULD READ MINDS"
A SUPERMAN
DC
PUBLICATION
IND
The BATMAN
Detective
REG. U. S. PAT. OFF.
DEC.
COMICS
10¢

Left
ORIGINAL ART TO COVER OF *DETECTIVE COMICS* NO. 70
December 1942, pencils and inks by Jerry Robinson.

Above
COLOR COVER OF *DETECTIVE COMICS* NO. 70
December 1942, pencils, inks, and colors by Jerry Robinson.

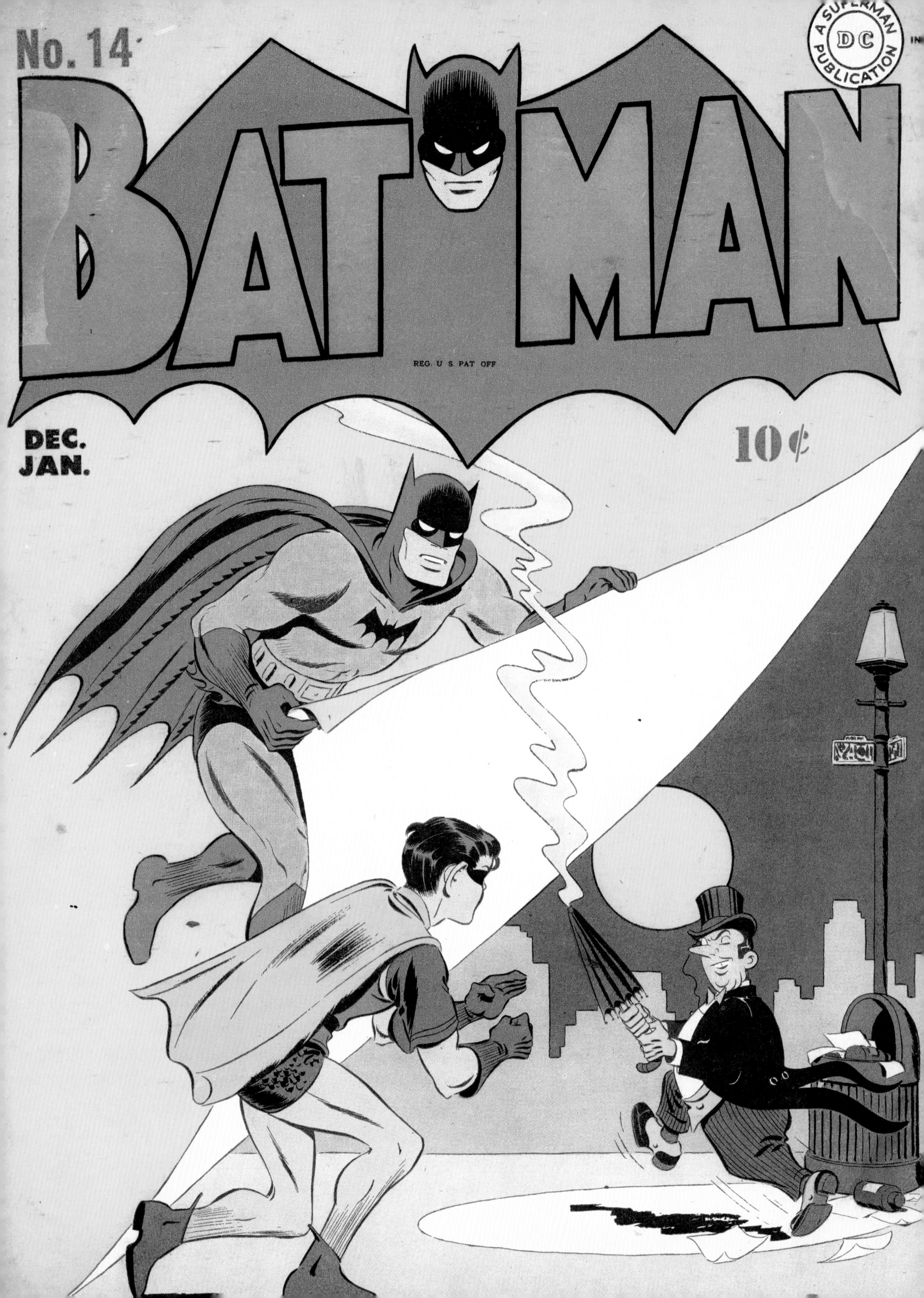
No. 14
A SUPERMAN DC PUBLICATION
BATMAN
REG. U S. PAT OFF
DEC.
JAN.
10¢

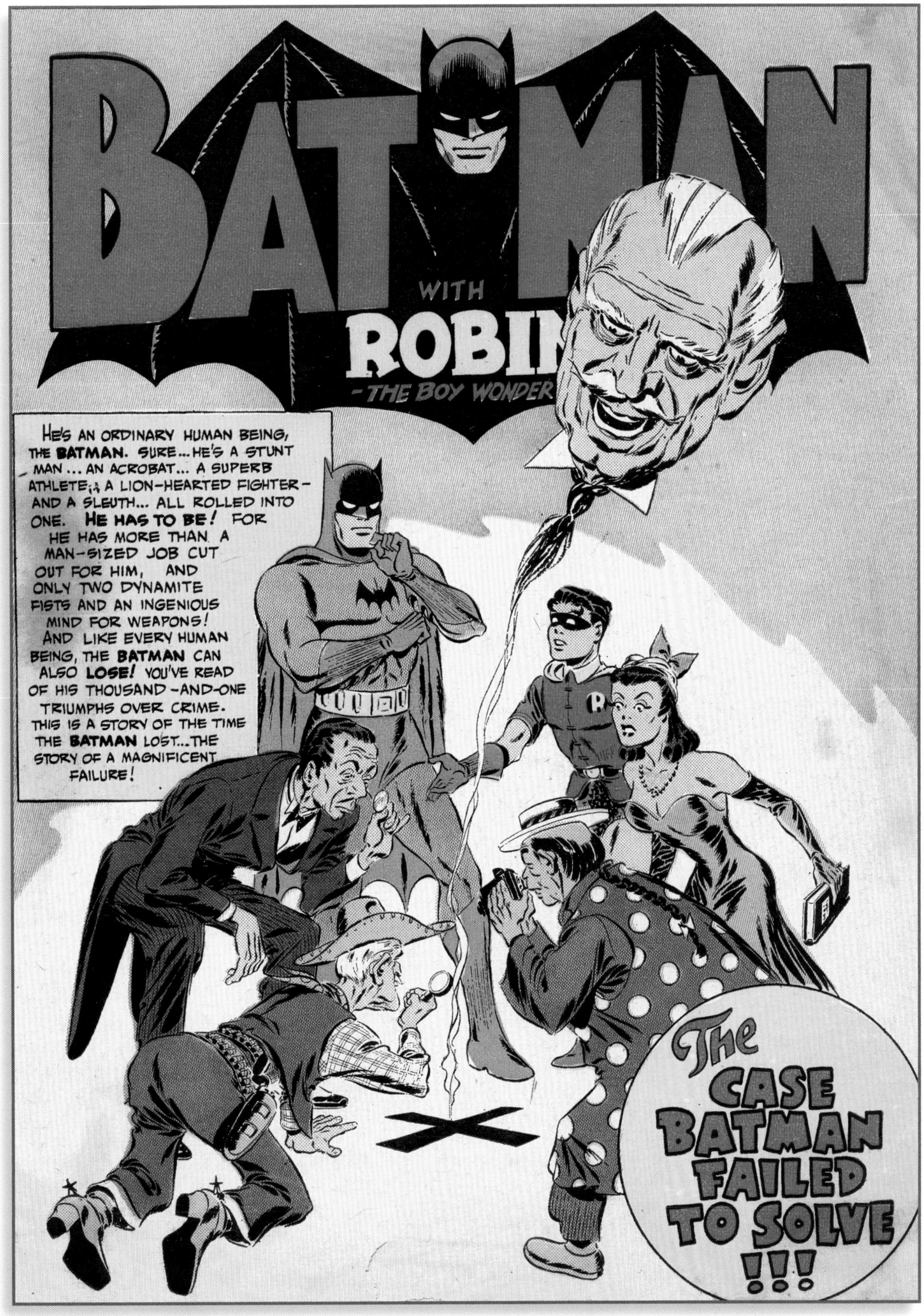
BATMAN
WITH
ROBIN
-THE BOY WONDER
HE'S AN ORDINARY HUMAN BEING, THE BATMAN. SURE...HE'S A STUNT MAN ... AN ACROBAT... A SUPERB ATHLETE; A LION-HEARTED FIGHTER - AND A SLEUTH... ALL ROLLED INTO ONE. HE HAS TO BE! FOR HE HAS MORE THAN A MAN-SIZED JOB CUT OUT FOR HIM, AND ONLY TWO DYNAMITE FISTS AND AN INGENIOUS MIND FOR WEAPONS! AND LIKE EVERY HUMAN BEING, THE BATMAN CAN ALSO LOSE! YOU'VE READ OF HIS THOUSAND-AND-ONE TRIUMPHS OVER CRIME. THIS IS A STORY OF THE TIME THE BATMAN LOST...THE STORY OF A MAGNIFICENT FAILURE!
The CASE BATMAN FAILED TO SOLVE !!!

Left
ORIGINAL ART TO SPLASH PAGE OF "THE CASE BATMAN FAILED TO SOLVE!!!" FROM *BATMAN* NO. 14
December 1942 – January 1943, pencils and inks by Jerry Robinson.

Above
COLOR SPLASH PAGE OF "THE CASE BATMAN FAILED TO SOLVE!!!" FROM *BATMAN* NO. 14
December 1942 – January 1943, pencils, inks, and colors by Jerry Robinson.

Following pages
ORIGINAL ART PAGES 3–4 AND 6–13 TO "THE CASE BATMAN FAILED TO SOLVE!!!" FROM *BATMAN* NO. 14
December 1942 – January 1943, pencils and inks by Jerry Robinson.

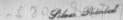

ROBIN, I CAN SEE YOU'VE BEEN SHIRKING YOUR CRIMINOLOGY STUDIES. WHY, EVERYONE KNOWS DANA DRYE, DEAN OF DETECTIVES, GREATEST OF THEM ALL!

"HERE'S A PICTURE OF DRYE IN 1880. SINGLE-HANDED HE ROUNDED UP THE NOTORIOUS GRAVES GANG!..."

"HERE'S DRYE IN 1910 WHEN HE CRACKED THE CONEY POISONING CASE. DRYE WORKED ON OVER A THOUSAND MURDERS AND NEVER FAILED!

DRYE 1910

AND NOW YOU'LL GET A CHANCE TO SEE WHAT HE LOOKS LIKE TODAY!

I BET WE COULD LEARN A LOT FROM DRYE, BATMAN... I'D LIKE TO TALK TO HIM!

AND AS A BRILLIANT NOVEMBER SUN STREAKS THRU SPARK-LING WINDOWS AT RIVER HOUSE, THE GREAT DETECTIVES OF THE WORLD ASSEMBLE...

HONORABLE MISS SEERS HAS GREAT REPUTATION IN 'FRISCO!

I'LL BE GOLDARNED! BATMAN! H'ARE YA!

GLAD TO SEE YOU, SHERIFF PLUNKETT.

I THINK WE'D BETTER SIT DOWN. DRYE IS COMING UP TO SPEAK!

YIPPEE! GOOD OLE DRYE!

BRAVO! BRAVO!

GOOD TO SEE YOU, DRYE!

FELLOW DETECTIVES, YOU ARE TRUE FRIENDS INDEED, VISITING ME THIS LAST TIME, WHEN I'M ABOUT TO RETIRE!

3

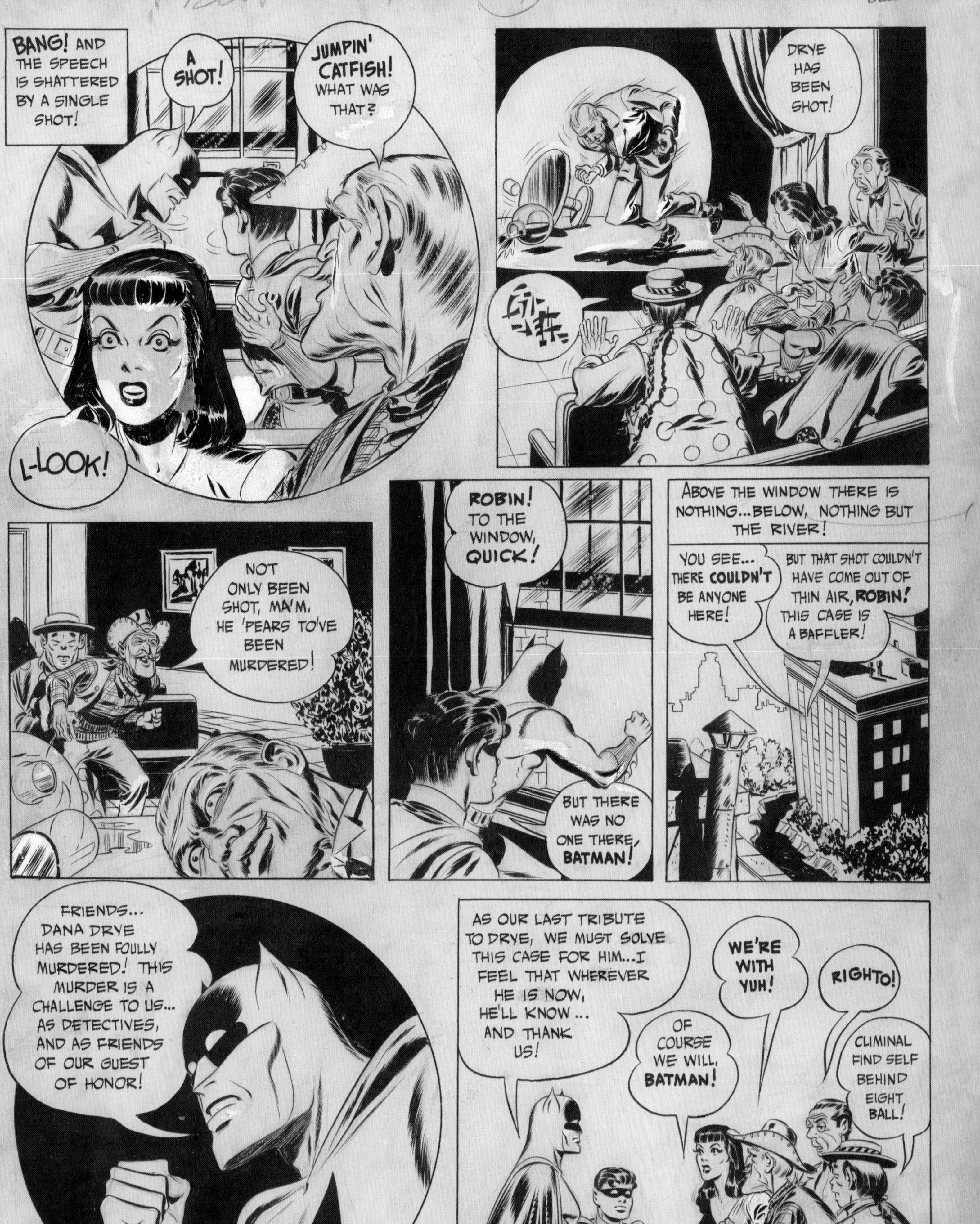
BANG! AND THE SPEECH IS SHATTERED BY A SINGLE SHOT!
A SHOT!
JUMPIN' CATFISH! WHAT WAS THAT?
L-LOOK!
DRYE HAS BEEN SHOT!
NOT ONLY BEEN SHOT, MA'M. HE 'PEARS TO'VE BEEN MURDERED!
ROBIN! TO THE WINDOW, QUICK!
BUT THERE WAS NO ONE THERE, BATMAN!
ABOVE THE WINDOW THERE IS NOTHING...BELOW, NOTHING BUT THE RIVER!
YOU SEE... THERE COULDN'T BE ANYONE HERE!
BUT THAT SHOT COULDN'T HAVE COME OUT OF THIN AIR, ROBIN! THIS CASE IS A BAFFLER!
FRIENDS... DANA DRYE HAS BEEN FOULLY MURDERED! THIS MURDER IS A CHALLENGE TO US... AS DETECTIVES, AND AS FRIENDS OF OUR GUEST OF HONOR!
AS OUR LAST TRIBUTE TO DRYE, WE MUST SOLVE THIS CASE FOR HIM...I FEEL THAT WHEREVER HE IS NOW, HE'LL KNOW ... AND THANK US!
OF COURSE WE WILL, BATMAN!
WE'RE WITH YUH!
RIGHTO!
CLIMINAL FIND SELF BEHIND EIGHT BALL!
4

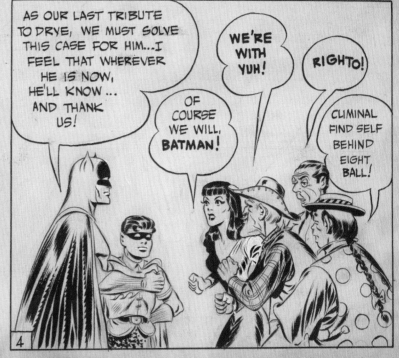

Batman #14

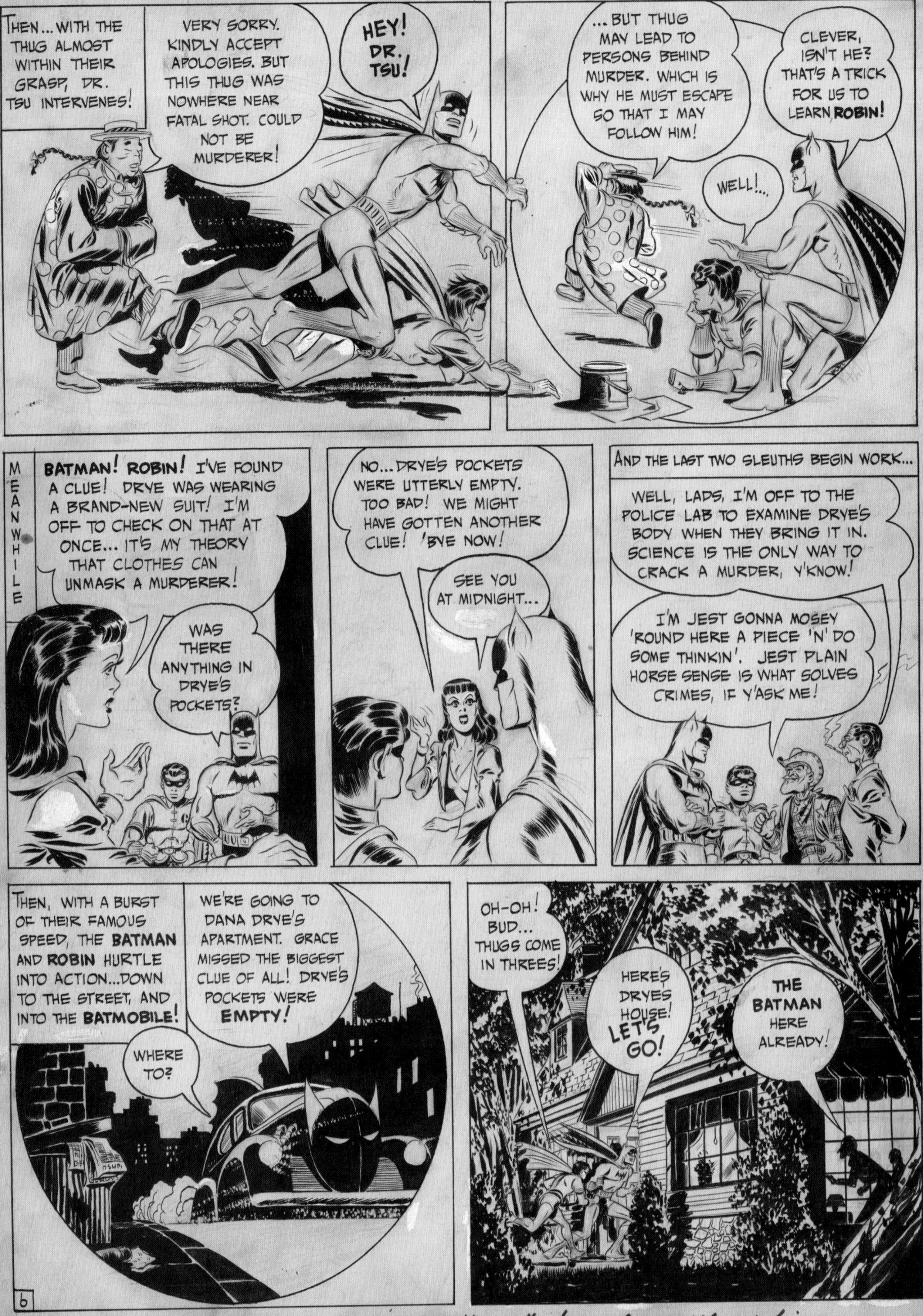
THEN... WITH THE THUG ALMOST WITHIN THEIR GRASP, DR. TSU INTERVENES!
VERY SORRY. KINDLY ACCEPT APOLOGIES. BUT THIS THUG WAS NOWHERE NEAR FATAL SHOT. COULD NOT BE MURDERER!
HEY! DR. TSU!
...BUT THUG MAY LEAD TO PERSONS BEHIND MURDER. WHICH IS WHY HE MUST ESCAPE SO THAT I MAY FOLLOW HIM!
CLEVER, ISN'T HE? THAT'S A TRICK FOR US TO LEARN, ROBIN!
WELL!...
MEANWHILE
BATMAN! ROBIN! I'VE FOUND A CLUE! DRYE WAS WEARING A BRAND-NEW SUIT! I'M OFF TO CHECK ON THAT AT ONCE... IT'S MY THEORY THAT CLOTHES CAN UNMASK A MURDERER!
WAS THERE ANYTHING IN DRYE'S POCKETS?
NO... DRYE'S POCKETS WERE UTTERLY EMPTY. TOO BAD! WE MIGHT HAVE GOTTEN ANOTHER CLUE! 'BYE NOW!
SEE YOU AT MIDNIGHT...
AND THE LAST TWO SLEUTHS BEGIN WORK...
WELL, LADS, I'M OFF TO THE POLICE LAB TO EXAMINE DRYE'S BODY WHEN THEY BRING IT IN. SCIENCE IS THE ONLY WAY TO CRACK A MURDER, Y'KNOW!
I'M JEST GONNA MOSEY 'ROUND HERE A PIECE 'N' DO SOME THINKIN'. JEST PLAIN HORSE SENSE IS WHAT SOLVES CRIMES, IF Y'ASK ME!
THEN, WITH A BURST OF THEIR FAMOUS SPEED, THE BATMAN AND ROBIN HURTLE INTO ACTION... DOWN TO THE STREET, AND INTO THE BATMOBILE!
WE'RE GOING TO DANA DRYE'S APARTMENT. GRACE MISSED THE BIGGEST CLUE OF ALL! DRYE'S POCKETS WERE EMPTY!
WHERE TO?
6
OH-OH! BUD... THUGS COME IN THREES!
HERE'S DRYES HOUSE! LET'S GO!
THE BATMAN HERE ALREADY!

from the collection of jerry robinson

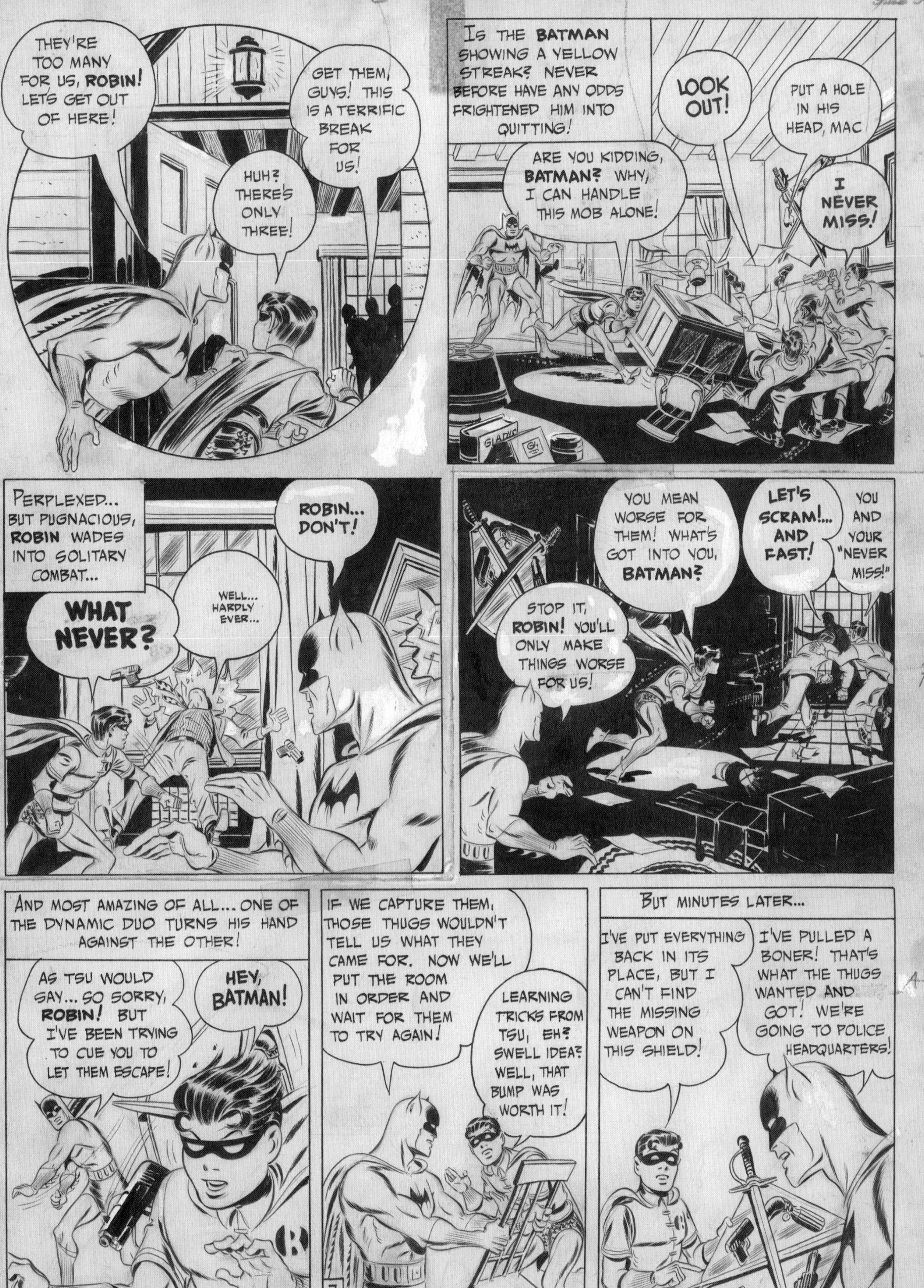

THEY'RE TOO MANY FOR US, ROBIN! LET'S GET OUT OF HERE!
GET THEM, GUYS! THIS IS A TERRIFIC BREAK FOR US!
HUH? THERE'S ONLY THREE!
IS THE BATMAN SHOWING A YELLOW STREAK? NEVER BEFORE HAVE ANY ODDS FRIGHTENED HIM INTO QUITTING!
LOOK OUT!
PUT A HOLE IN HIS HEAD, MAC
ARE YOU KIDDING, BATMAN? WHY, I CAN HANDLE THIS MOB ALONE!
I NEVER MISS!
GLADYS
PERPLEXED... BUT PUGNACIOUS, ROBIN WADES INTO SOLITARY COMBAT...
ROBIN... DON'T!
WHAT NEVER?
WELL... HARDLY EVER...
YOU MEAN WORSE FOR THEM! WHAT'S GOT INTO YOU, BATMAN?
LET'S SCRAM!... AND FAST!
YOU AND YOUR "NEVER MISS!"
STOP IT, ROBIN! YOU'LL ONLY MAKE THINGS WORSE FOR US!
AND MOST AMAZING OF ALL... ONE OF THE DYNAMIC DUO TURNS HIS HAND AGAINST THE OTHER!
AS TSU WOULD SAY... SO SORRY, ROBIN! BUT I'VE BEEN TRYING TO CUE YOU TO LET THEM ESCAPE!
HEY, BATMAN!
IF WE CAPTURE THEM, THOSE THUGS WOULDN'T TELL US WHAT THEY CAME FOR. NOW WE'LL PUT THE ROOM IN ORDER AND WAIT FOR THEM TO TRY AGAIN!
LEARNING TRICKS FROM TSU, EH? SWELL IDEA? WELL, THAT BUMP WAS WORTH IT!
7
BUT MINUTES LATER...
I'VE PUT EVERYTHING BACK IN ITS PLACE, BUT I CAN'T FIND THE MISSING WEAPON ON THIS SHIELD!
I'VE PULLED A BONER! THAT'S WHAT THE THUGS WANTED AND GOT! WE'RE GOING TO POLICE HEADQUARTERS!

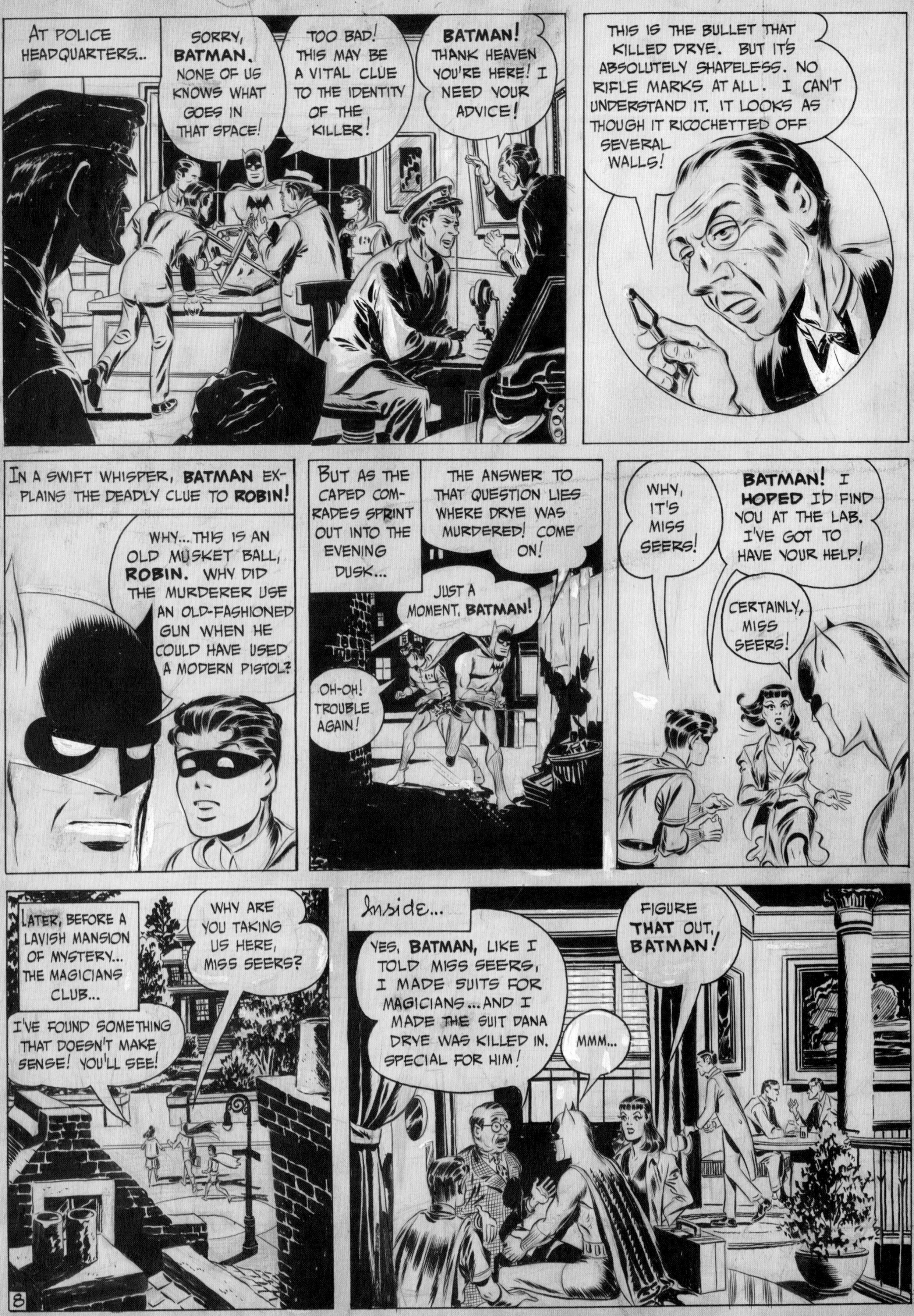

Batman #14
AT POLICE HEADQUARTERS...
SORRY, BATMAN. NONE OF US KNOWS WHAT GOES IN THAT SPACE!
TOO BAD! THIS MAY BE A VITAL CLUE TO THE IDENTITY OF THE KILLER!
BATMAN! THANK HEAVEN YOU'RE HERE! I NEED YOUR ADVICE!
THIS IS THE BULLET THAT KILLED DRYE. BUT IT'S ABSOLUTELY SHAPELESS. NO RIFLE MARKS AT ALL. I CAN'T UNDERSTAND IT. IT LOOKS AS THOUGH IT RICOCHETTED OFF SEVERAL WALLS!
IN A SWIFT WHISPER, BATMAN EXPLAINS THE DEADLY CLUE TO ROBIN!
WHY... THIS IS AN OLD MUSKET BALL, ROBIN. WHY DID THE MURDERER USE AN OLD-FASHIONED GUN WHEN HE COULD HAVE USED A MODERN PISTOL?
BUT AS THE CAPED COMRADES SPRINT OUT INTO THE EVENING DUSK...
THE ANSWER TO THAT QUESTION LIES WHERE DRYE WAS MURDERED! COME ON!
JUST A MOMENT, BATMAN!
OH-OH! TROUBLE AGAIN!
WHY, IT'S MISS SEERS!
BATMAN! I HOPED I'D FIND YOU AT THE LAB. I'VE GOT TO HAVE YOUR HELP!
CERTAINLY, MISS SEERS!
LATER, BEFORE A LAVISH MANSION OF MYSTERY... THE MAGICIANS CLUB...
WHY ARE YOU TAKING US HERE, MISS SEERS?
I'VE FOUND SOMETHING THAT DOESN'T MAKE SENSE! YOU'LL SEE!
Inside...
YES, BATMAN, LIKE I TOLD MISS SEERS, I MADE SUITS FOR MAGICIANS... AND I MADE THE SUIT DANA DRYE WAS KILLED IN. SPECIAL FOR HIM!
FIGURE THAT OUT, BATMAN!
MMM...
8
Magicians The

Panel 1: AND AS THE **BATMAN** PONDERS THE ENIGMA, AN UNEXPLAINED ATTACK ARRIVES FROM NOWHERE!

WHY IN THE WORLD DID DRYE HAVE A MAGICIAN'S SUIT MADE?

SORRY TO INTERRUPT, **BATMAN**, BUT COMPANY'S COMING!

THERE THEY ARE, GUYS!

Panel 2: O.K., BOYS... THERE AIN'T GOIN' TO BE ANY ROUGH STUFF... THE **BATMAN** KNOWS IT DON'T PAY TO TANGLE WITH US!

YEAH ...YOU OUGHT TO WISE UP, TOO, KID... YA MIGHT GET HURT!

HOW ABOUT IT, **BATMAN**? IS IT THE REAL MCCOY THIS TIME, CAN WE LET THEM HAVE IT?

YOU'RE RIGHT, GENTLEMEN. WE DON'T WANT TO GET HURT!

LET THEM HAVE IT, **ROBIN**!

Panel 3: AND THIS IS TO MAKE SURE WE DON'T GET HURT!

?

RIGHT! JUST KEEP 'EM SOCKIN'!

Panel 4: AND NOW TO CHECK YOU OUT... IN THE CHECK ROOM!

Panel 5: YEEOW! I'M SEEIN' THINGS!

CHECK ROOM

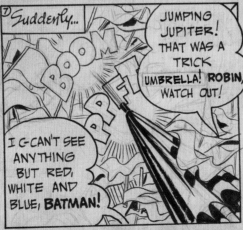

Panel 6: AN UMBRELLA IS GOOD PROTECTION FOR A RAIN OF LEAD!

Panel 7: *Suddenly...*

BOOM

I C-CAN'T SEE ANYTHING BUT RED, WHITE AND BLUE, **BATMAN**!

JUMPING JUPITER! THAT WAS A TRICK UMBRELLA! ROBIN, WATCH OUT!

Panel 8: NOW'S OUR CHANCE! QUICK... WHEN THEY'RE NOT LOOKING!

WE'LL TAKE 'EM BACK TO RIP'S OFFICE!

I'LL GET THAT SUITCASE!

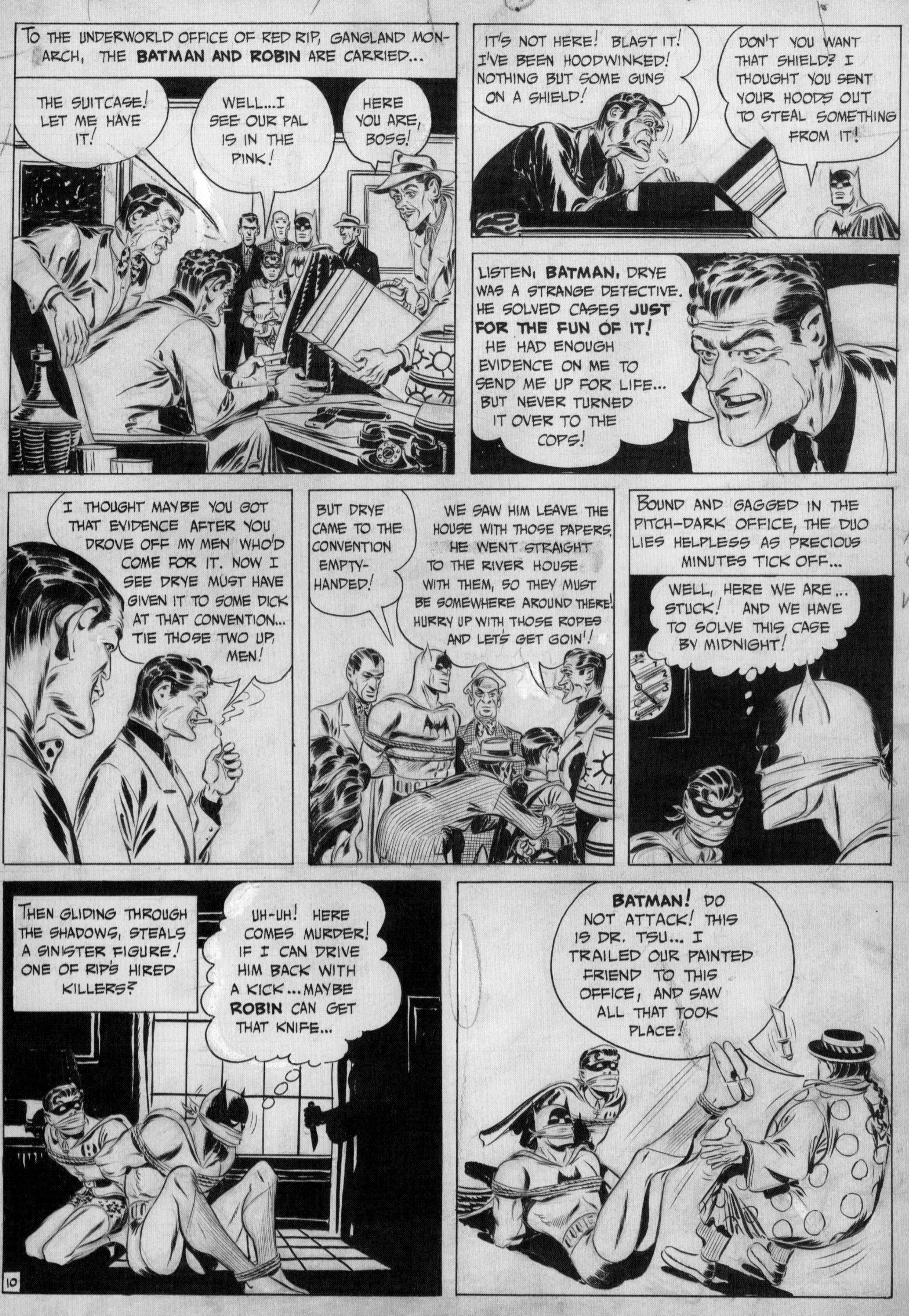

TO THE UNDERWORLD OFFICE OF RED RIP, GANGLAND MONARCH, THE BATMAN AND ROBIN ARE CARRIED...
THE SUITCASE! LET ME HAVE IT!
WELL...I SEE OUR PAL IS IN THE PINK!
HERE YOU ARE, BOSS!
IT'S NOT HERE! BLAST IT! I'VE BEEN HOODWINKED! NOTHING BUT SOME GUNS ON A SHIELD!
DON'T YOU WANT THAT SHIELD? I THOUGHT YOU SENT YOUR HOODS OUT TO STEAL SOMETHING FROM IT!
LISTEN, BATMAN, DRYE WAS A STRANGE DETECTIVE. HE SOLVED CASES JUST FOR THE FUN OF IT! HE HAD ENOUGH EVIDENCE ON ME TO SEND ME UP FOR LIFE... BUT NEVER TURNED IT OVER TO THE COPS!
I THOUGHT MAYBE YOU GOT THAT EVIDENCE AFTER YOU DROVE OFF MY MEN WHO'D COME FOR IT. NOW I SEE DRYE MUST HAVE GIVEN IT TO SOME DICK AT THAT CONVENTION... TIE THOSE TWO UP, MEN!
BUT DRYE CAME TO THE CONVENTION EMPTY-HANDED!
WE SAW HIM LEAVE THE HOUSE WITH THOSE PAPERS. HE WENT STRAIGHT TO THE RIVER HOUSE WITH THEM, SO THEY MUST BE SOMEWHERE AROUND THERE! HURRY UP WITH THOSE ROPES AND LET'S GET GOIN'!
BOUND AND GAGGED IN THE PITCH-DARK OFFICE, THE DUO LIES HELPLESS AS PRECIOUS MINUTES TICK OFF...
WELL, HERE WE ARE... STUCK! AND WE HAVE TO SOLVE THIS CASE BY MIDNIGHT!
THEN GLIDING THROUGH THE SHADOWS, STEALS A SINISTER FIGURE! ONE OF RIP'S HIRED KILLERS?
UH-UH! HERE COMES MURDER! IF I CAN DRIVE HIM BACK WITH A KICK...MAYBE ROBIN CAN GET THAT KNIFE...
BATMAN! DO NOT ATTACK! THIS IS DR. TSU... I TRAILED OUR PAINTED FRIEND TO THIS OFFICE, AND SAW ALL THAT TOOK PLACE!
10

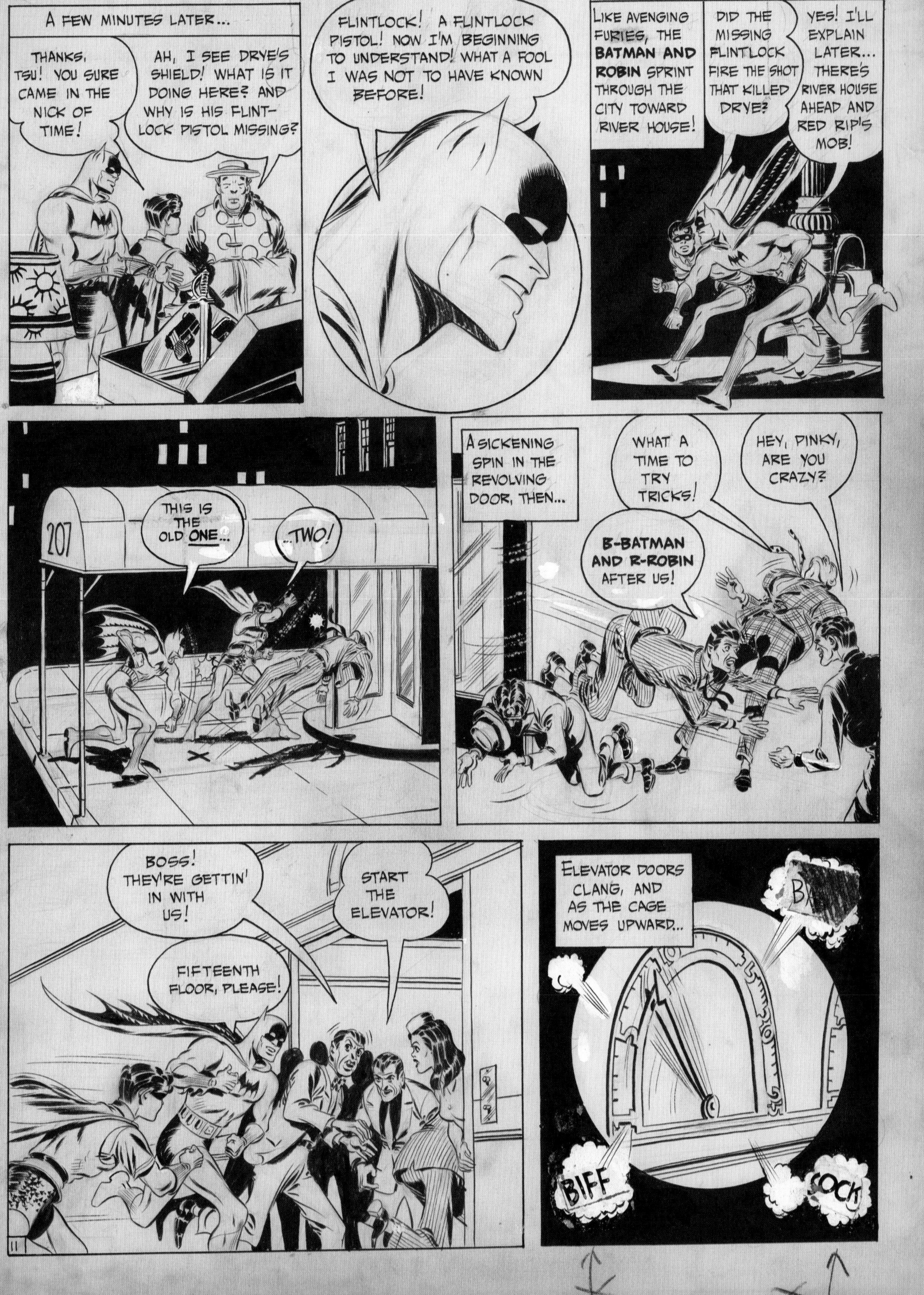
A FEW MINUTES LATER...
THANKS, TSU! YOU SURE CAME IN THE NICK OF TIME!
AH, I SEE DRYE'S SHIELD! WHAT IS IT DOING HERE? AND WHY IS HIS FLINT-LOCK PISTOL MISSING?
FLINTLOCK! A FLINTLOCK PISTOL! NOW I'M BEGINNING TO UNDERSTAND! WHAT A FOOL I WAS NOT TO HAVE KNOWN BEFORE!
LIKE AVENGING FURIES, THE BATMAN AND ROBIN SPRINT THROUGH THE CITY TOWARD RIVER HOUSE!
DID THE MISSING FLINTLOCK FIRE THE SHOT THAT KILLED DRYE?
YES! I'LL EXPLAIN LATER... THERE'S RIVER HOUSE AHEAD AND RED RIP'S MOB!
207
THIS IS THE OLD ONE...
...TWO!
A SICKENING SPIN IN THE REVOLVING DOOR, THEN...
WHAT A TIME TO TRY TRICKS!
HEY, PINKY, ARE YOU CRAZY?
B-BATMAN AND R-ROBIN AFTER US!
BOSS! THEY'RE GETTIN' IN WITH US!
START THE ELEVATOR!
FIFTEENTH FLOOR, PLEASE!
11
ELEVATOR DOORS CLANG, AND AS THE CAGE MOVES UPWARD...
BIFF

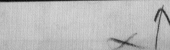

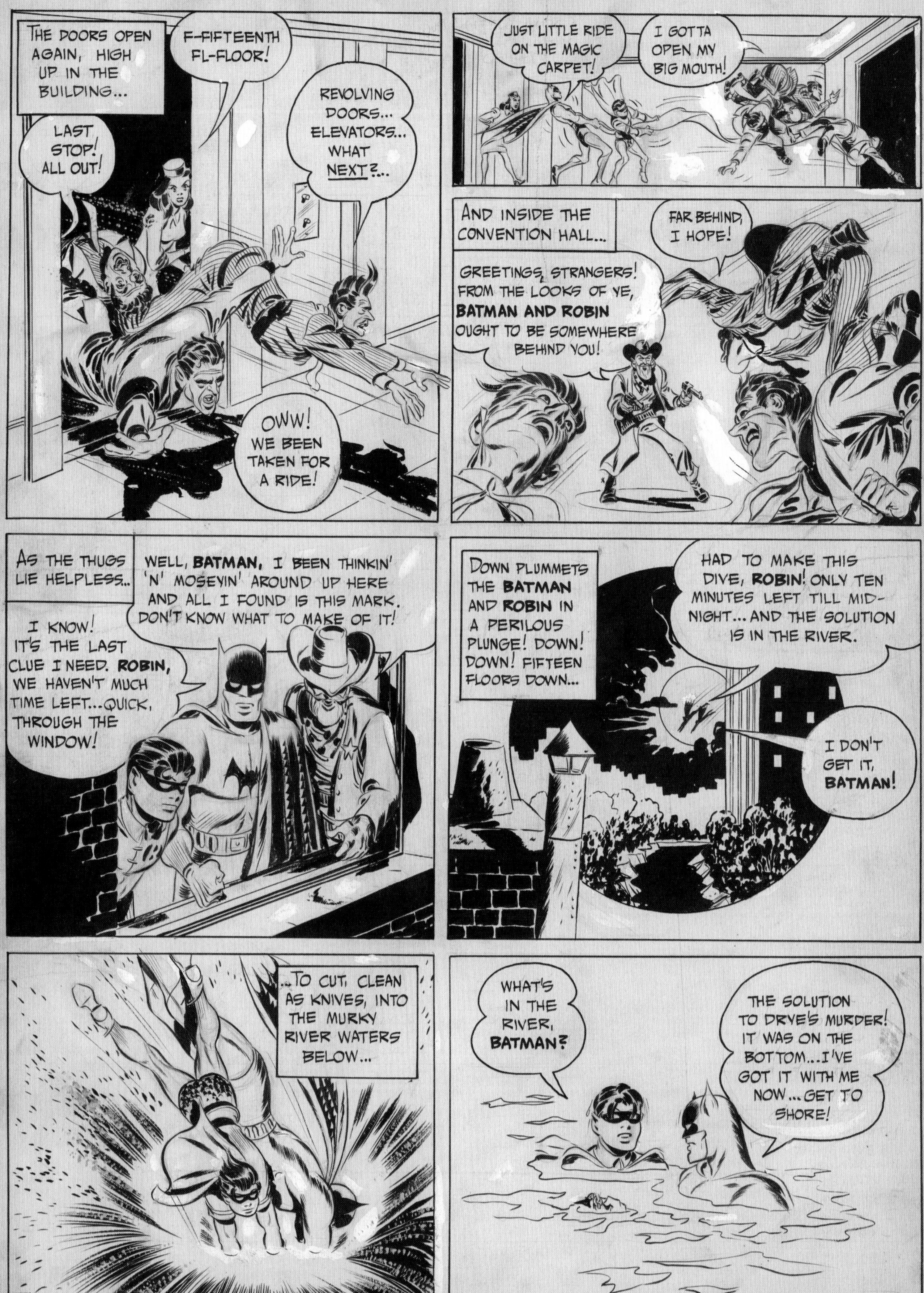

THE DOORS OPEN AGAIN, HIGH UP IN THE BUILDING...
F-FIFTEENTH FL-FLOOR!
LAST STOP! ALL OUT!
REVOLVING DOORS... ELEVATORS... WHAT NEXT?...
OWW! WE BEEN TAKEN FOR A RIDE!
JUST LITTLE RIDE ON THE MAGIC CARPET!
I GOTTA OPEN MY BIG MOUTH!
AND INSIDE THE CONVENTION HALL...
FAR BEHIND, I HOPE!
GREETINGS, STRANGERS! FROM THE LOOKS OF YE, BATMAN AND ROBIN OUGHT TO BE SOMEWHERE BEHIND YOU!
AS THE THUGS LIE HELPLESS...
WELL, BATMAN, I BEEN THINKIN' 'N' MOSEYIN' AROUND UP HERE AND ALL I FOUND IS THIS MARK. DON'T KNOW WHAT TO MAKE OF IT!
I KNOW! IT'S THE LAST CLUE I NEED. ROBIN, WE HAVEN'T MUCH TIME LEFT...QUICK, THROUGH THE WINDOW!
DOWN PLUMMETS THE BATMAN AND ROBIN IN A PERILOUS PLUNGE! DOWN! DOWN! FIFTEEN FLOORS DOWN...
HAD TO MAKE THIS DIVE, ROBIN! ONLY TEN MINUTES LEFT TILL MIDNIGHT... AND THE SOLUTION IS IN THE RIVER.
I DON'T GET IT, BATMAN!
...TO CUT, CLEAN AS KNIVES, INTO THE MURKY RIVER WATERS BELOW...
12
WHAT'S IN THE RIVER, BATMAN?
THE SOLUTION TO DRYE'S MURDER! IT WAS ON THE BOTTOM...I'VE GOT IT WITH ME NOW... GET TO SHORE!

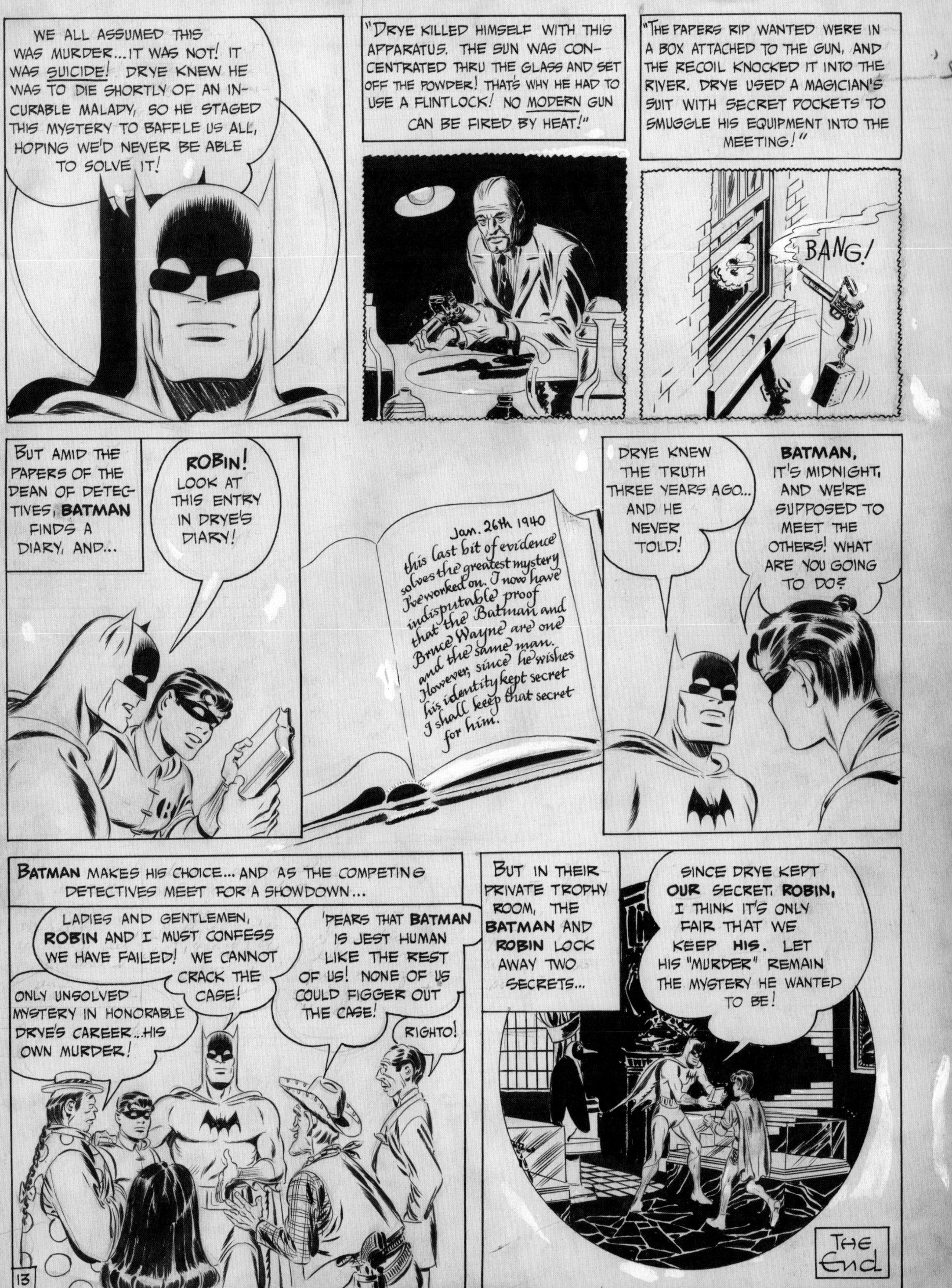

WE ALL ASSUMED THIS WAS MURDER... IT WAS NOT! IT WAS SUICIDE! DRYE KNEW HE WAS TO DIE SHORTLY OF AN INCURABLE MALADY, SO HE STAGED THIS MYSTERY TO BAFFLE US ALL, HOPING WE'D NEVER BE ABLE TO SOLVE IT!
"DRYE KILLED HIMSELF WITH THIS APPARATUS. THE SUN WAS CONCENTRATED THRU THE GLASS AND SET OFF THE POWDER! THAT'S WHY HE HAD TO USE A FLINTLOCK! NO MODERN GUN CAN BE FIRED BY HEAT!"
"THE PAPERS RIP WANTED WERE IN A BOX ATTACHED TO THE GUN, AND THE RECOIL KNOCKED IT INTO THE RIVER. DRYE USED A MAGICIAN'S SUIT WITH SECRET POCKETS TO SMUGGLE HIS EQUIPMENT INTO THE MEETING!"
BANG!
BUT AMID THE PAPERS OF THE DEAN OF DETECTIVES, BATMAN FINDS A DIARY, AND...
ROBIN! LOOK AT THIS ENTRY IN DRYE'S DIARY!
Jan. 26th 1940 this last bit of evidence solves the greatest mystery I've worked on. I now have indisputable proof that the Batman and Bruce Wayne are one and the same man. However, since he wishes his identity kept secret I shall keep that secret for him.
DRYE KNEW THE TRUTH THREE YEARS AGO... AND HE NEVER TOLD!
BATMAN, IT'S MIDNIGHT, AND WE'RE SUPPOSED TO MEET THE OTHERS! WHAT ARE YOU GOING TO DO?
BATMAN MAKES HIS CHOICE... AND AS THE COMPETING DETECTIVES MEET FOR A SHOWDOWN...
LADIES AND GENTLEMEN, ROBIN AND I MUST CONFESS WE HAVE FAILED! WE CANNOT CRACK THE CASE!
'PEARS THAT BATMAN IS JEST HUMAN LIKE THE REST OF US! NONE OF US COULD FIGGER OUT THE CASE!
ONLY UNSOLVED MYSTERY IN HONORABLE DRYE'S CAREER... HIS OWN MURDER!
RIGHTO!
BUT IN THEIR PRIVATE TROPHY ROOM, THE BATMAN AND ROBIN LOCK AWAY TWO SECRETS...
SINCE DRYE KEPT OUR SECRET, ROBIN, I THINK IT'S ONLY FAIR THAT WE KEEP HIS. LET HIS "MURDER" REMAIN THE MYSTERY HE WANTED TO BE!
THE End
13

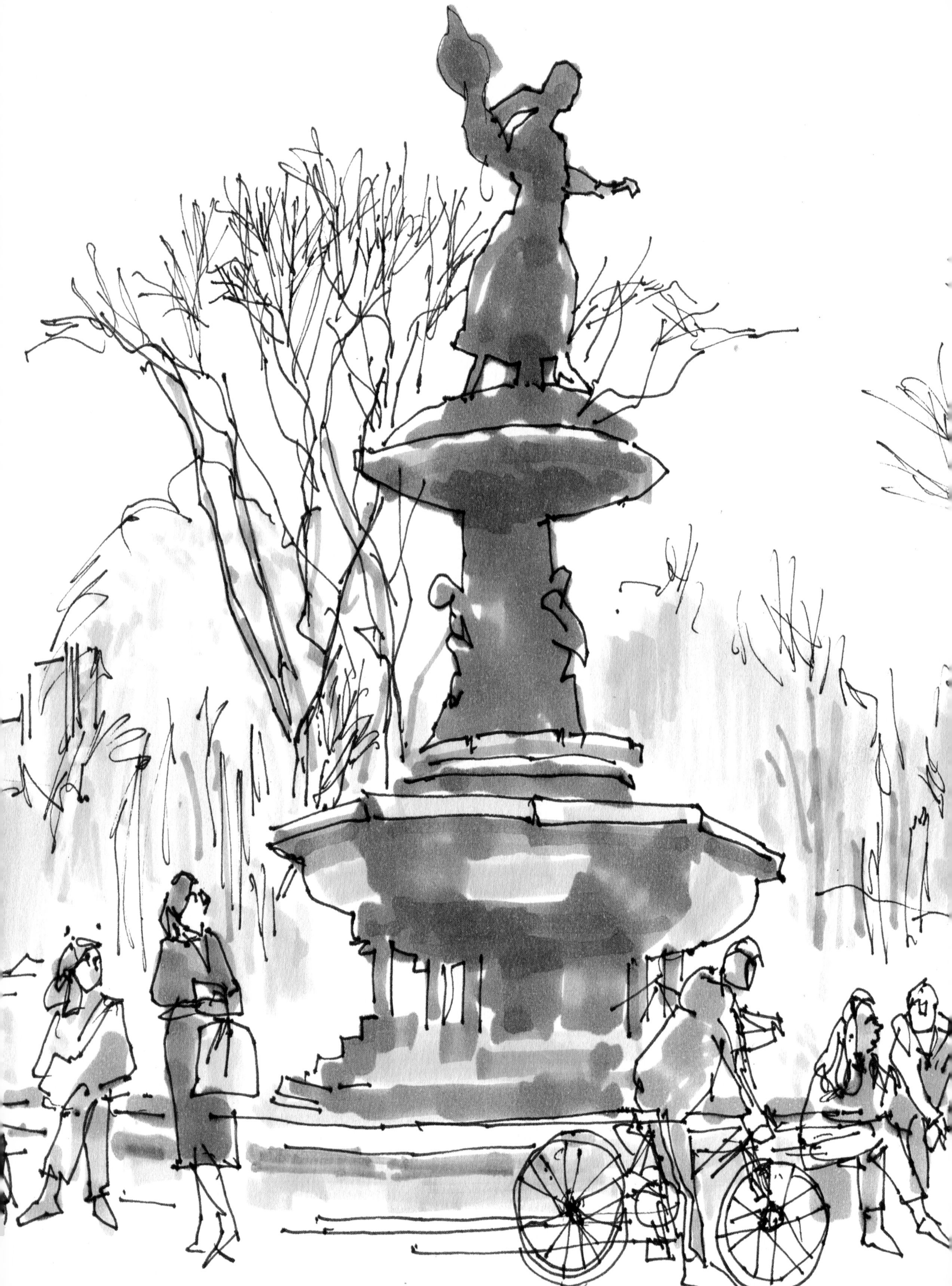

CHAPTER 4: OF WINE, BERBERS, GONDOLAS, AND FRAUD

We were thirty thousand feet over the Atlantic. It was my first flight to Europe, and it was to be the most memorable. Imagine five irrepressible cartoonists crowded into the cockpit joking with the pilot and copilot and taking turns at the controls. It was the mid-1950s, and you could do things like that. We were all members of the National Cartoonists Society, and our mission for the Department of Defense was to entertain American troops at bases scattered throughout Europe and northern Africa.

Left
STATUE ON FOUNTAIN SKETCH
Ink and gray marker by Jerry Robinson.

BERRY

Our group included Mike Berry, a world traveler, gourmet, and wine connoisseur whose stylish drawings, often of sexy women, appeared in *Esquire* and other slick magazines. After a briefing in Paris, we flew to Rome for the start of the tour. We checked in at our base, and within hours, Mike, with obvious delight, led me to a narrow street near the Spanish Steps. We made our way through the groups of students and tourists lining the walk. He guaranteed me the finest glass of wine in Italy—for ten cents! On such important forays as springing for a special ten-cent glass of wine, Mike was as splendidly groomed as one of the social elites he portrayed in his cartoons. He sported an English tweed jacket and gray slacks that complemented his slight but carefully tailored moustache.

He stopped suddenly before a nondescript doorway. There was no sign or other evidence of it being a bar. Drawing back a drab curtain, Mike ushered me into a small room with just a wooden stand and a kaleidoscope of all manner of bottles of wine and liquors lining the walls to the ceiling. Mike was warmly greeted by the proprietor, a plump woman with a radiant smile. Although he claimed not to have been there for years, Mike simply said, "And a glass for my friend." She selected a bottle and carefully poured two glasses. It was delicious.

"It's Frascati," he explained. "It came from the Rome hills. It's the only place in the world where you can truly appreciate its bouquet," Mike assured me. "It doesn't travel." I've since had Frascati elsewhere, and Mike was right: it never has been as good. And certainly not as cheap. For the rest of the trip, I dutifully followed Mike's advice as to where and what to eat and drink.

DiPRETA

Tony DiPreta, another in our intrepid group, had taken over the comic strip escapades of *Joe Palooka*, the hapless boxer created years before by Ham Fisher. Tony was a tough little guy who looked as if he could be a professional prizefighter himself, but he was in fact gentle and retiring in nature.

Our tour took us to the port city of Rabat, the Moroccan capital. We landed at Rabat Salé Air Base, a former French airfield taken over by the United States during World War II for the Seventeenth Air Force, which oversaw the Strategic Air Command (SAC). With the withdrawal of the USAF in the 1960s, the facility became an air base for the Royal Moroccan Air Force. Strategically, in that region it's more important to know who controls the airport than who controls the palace.

Some of my most enjoyable times on Defense Department tours—throughout Europe and northern Africa twice and Japan and Korea once—were when I had some time off to wander on my own with my Canon and my Rollei. Morocco was a photographer's dream: clear, azure skies (at least they were in the 1950s), pure white or pastel walls gleaming in the sun, and the fascinating Arab and Jewish medinas sitting almost side by side. Most Moroccan cities have preserved their medinas, a part of the original walled medieval cities.

I headed for the medinas whenever I could in Rabat, Casablanca (Morocco's largest city), and Marrakesh. I was in my element—the narrow, winding streets teeming with life and lined with tiny shops filled with goods, the merchants and artisans in front, weaving, sewing, making shoes and belts, hammering metal plates, cooking, or engaged in a myriad of other activities. There were small, handsomely tiled mosques. I photographed elderly Jewish men sitting on a cobbled street next to an ancient synagogue wall. The narrow streets and alleyways prevented the use of automobiles, making the medina an oasis of car-free living. Pack mules and donkeys, carts, bicycles, and mopeds took their place. Rooftops of stone buildings were used for washing and drying clothes and outdoor eating. They also made excellent vantage points to photograph the colorful street life below. The most exciting display I've ever seen was on a street where folks dyed wool in long strands to be woven into cloth. With the sun shining through colors from canary yellow and emerald green to scarlet red and cobalt blue, it was a dazzling sight when the wool was strung out to dry.

Our escort officer warned us of the Berbers, the fiercest of the country's many tribes, who were camped just outside the city for their traditional visit during the holy days. They were reputed to have handsome horses and elaborately adorned tents. Tony and I were determined to see them, but there was a catch. Morocco was in the process of eliminating the remnants of French rule, and one of their methods was to separate the skin from any Frenchmen they could put a blade to. One such operation had been reported only a few days earlier in the city of Fez. Understandably, we were a bit nervous and quickly identified ourselves as American, not French, if anyone even looked in our direction.

Not to be deterred, Tony and I decided to hire a taxi to drive us to the Berber camp. This proved to be no easy task. Neither one of us spoke Arabic or, heaven forbid, French. We found a driver who finally understood where we wanted to go when Tony drew his hand across his throat, gurgling, "You know, *Berbers!*" The driver turned somewhat green. Only for photographs, I assured him, indicating the long-distance lens on my Canon. Finally, US currency won him over; he waved us in, and we took off.

We soon saw the gleaming gold balls at the tops of dozens of Berber tents half a mile away, in the middle of a desolate field. The driver refused to go any closer. We persuaded him to take a road that would bring us to the other side of the field, a bit closer to the camp.

To our horror, the road narrowed and, before we realized what was happening, it led us directly into the camp. Horsemen swung around with fierce looks, their hands on ominous ornamented swords. My journalistic instincts took over. I gingerly clicked off a few frames by aiming the lens just above the level of the window while staring straight ahead. As you might imagine, we were petrified. Fortunately, so was the driver. He kept his foot frozen to the gas pedal, and we sailed through the encampment without pause until we reached the far road on the other side of the field.

Tony and I, shaken but with our skins intact, met our less adventurous colleagues when we returned. "Oh, we were just visiting the Berbers—they're really quite friendly!" Before they had a chance to give voice to the doubts evident in their incredulous looks, we disappeared through the lobby and into our rooms.

One afternoon I decided to take photos around the palace, which loomed in the center of a vast, unadorned field. There were a few groups of what appeared to be visiting tribesmen seated on the ground. Mindful of our briefing about the Berbers, I gave them a wide berth, just in case they were of the same tribe. No one challenged me as I went for a close-up of the palace's elaborate gate and the handsomely outfitted guard. I'd taken just a shot or two when the gate suddenly opened and several of the king's horse guards trotted out, followed by Mohammad V in an ornate carriage suitable for the new king (Morocco had become independent only the year before). I learned later that it was the king's custom each day during Ramadan to go to a special mosque for prayer. I should note for historical purposes that the future King Hassan II, then twenty-eight, followed his father's carriage on a splendid white horse. As the carriage passed by, the direct descendant of *the* Mohammad stared at what was obviously an impertinent American running alongside taking his picture.

> **HORSEMEN SWUNG AROUND, WITH FIERCE LOOKS AND THEIR HANDS ON OMINOUS ORNAMENTED SWORDS.**

After several performances in and near Rabat, we took our show on the road. We performed at military bases along the coast to Tiznit from Casablanca (where I visited the site of the historic World War II meeting of FDR, Churchill, and de Gaulle). We then flew to Marrakesh for what was to be the last stop before our tour in Spain. Our escort officer announced that an additional show would be added to our schedule—at an advanced radar site in the desert near the Algerian border. The base's mission was to protect our Atlantic naval fleet. The only catch was that to get there we had to fly over the treacherous Atlas Mountains. Looming fourteen thousand feet high, they separate the Sahara from the Atlantic and Mediterranean coastlines.

As if this were not daunting enough, the mountains were also the stronghold of the Berbers. A flight to the desert base had to be on a small six-passenger propeller plane that could land on an unpaved runway with limited equipment (no wonder the base got little live entertainment). We qualified because we were a group of only six, and all we needed for the show was six easels, a roll of paper, and chalk.

In a case of saving the worst news for last, we were warned that if the plane went down in the mountains for any reason, there was little chance we would be found by anyone but the Berbers.

The next day, with some trepidation—no, with great trepidation—the volunteers crowded into what looked like an antique and entirely inadequate airplane last flown by Wiley Post to Alaska with Will Rogers. That impression was quickly disproved when we took off. It was a bright, sunny day, and the view from the tiny plane was spectacular. But we did sigh in relief when the last mountain peak was behind us, and only the vast Sahara stretched ahead. Finally, a few small buildings appeared on the horizon. We soon landed and were greeted profusely by the commanding officer. After we had lunch with his staff, he proudly gave us a briefing on the base. Isolated in the middle of the desert, it was basically self-sufficient. More than ninety men manned the base on tours lasting six months to a year. There were cooks, a barber, a doctor, two nurses, a pharmacist, and technicians—all to support the six men who manned the radar in eight-hour shifts around the clock.

> **WE DID SIGH IN RELIEF, HOWEVER, WHEN THE LAST MOUNTAIN PEAK WAS BEHIND US AND ONLY THE VAST SAHARA STRETCHED AHEAD.**

We had a few hours before the show was to start at eight o'clock that evening. Two jeeps pulled up to show us around the site. I couldn't imagine what could be of interest—I saw nothing but sand and an occasional dune in all directions—but I was in for a surprise. We took off and before long came across a family of nomadic Bedouins with a couple of scrawny camels. They had apparently stopped for a rest during their trek across the Sahara and had shielded themselves from the sun with a small tent. As none of our sheltered group had ever seen a genuine Bedouin before—or a real camel, scrawny or otherwise, outside of a zoo—we were excited about even this small glimpse of real desert life. But our escorts had another sight for us a few miles on. Before we knew it, the jeeps came to a stop before a huge, yawning crater, perhaps a hundred yards across and twenty-five feet at its deepest. Although it was in the center of a patch of dirt where there was little sand, it was surprising that sand hadn't filled it up over the years. Or was it the result of a recent meteorite? Or perhaps a violent sandstorm had uncovered the crater? No one knew how long it had been there.

That night, the small theater was packed. Eighty-eight men were in the audience—everyone on base except those who were manning the radar. It was great. They were starved for entertainment. I don't think the base had been visited in over a year. They howled at every gag, good or bad. They loved the skits—the more outrageous the better. And of course our New York model added the needed sex appeal. Bill Holman, our intrepid leader, was in rare form. It was one of the funniest shows we ever did on the tour. We ad-libbed more than usual. Swept up in the euphoria of the occasion, we felt liberated from all restraints. The show, usually two hours long, ran for three and a half.

The head honcho was so appreciative that he threw a party for us afterward. Sometime after two in the morning, when everyone was pretty well soused, he casually remarked, "I feel sorry for those poor slobs on radar," referring to the six on duty who'd missed the show. Holman quickly volunteered to do the entire show for those six men when they got off duty, even though we were due to take off at seven in the morning.

"They don't come off duty till four," said one officer.

"No problem," said Bill. "We'll just party till then."

published in the *Sunday News* in New York, as was *Smokey Stover*. In addition to competing for readers, they both sought the hand of the lovely Dolores, who lived in apartment 1506. When Holman inserted "1506 nix nix," it was a warning to his friend Al to stay away from Dolores.

Holman won that fight. He and Dolores got married and lived happily ever after.

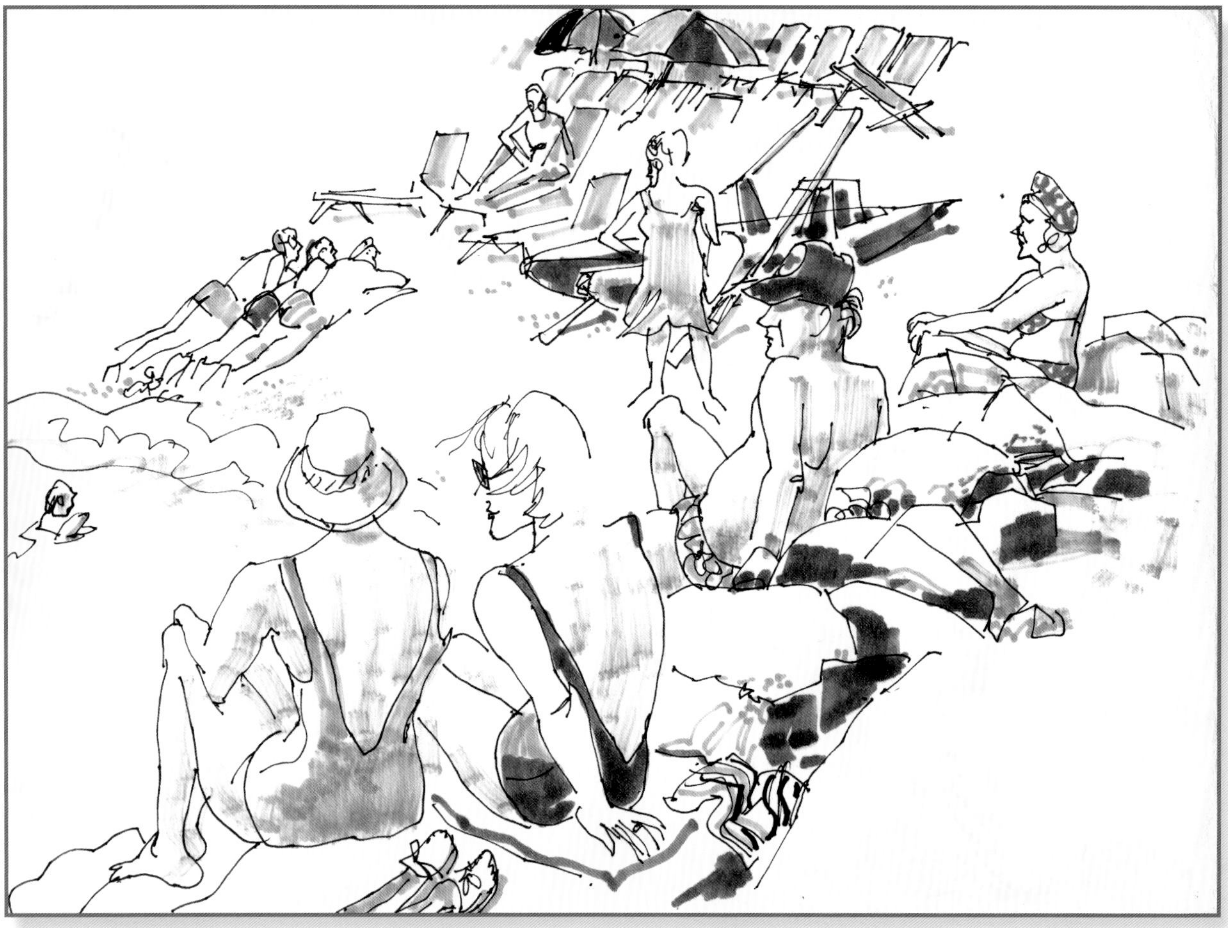

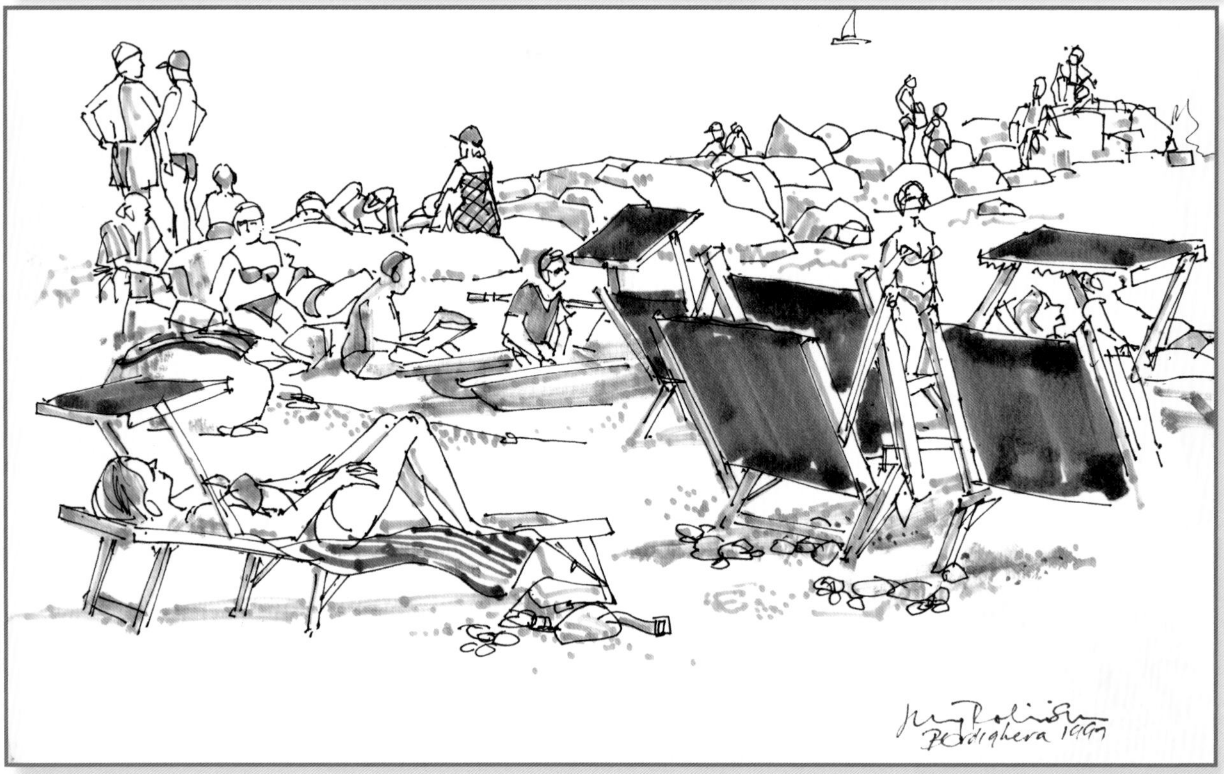
Bordighera 1997

Top
BEACH SKETCH
Bordighera, Italy, 1997, ink and gray marker by Jerry Robinson.

Bottom
BEACH SKETCH
Bordighera, Italy, 1997, ink and gray marker by Jerry Robinson.

CHAPTER 6:
THEATRE LIFE: BACKSTAGE WITH PLAYBILL

In the late 1970s and early '80s, I had a really great gig: covering Broadway for *Playbill*, the venerable theater program magazine. First published in 1884 for a single New York theater, *Playbill* is now distributed at all Broadway and off-Broadway productions. In recent years it has expanded to produce the programs for such classic arts venues as the Metropolitan Opera and Carnegie Hall, as well as for theaters in major cities throughout the country. Though its circulation was down from a high of about four million per month, it still reached a wide audience. I was excited to have the rare opportunity to meet major performers and sketch the fascinating backstage life.

Left
PLAYBILL MAGAZINE ILLUSTRATION, ANN MILLER, *SUGAR BABIES*
1980, pencils and inks
by Jerry Robinson.

Playbill arranged for Gro and me to have sixth-row center-orchestra seats for new Broadway productions. In the days following seeing the show I would sketch the principal actors backstage. Each issue of *Playbill* featured *Theatre Life with Robinson*, a page of my impressions of the show. The name was inspired by *Life with Robinson*, the syndicated daily cartoon of political and social satire that I did for about forty years.

One of the first shows I covered was *Sugar Babies* with Mickey Rooney and Ann Miller—stars of stage, screen, and TV. Mickey was a born performer. His vaudevillian parents wrote him into their routine at the advanced age of seventeen months, dressed in a tailored tuxedo. In his eighty-year career, he garnered the actor's trifecta: an honorary Academy Award, an Emmy, and two Golden Globes. He is perhaps best known for his role as Andy Hardy. Judy Garland played the love interest in several of the Hardy movies, and they costarred as a song-and-dance team in the Oscar-nominated *Babes in Arms* (1939) and other hit musicals. Mickey was Hollywood's biggest box-office draw in 1939, 1940, and 1941.

Sketching Mickey in his dressing room was a feat in itself, as he didn't hold still for a minute. There were endless phone calls, chorus girls drifting in and out, agents, PR reps, visitors, friends, fans, and entrepreneurs pitching Mickey one elaborate scheme after another. The first day I was with him, he got a call from someone with the idea of a chain of Mickey Rooney restaurants. I heard Mickey tell the caller, "I have absolutely the best designer . . . My good friend, Jerry Robinson! He'll design a fabulous neon sign, the logo, and the menu." This was after I'd met with Mickey that day for only a short time, and he had no knowledge of what I did, other than my *Theatre Life* drawings for *Playbill*.

While still on the phone, he turned to me. "Quick, what's on the menu at the Mickey Rooney restaurant?" After a couple of minutes I came up with a few suggestions. The only dish I can recall now was Mickey Rooney Special Short Ribs. "Fantastic! I told you he was a genius! *Mickey Rooney Special Short Ribs!*" Excited by the menu, I designed the restaurant's logo and neon sign in full color. When I brought them in, he said, "That's great, kid, but the project is on hold." The Mickey Rooney restaurant chain never materialized.

One call to Mickey was interrupted by another—from his agent, bookie, manager, and a myriad of others. Getting Mickey to pose for a drawing for more than twenty seconds was impossible. In desperation, I took a three-cornered hat that he wore in one of the skits and placed it on his head. "Great, Mickey, that looks great!" That did it! As if he was onstage with the spotlight on him, he struck a typical Rooney pose and grin. "Just hold that!" I pleaded. For the first time he was still for about two minutes, long enough for me to do a quick sketch that I was able to finish at my studio. I returned the next day, and Mickey was very pleased with the drawing.

> **THE CHILD ACTOR, JOE YULE JR., NEE MICKEY MCGUIRE, WAS FORCED TO CHANGE HIS NAME AGAIN, THIS TIME TO MICKEY ROONEY."**

I also brought him a copy of my book *The Comics*. I read him a section from the chapter "The Golden Age: 1910–1919" about Fontaine Fox's *Toonerville Trolley*, a popular newspaper feature that perhaps only a few Rooney aficionados would be familiar with. The comic strip first was syndicated in 1913, only nine years before I was born, so it reflected some of my own childhood. The strip centered around a swaying, rattletrap trolley conducted by a wistful old codger with an Airedale beard. The skipper knew every passenger by name and enlivened the ride with local chitchat. We still had trolley cars in Trenton when I grew up, but I can't say the conductor knew every passenger's name.

Fox's inspiration for the strip came while on a visit to a cartoonist colleague, Charles Voight, creator of the strip *Betty*, in Pelham, New York. When Fox asked for directions, the conductor stopped the trolley and climbed to the top of a knoll to point out the Voight home. Among the droll passengers Fox created were Powerful Katrinka, the Terrible Tempered Mr. Bang, Aunt Eppie Hogg, the traveling salesman Suitcase Simpson, and the kid gang of Little Scorpions led by Mickey "Himself" McGuire. The idiosyncratic feature ran until 1955, when, after forty-two years of service, the Toonerville Trolley, with its stovepipe mast, took its last run when Fox retired.

I read Mickey the following excerpt from my book:

> *Fox was scrupulous in keeping their behavior [the cast of* Toonerville Trolley*] in character. "I own their bodies, but I do not own their souls," he once wrote. Derby-wearing Mickey McGuire became so identified as the impish tough guy that the young child actor Joe Yule, Jr. [who played the role in the popular film shorts] took the character's name. Fox had to go to court to establish his copyright to the character. Yule then became Mickey Rooney.*

Mickey was so delighted with my knowledge of his early career that he began referring to me as his "very dear friend."

I was also in for a fascinating time with Mickey's costar, Ann Miller (whose performance in *Sugar Babies* earned her a Tony nomination). Ann was sometimes billed as the world's fastest tap dancer; her publicist claimed she could tap five hundred times per minute. Ann, then well into her fifties and sporting her distinctive black bouffant hairstyle, graciously posed for me in her dressing room. She was seated in an easy chair in a revealing costume that displayed her justifiably famous legs to the best advantage. I liked to do some prior research on a star's career to keep the conversation going, if need be, while I drew. I had learned her father was a noted criminal defense attorney whose clients included the notorious Barrow Gang, Machine Gun Kelly, and Baby Face Nelson. And her maternal grandmother was Cherokee. She had major roles in the MGM hit musicals *Kiss Me Kate*, *Easter Parade*, and *On the Town*. There's no better way to focus a performer's attention than to talk about his or her career. So I made sure I knew most of Ann's major film credits.

I immediately noticed in her dressing room an abundance of lions. Stuffed lions, photographs of lions, paintings of lions—I fully expected a live one to come out of the closet, and in a way one did. "You must love lions," I said to Ann.

"I do," she quickly replied. "A lion once saved my life!" I assumed she must have appeared in a film with one. "Oh, no, it was when I was Queen Hatshepsut in ancient Egypt. A lion saved me from being eaten by a wild beast!" she explained in her high-pitched, almost innocent, sweet voice.

I had a reply on the tip of my tongue to the effect that her experience was nothing compared to the time I was nearly crucified by the Romans next to Jesus but was rescued by a giraffe. Luckily I didn't say this before Ann went on to describe her other lives. Her multiple reincarnations ranged from the time of the Vikings to the Spanish Inquisition.

Among the other performers I sketched were Tony Perkins and Mia Farrow, who were appearing in *Romantic Comedy*. I had met Tony, a serious, quiet man offstage, several times during summers on Cape Cod. He was best known for his role as Norman Bates in the classic thriller *Psycho*. But I was in for a surprise when I met Mia Farrow (real name Maria de Lourdes Villiers-Farrow—try putting that on a marquee), who had starred in *Rosemary's Baby* and *The Great Gatsby*.

Mia looked like a charming seventeen-year-old waif. One day, as I was sketching her curled up on a couch in her dressing room, she introduced me to her mother, who had arrived with Mia's latest adopted baby in her arms and several other youngsters trailing behind. (Mia was to have fifteen kids all told, eleven adopted.) I instantly recognized her mother, who was still beautiful, although it had probably been almost fifty years since I had first seen her in a film, scantily clad and perched in a jungle tree with Johnny Weissmuller in the classic *Tarzan the Ape Man*. Yes, it was Maureen O'Sullivan, my boyhood fantasy!

Oh! Calcutta! was billed as "The World's Longest Running Erotic Stage Musical" (I didn't know any other long-running erotic musicals). It was certainly the most revealing—complete nudity. The cast of nine attractive young men and women was the sole reason it survived—a show for voyeurs and tourists. It originally opened in June 1969, when baring it all had not been seen on Broadway or hardly anywhere else since the demise of burlesque.

The reviews, to put it mildly, were not enthusiastic. Clive Barnes in *The New York Times* wrote, "The humor is so doggedly sophomoric and soporific that from internal evidence alone I would go to court and testify that in my opinion such highly literate men could not have been responsible." Indeed, the individual skit credits were not listed. Two pieces on the program, however, did have genuine wit and were worthy of better direction. One was "Delicious Indignities," and the other was "Jack and Jill," which I later learned was written by Jules Feiffer as an exercise preliminary to his writing the screenplay for *Carnal Knowledge*.

As usual, covering *Oh! Calcutta!* meant sketching the cast in their dressing rooms. I was totally unprepared when I entered the one communal dressing room, where the entire cast, male and female, were at their individual makeup tables or preparing for the next performance, all as completely nude as they were onstage. Here I was drawing them, and I was the one who felt embarrassed!

They seemed to be oblivious to the fact I was the only clothed person. Before long it seemed perfectly natural to me as well.

The years with *Playbill* magazine were an unforgettable experience. Not only did my family and I see some terrific theater, but I also got to hang out with some of the great performers. Seeing the productions from the view of the producers, directors, actors, and even stagehands gave me an appreciation of the enormous talent, dedication, money, and effort that go into a Broadway show. A few that I covered were *Hamlet* with William Hurt, *Evita* with Patti LuPone and Mandy Patinkin, Duke Ellington's *Sophisticated Ladies* with Gregory Hines, *The Elephant Man* with David Bowie, Michael Bennett's *A Chorus Line*, Bob Fosse's *Dancin'*, and *Barnum* with Jim Dale (who really enjoyed performing). Among the actors I found to be personally impressive and masters of their craft were Kevin Kline, John Cullum, and Raul Julia.

My time with *Playbill* was my unique way of continuing a family tradition in the theater. Two of my mother's brothers, Harry and Arthur, were in vaudeville at the turn of the twentieth century. After some tours of the vaudeville circuit, their act stalled out, but Harry went on to a successful career as an emcee, an announcer on the WMCA radio station, and a noted after-dinner speaker and entertainer. He was a tall, handsome man with a melodious voice. I remember when I was about ten or eleven, the family crowded around the Emerson radio to hear Uncle Harry on some program. Despite our straining to hear, we could make out very little of it over the static, and when we did hear something, we would shout, "That's Uncle Harry! That's Uncle Harry!" When he visited us in Trenton, it was a grand occasion. He billed himself as a superb cook, which meant Uncle Harry delighted in his specialty: cooking the steak to perfection and majestically serving it while my mother (who was also excellent in the kitchen) prepared the rest of the dinner.

My aunt Virginia, Uncle Harry's wife, was an actress with the professional name Virginia Fairfax. She had appeared on Broadway as well as in films. When I first came to New York, my uncle had long since passed on, and I stayed with her for some months. As fate would have it, she lived on Crescent Avenue in the Bronx, only a few blocks from Bob Kane, with whom I was to begin working on *Batman*.

I loved to hear Virginia's reminiscences of her early days in the theater and movies. She had a role in *The Smiling Lieutenant*, starring Maurice Chevalier and Academy Award winner Claudette Colbert. One of Aunt Virginia's friends was another vaudevillian, Marie Dressler, a fine character actor and Academy Award winner for her role as Min in *Min and Bill* with Wallace Beery. I wish I had thought of finding a tape recorder to preserve her wonderful stories. But I was too absorbed at age seventeen and eighteen, juggling my studies at Columbia with my new career as a *Batman* artist and drinking in the New York life and culture in which I was suddenly immersed.

Above

MICKEY ROONEY, *SUGAR BABIES*

1980, pencils and inks by Jerry Robinson.

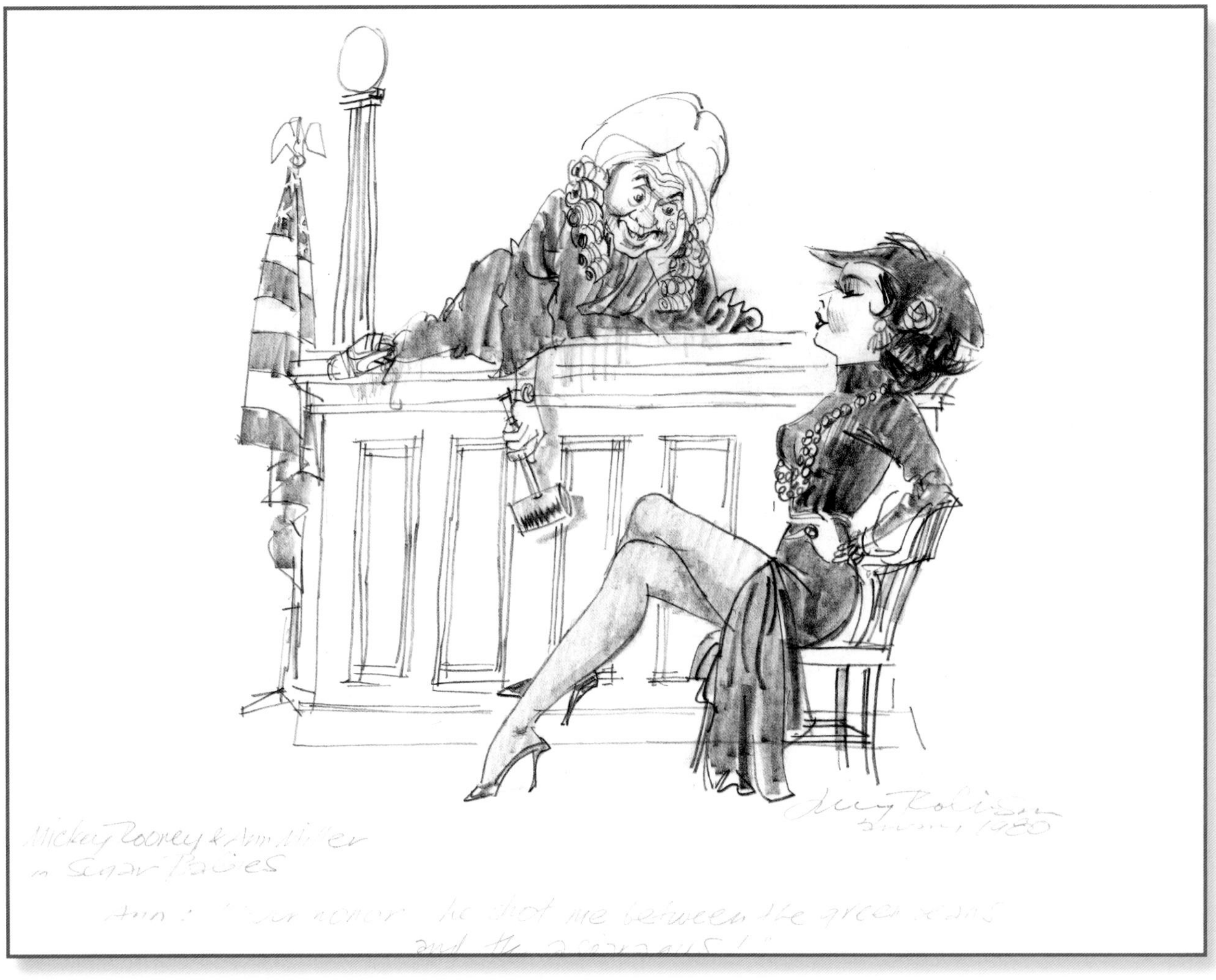
Mickey Rooney & Ann Miller
in Sugar Babies
Jerry Robinson

Above
MICKEY ROONEY AND ANN MILLER,
SUGAR BABIES
1980, pencils by Jerry Robinson.

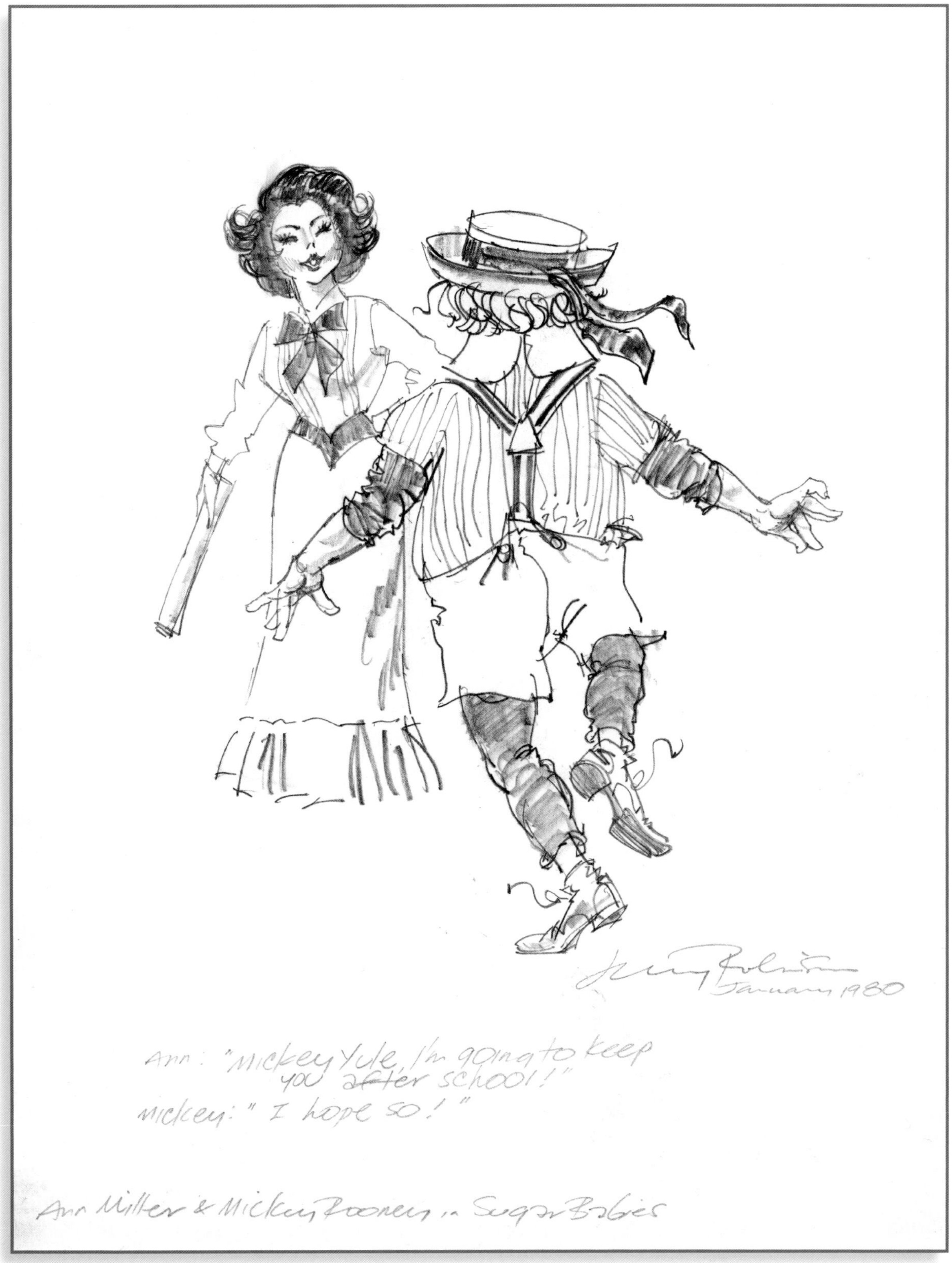
Jerry Robinson
January 1980
Ann: "Mickey Yule, I'm going to keep you after school!"
Mickey: " I hope so! "
Ann Miller & Mickey Rooney in Sugar Babies

Above
ANN MILLER AND MICKEY ROONEY,
SUGAR BABIES
1980, pencils by Jerry Robinson.

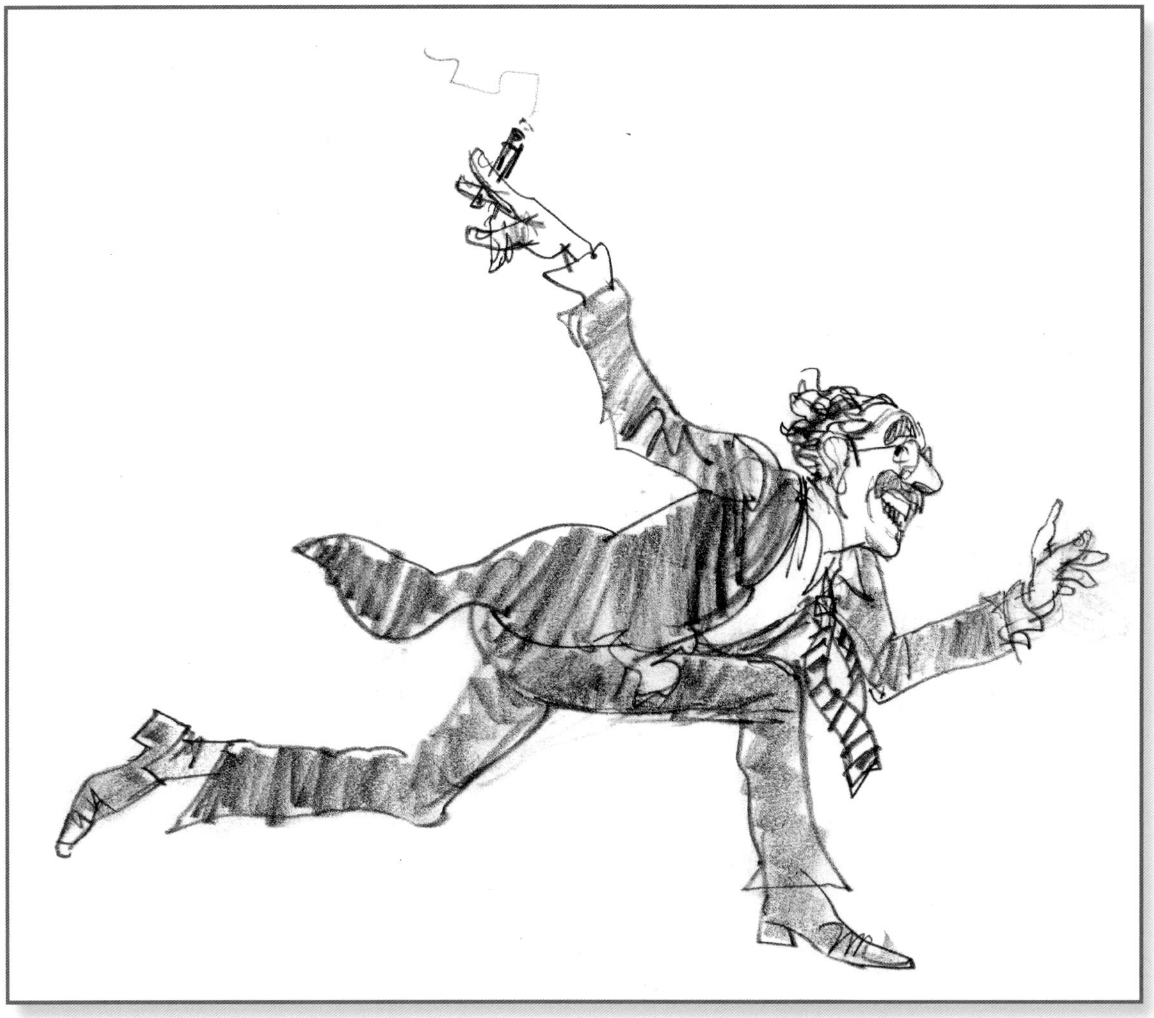

Above
GROUCHO MARX SKETCH
Pencils by Jerry Robinson.

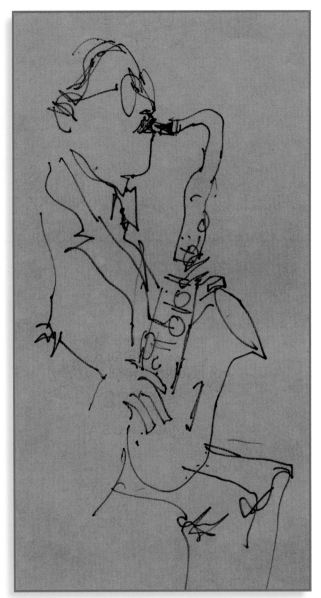

Above
ORCHESTRA MUSICIANS ON BROADWAY
Pencils and inks by Jerry Robinson.

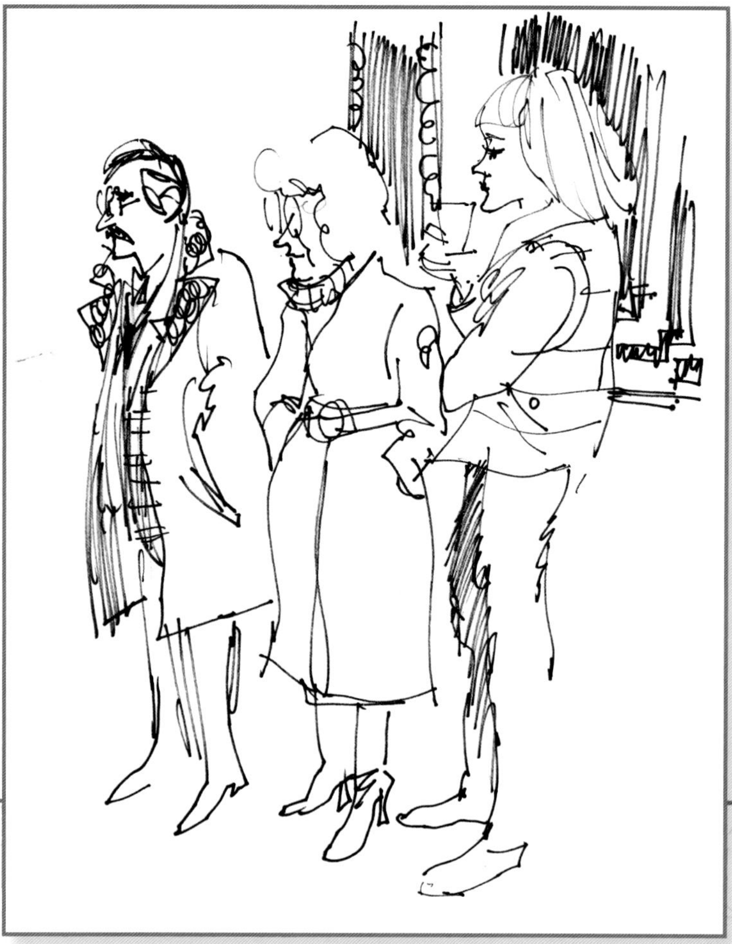

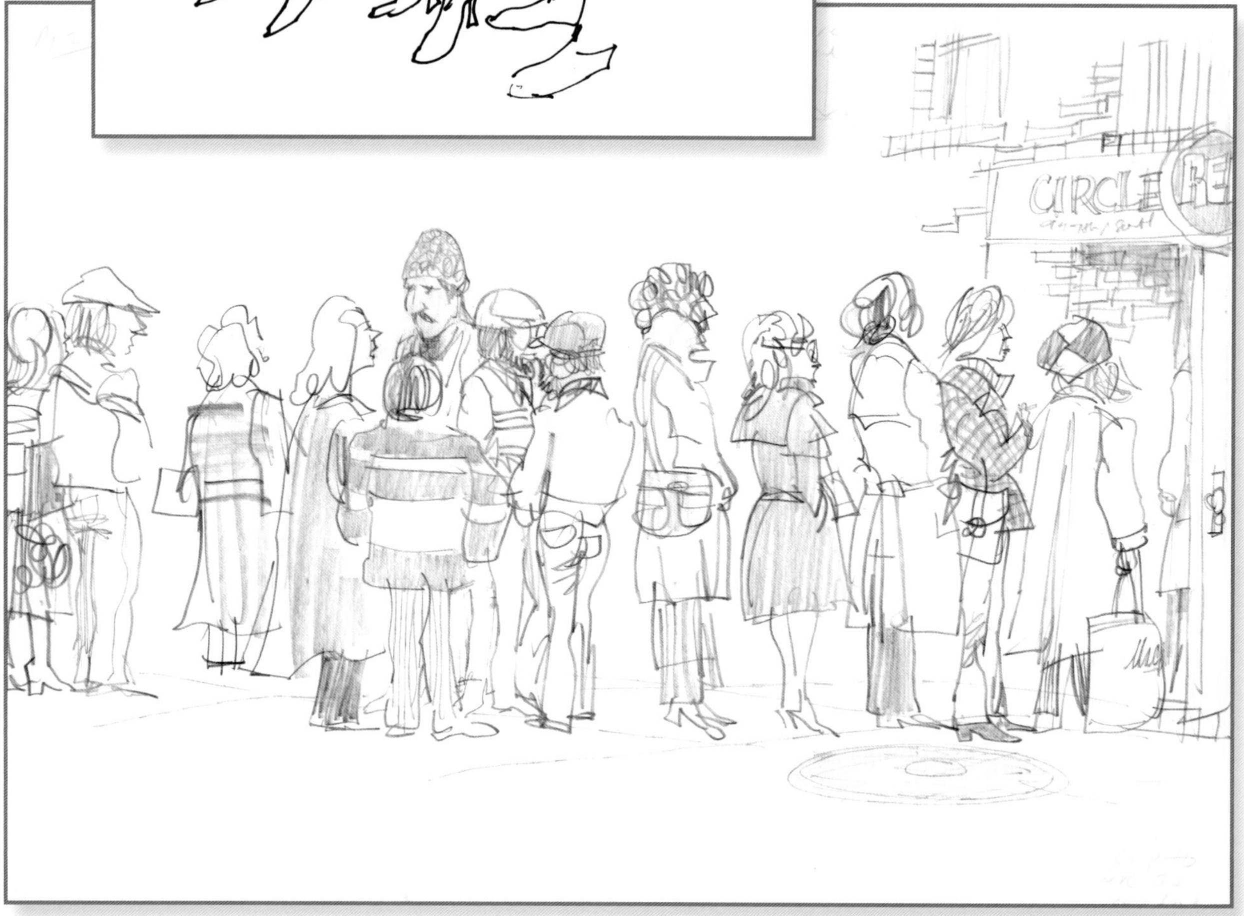

CIRCLE

Above
PEOPLE IN LINE AT THE THEATER
Pencils and inks by Jerry Robinson.

jerry Robinson

Theatre drawings from Playbill

COCKTAILS
SATURDAY, AUGUST 23
6 TO 8 PM

TO SEPTEMBE

LEFT BANK GALLERY

COMMERCIAL STREET, WELLFLE

Above

THEATRE DRAWINGS FROM PLAYBILL
EXHIBITION INVITATION, CAPE COD
Pencils by Jerry Robinson.

Handbook for SPACE TRAVELERS

Walter B. Hendrickson, Jr.

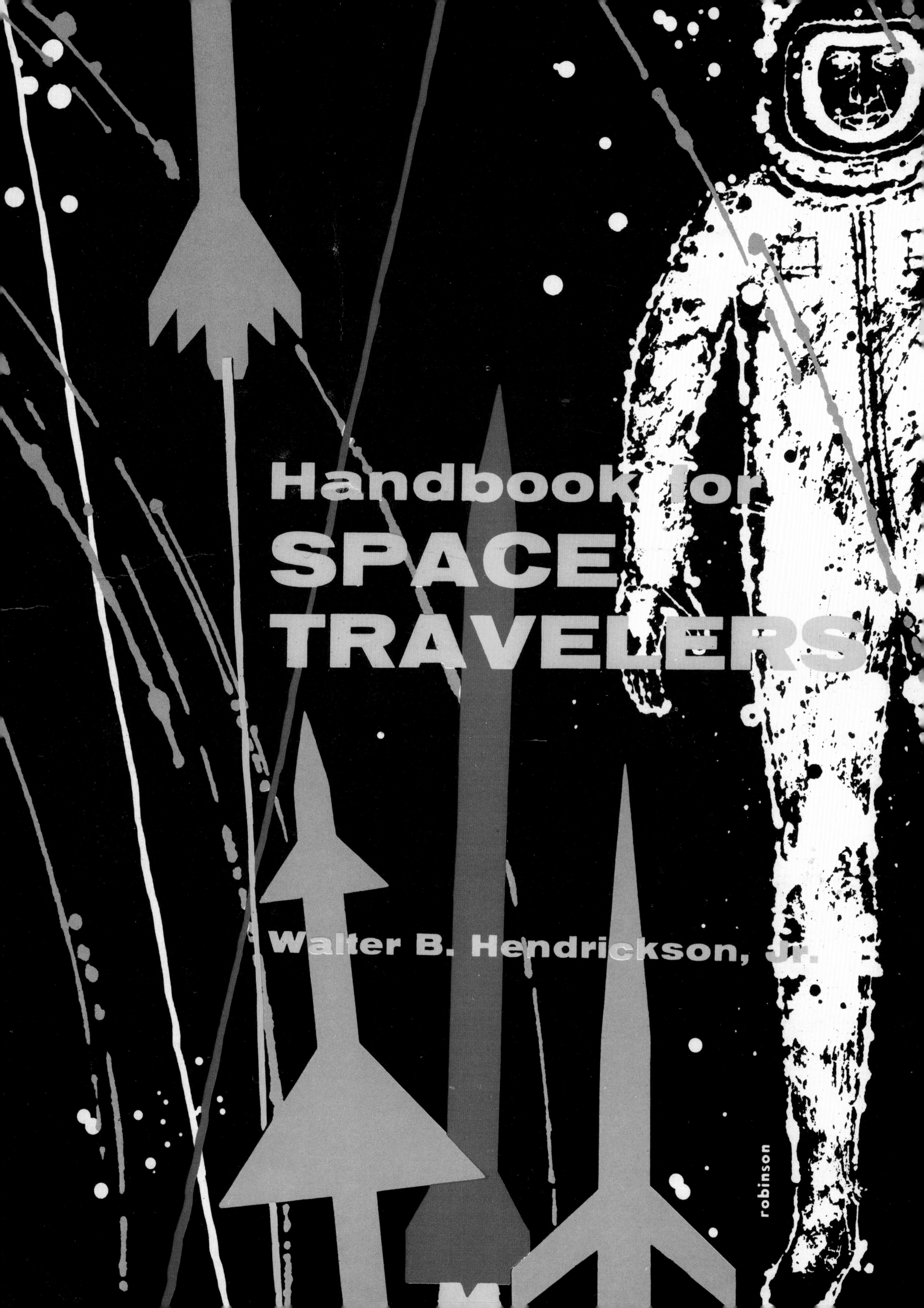
robinson

Chapter 7: Additional Comics, Books, and Magazine Art

Notes by Jens Robinson

My father, Jerry Robinson, was a cartooning legend—so it is so written in many an article and on many a plaque and award statue. While he was best known for conceiving of the Joker—the first and most revered supervillain in the comics and one of the world's most iconic pop culture characters—Jerry's numerous accomplishments over a six-decade career in cartoons and comics went far beyond the world of the Caped Crusader. Second only to Batman co-creators Bill Finger and Bob Kane, Jerry put a monumental stamp on the Batman mythos that went well beyond the Joker and is increasingly recognized by fans and experts. Jerry created, designed, or significantly refined well-known Batman iconography, from the winged bat logo to the Batplane. Although largely responsible for the initial appearances of key characters, including Alfred and Robin, he always unreservedly gave credit to Bill Finger as co-creator of everything *Batman*. And he was thrilled to present the first Bill Finger Award, an annual honor Jerry initiated with the San Diego Comic-Con.

Left
BOOK COVER FOR *HANDBOOK FOR SPACE TRAVELERS*
1959, illustrated by Jerry Robinson.

Any question of who created the Joker seems definitively settled by statements from DC Comics editor and historian E. Nelson Bridwell and Bill Finger himself. In an interview with Bridwell, Finger stated that Jerry Robinson created the Joker. Bridwell wrote, "As Bob Kane recalls Bill Finger as the Joker's creator and Bill told me it was Jerry Robinson's idea, I think we can accept Jerry as having come up with the concept" (*Comics Interview* #38, 1986).

Jerry had a primary role in the development of Robin, whom he named after Robin Hood (not Robinson, as is sometimes thought). N. C. Wyeth's illustrations of Robin Hood inspired Jerry's first Robin costume design in *Detective Comics* #38 in 1940. Although his inks of Bob Kane's pencils of Catwoman in *Batman* #1 left little of the Robinson stamp, his influence on the look of the Joker elsewhere in that spring 1940 issue placed an indelible mark on the character he had dreamed up for a creative writing course at Columbia University, where he took night classes. Jerry's early cover images of the Scarecrow, the Penguin (*Detective Comics* #67), Two-Face (*Detective Comics* #68), and the Alice in Wonderland–inspired Tweedledum and Tweedledee (*Detective Comics* #74) were truly formative contributions to those characters' look and feel.

Before leaving the superhero genre to branch out to other areas, he created Atoman, London (and his alter ego, radio broadcaster Marc Holmes), and Jet Scott, each a pivotal character of his time. Atoman (published by Spark Publications) was one of the earliest heroes to springboard from the atomic and nuclear advancements of the Cold War. London (who debuted in 1941, in *Daredevil Comics*, published by MLJ) is recognized for his innovative story line that tracked the current events of the day, namely the London Blitz. *Jet Scott*, written by Sheldon Stark, was a near-sci-fi adventure that amounted to a richly illustrated preview of coming scientific breakthroughs, such as man's going to the moon.

The collaboration between my father and his good friend and artistic partner Mort Meskin produced a prime run of another hero, the Black Terror (created by Richard E. Hughes and Don Gabrielson). Jerry's other noted collaborations with Meskin were on the characters of Fighting Yank, Green Hornet, Johnny Quick, and Vigilante.

Jerry's early 1940s comic book work was historic and groundbreaking because it was contemporaneous with the early growth of the medium itself. However, in the next decade, while working with Stan Lee at Timely/Atlas Comics, Jerry produced what has been called his finest (though most underappreciated) work in the comics. During several points in his career, Jerry was also a dedicated teacher of the cartoon arts; one of his prized students was Steve Ditko, who later co-created Spider-Man for Marvel Comics.

> JERRY WAS DEDICATED THROUGHOUT HIS CAREER TO ELEVATING THE ART FORM TO ITS DESERVED STATUS AS FINE ART.

According to historian Ger Apeldoorn, Jerry Robinson's "rightful place in comics history [is] as one of the 'inventors' of modern comics." Although Jerry's "work on *Batman* was more historically important . . . [he was] an artist at the peak of his abilities, a man who taught comics to a generation of new artists and clearly knew what he was doing. Robinson was far ahead of his colleagues at that point, many of whom were still finding their style."

I believe there has not been a comics genre that Jerry did not work in and master: crime, with its heroes fighting for justice; religion, with stories and references from the Bible; romance; fantasy, including horror and science fiction; war; and Western.

He had a full career in book and advertising illustration alone. My favorite of his book covers is the 1959 Hugo Award–winning novel *Starship Troopers* by Robert Heinlein. Among his many children's books is *Professor Egghead's Best Riddles*, a 1973 collaboration with author Rose Wyler. I remember loving as a child learning science through his whimsical artwork.

Following his 1950s work on *Jet Scott*, in the 1960s Jerry's comic strip and comic panel career took a humorous turn with *True Classroom Flubs & Fluffs*, the popular reader-participation Sunday page that ran in the *New York News*. His political cartoon career spanned three decades, as *Still Life*, the daily panel in which inanimate objects commented on the news, morphed into *Life with Robinson*, a larger panel that allowed him more artistic freedom.

My father's love of the theater and a chance connection led him to land one of his favorite gigs: sketching Broadway shows—from prime seats as well as backstage—for *Playbill* magazine in the late 1970s and early 1980s.

In his later career, he transformed the way political cartoonists worldwide were distributed outside their own countries by founding Cartoonists & Writers Syndicate, later known also as CartoonArts International. His book *The 1970s: Best Political Cartoons of the Decade* inspired the syndicated feature *Views of the World*, presenting the finest work by political cartoonists from leading publications from every continent except Antarctica. This venture was born of positive reviews of his book that took special note of the many outstanding political cartoons from outside the United States. Over the next decade, other features emerged, including international humor cartoons and caricatures, as well as offshoot features focusing on specific regions of the world and topics in the news.

My father assembled one of the most remarkable private collections of original comic and cartoon art. Portions of the collection have been exhibited in museums and fine art galleries around the world, and on the occasions when he decided to put an individual piece up for auction, it usually broke previous sales records.

The comic book and original comic art collecting community has paid tribute to Jerry's early role in creating the hobby. He had the foresight to save many outstanding works of original comic art that would have been destroyed at the printers. Without an investment strategy but with a sense of the cultural importance of the material, he salvaged, preserved, and traded for the pieces he liked best—both his own work and that of his friends and colleagues, including Charlie Biro, Will Eisner, Jack Kirby, Joe Simon, Bernie Klein, Mort Meskin, Fred Ray, and Jerry Siegel and Joe Shuster.

Jerry was dedicated throughout his career to elevating the art form to its deserved status as fine art. He worked on comic art shows in major museums and leading galleries in New York City and around the world. In 1972 Jerry curated an exhibition at the Graham Gallery on Madison Avenue, the first cartoon art show at a major New York art gallery. In 2004 he curated *The Superhero: The Golden Age of Comic Books* for the Breman Museum in Atlanta, which later went on a world tour. And in 2017, the core of his Golden Age comic art collection, featuring many of the finest examples of classic Batman and Superman art, will be shown in *The Art of DC* at Art Ludique Le Musée in Paris. Besides his own artwork, the pieces include some of the best examples of the iconic artists Jack Kirby, Fred Ray, and Mort Meskin.

Among his numerous accomplishments and awards, my father was most proud of his lifelong fight for creators' rights, most notably on behalf of his friends, the Superman co-creators Jerry Siegel and Joe Shuster, and of oppressed political cartoonists abroad.

Siegel and Shuster were the almost forgotten creators of Superman, who, second to Batman, was the most successful superhero in history. Jerry, along with DC Comics star artist Neal Adams, took up the cause of creating public awareness and private pressure to improve the bargaining position of the Superman creators. The result was lifetime stipends and the permanent placement of their names as co-creators of the property in publications and onscreen.

In the case of Uruguayan political cartoonist Francisco Laurenzo Pons, Jerry spearheaded the cause of a human rights case from the files of Amnesty International. He rallied the Association of American Editorial Cartoonists (an organization for which he had served as president) around Pons, who had been imprisoned and tortured for his views in opposition to the regime. The artist was eventually freed. Our syndicate also placed work by dissident cartoonists from the former Soviet Union in *The New York Times* and other leading American newspapers, and Jerry brought their royalties with him into the USSR over the course of several visits to Moscow.

Right
SPLASH PAGE OF "DANGER IN THE AIR!" FROM *THE BLACK TERROR* NO. 23
June 1948, pencils and inks by Jerry Robinson and Mort Meskin

Artist. Writer. Political cartoonist. Comic strip cartoonist. Comic book creator. Syndicate founder. Collector. Curator. Teacher. Husband. He was all of those things. However, my take on his greatest legacies was Fighter for Artists' Rights and Father.

"Jerry Robinson was a creative and business force in the comic book and related cartoon industries. From the early days, he was aware that this was an emerging new American art form, and would dedicate his life as its ambassador to elevate comics in the eyes of both the general public and art critics.

Perhaps Jerry's most important contribution to humanity was his commitment to his fellow creators and cartoonists, especially when life dictated that they could not protect or defend themselves. Jerry fought for the rights and welfare of cartoonists, artists, and writers who created the modernday mythology of comic book superheroes."

Michael Uslan
Executive producer of the *Batman* films

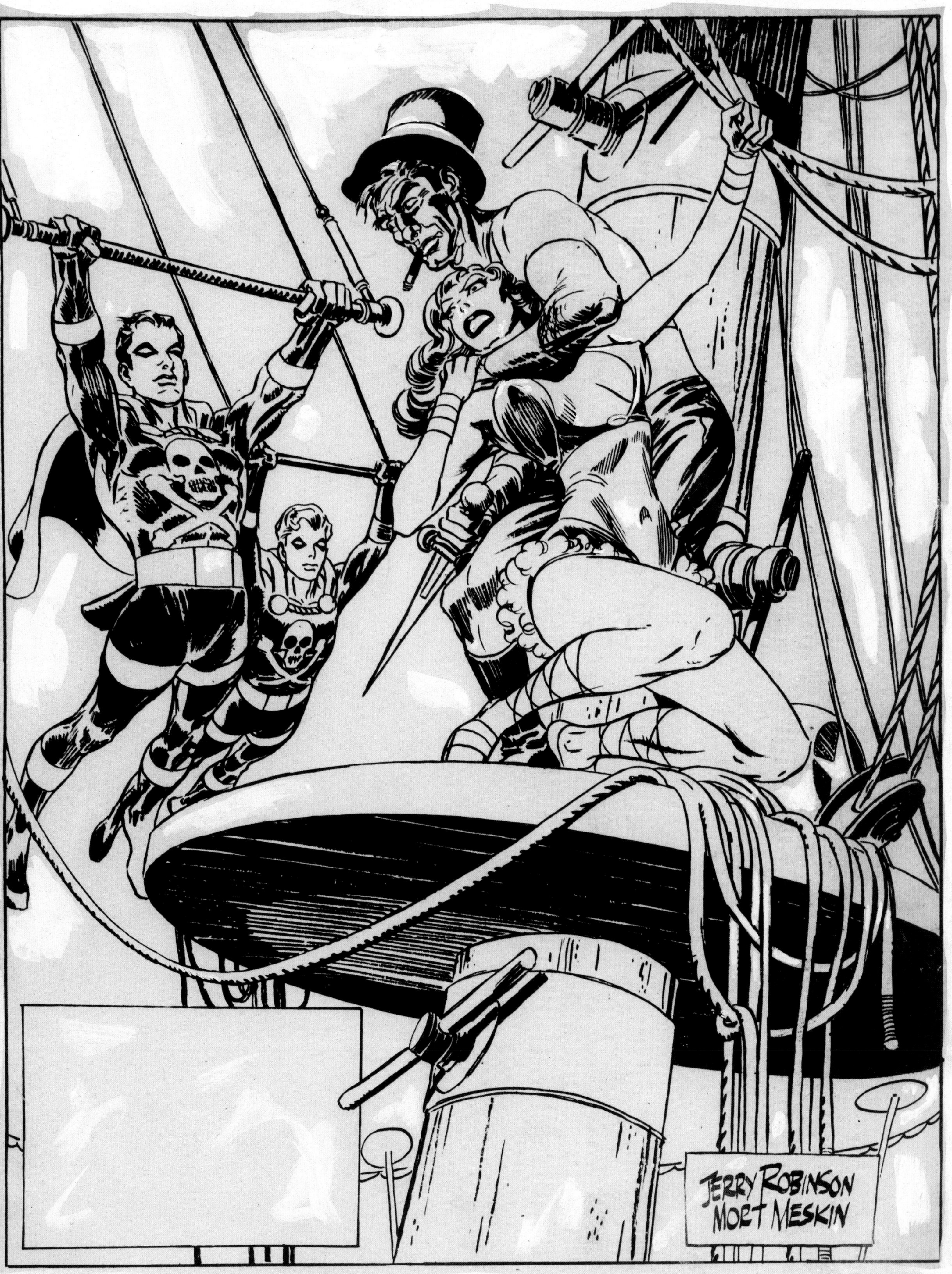
JERRY ROBINSON
MORT MESKIN

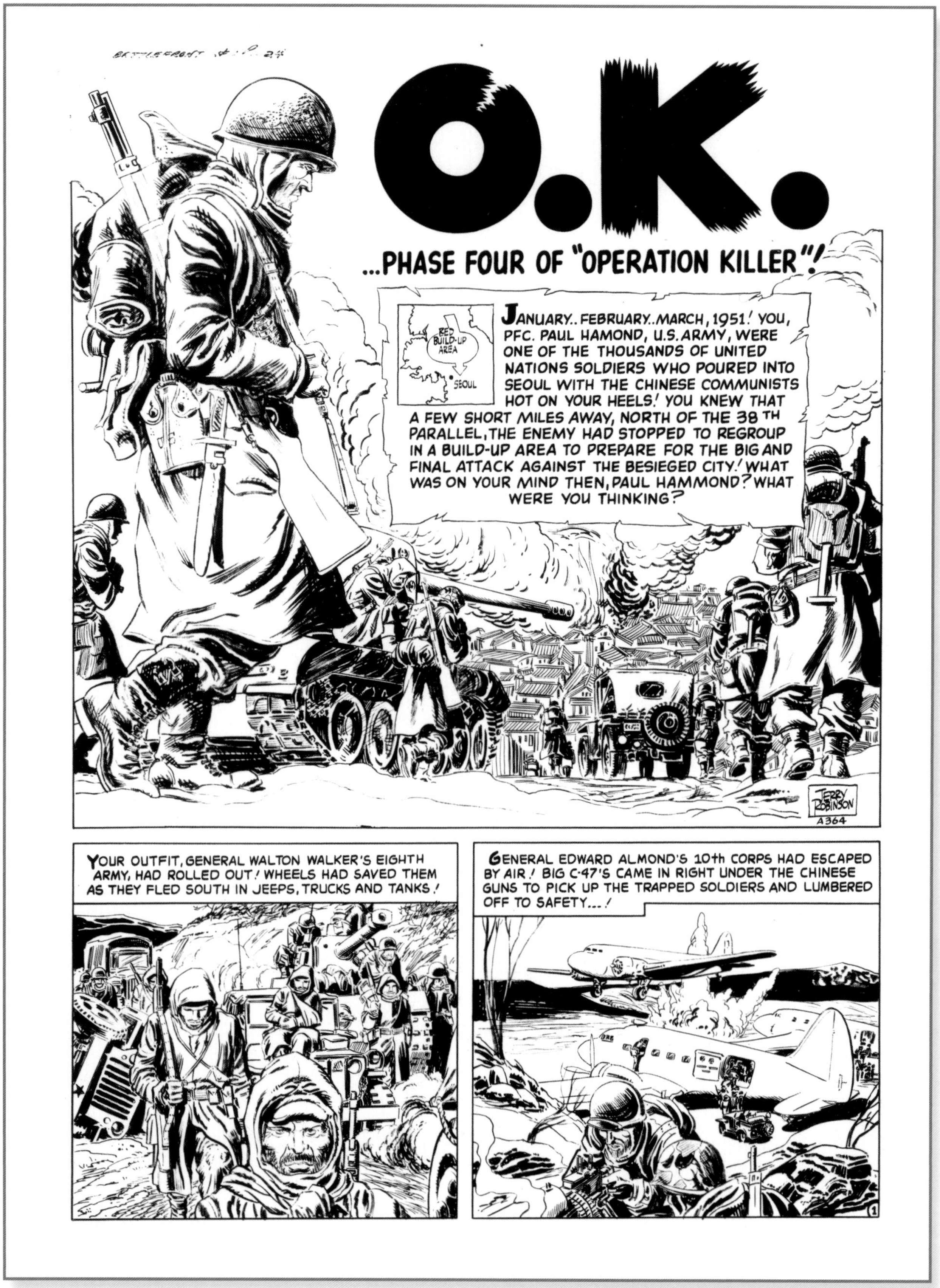
BATTLEFRONT #1
O.K.
...PHASE FOUR OF "OPERATION KILLER"!
RED BUILD-UP AREA
SEOUL
JANUARY.. FEBRUARY..MARCH, 1951! YOU, PFC. PAUL HAMOND, U.S. ARMY, WERE ONE OF THE THOUSANDS OF UNITED NATIONS SOLDIERS WHO POURED INTO SEOUL WITH THE CHINESE COMMUNISTS HOT ON YOUR HEELS! YOU KNEW THAT A FEW SHORT MILES AWAY, NORTH OF THE 38 TH PARALLEL, THE ENEMY HAD STOPPED TO REGROUP IN A BUILD-UP AREA TO PREPARE FOR THE BIG AND FINAL ATTACK AGAINST THE BESIEGED CITY! WHAT WAS ON YOUR MIND THEN, PAUL HAMMOND? WHAT WERE YOU THINKING?
JERRY ROBINSON
A364
YOUR OUTFIT, GENERAL WALTON WALKER'S EIGHTH ARMY, HAD ROLLED OUT! WHEELS HAD SAVED THEM AS THEY FLED SOUTH IN JEEPS, TRUCKS AND TANKS!
GENERAL EDWARD ALMOND'S 10th CORPS HAD ESCAPED BY AIR! BIG C-47'S CAME IN RIGHT UNDER THE CHINESE GUNS TO PICK UP THE TRAPPED SOLDIERS AND LUMBERED OFF TO SAFETY...!
1

Above

SPLASH PAGE OF "O.K.: PHASE FOUR OF 'OPERATION KILLER'!" FROM *BATTLEFRONT* NO. 1

June 1952, pencils and inks by Jerry Robinson.

Right

ROUGH SPLASH PAGE OF "FOLLOW -UP" FROM *BATTLEFRONT* NO. 3

August 1952, pencils by Jerry Robinson.

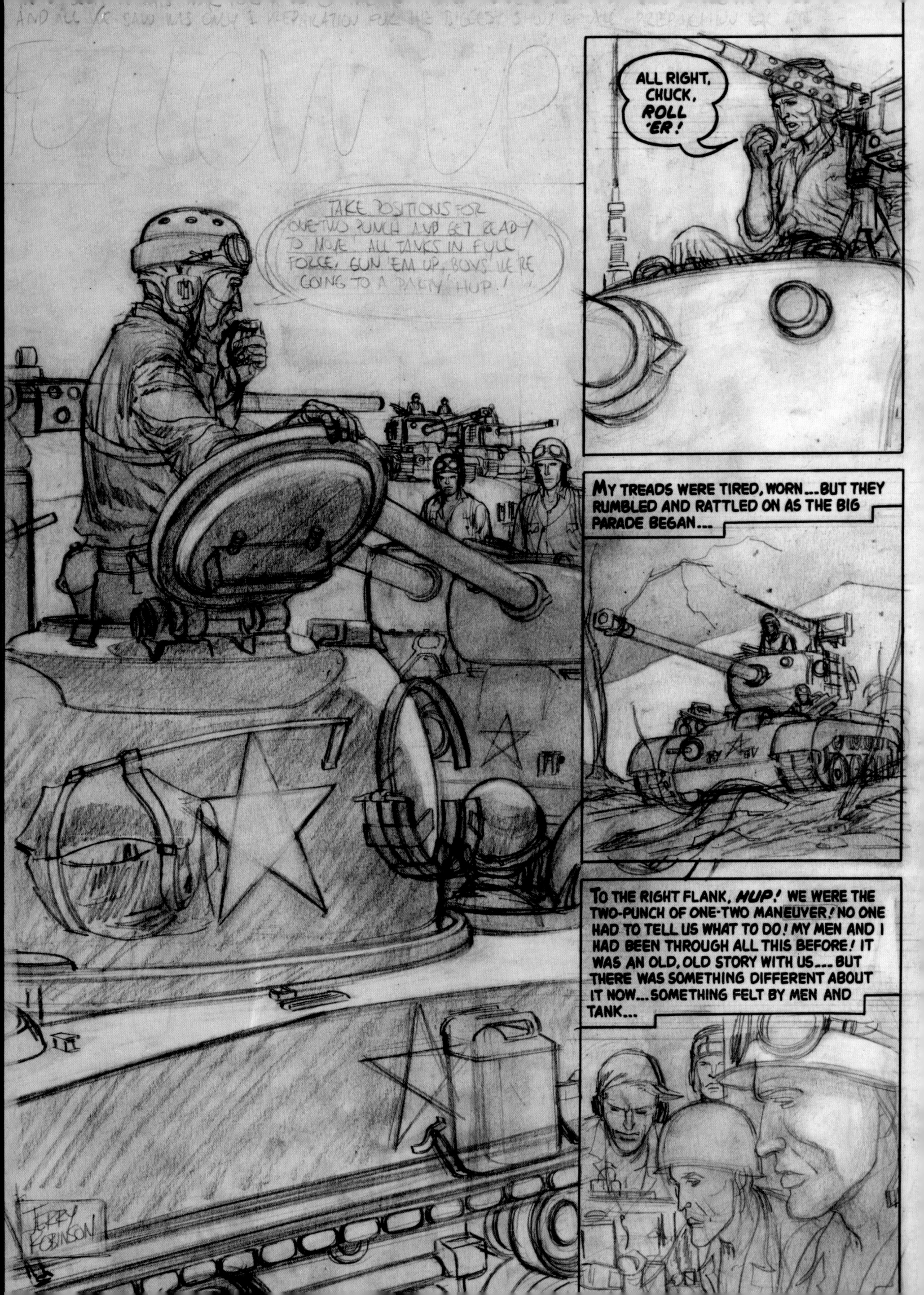

TAKE POSITIONS FOR ONE-TWO PUNCH AND GET READY TO MOVE! ALL TANKS IN FULL FORCE, GUN 'EM UP, BOYS, WE'RE GOING TO A PARTY! HUP!
ALL RIGHT, CHUCK, ROLL 'ER!
MY TREADS WERE TIRED, WORN... BUT THEY RUMBLED AND RATTLED ON AS THE BIG PARADE BEGAN...
TO THE RIGHT FLANK, HUP! WE WERE THE TWO-PUNCH OF ONE-TWO MANEUVER! NO ONE HAD TO TELL US WHAT TO DO! MY MEN AND I HAD BEEN THROUGH ALL THIS BEFORE! IT WAS AN OLD, OLD STORY WITH US... BUT THERE WAS SOMETHING DIFFERENT ABOUT IT NOW... SOMETHING FELT BY MEN AND TANK...
JERRY ROBINSON

Above

ILLUSTRATION FOR *LOOK*
MAGAZINE OF THE PROJECTED
UNITED STATES INVASION OF JAPAN
BEFORE ATOMIC BOMBING
OF HIROSHIMA

Ink and wash illustration by Jerry Robinson.

Right and following spread

ATOMAN ORIGINAL INKED
ART AND BLUE PENCILS

By Jerry Robinson.

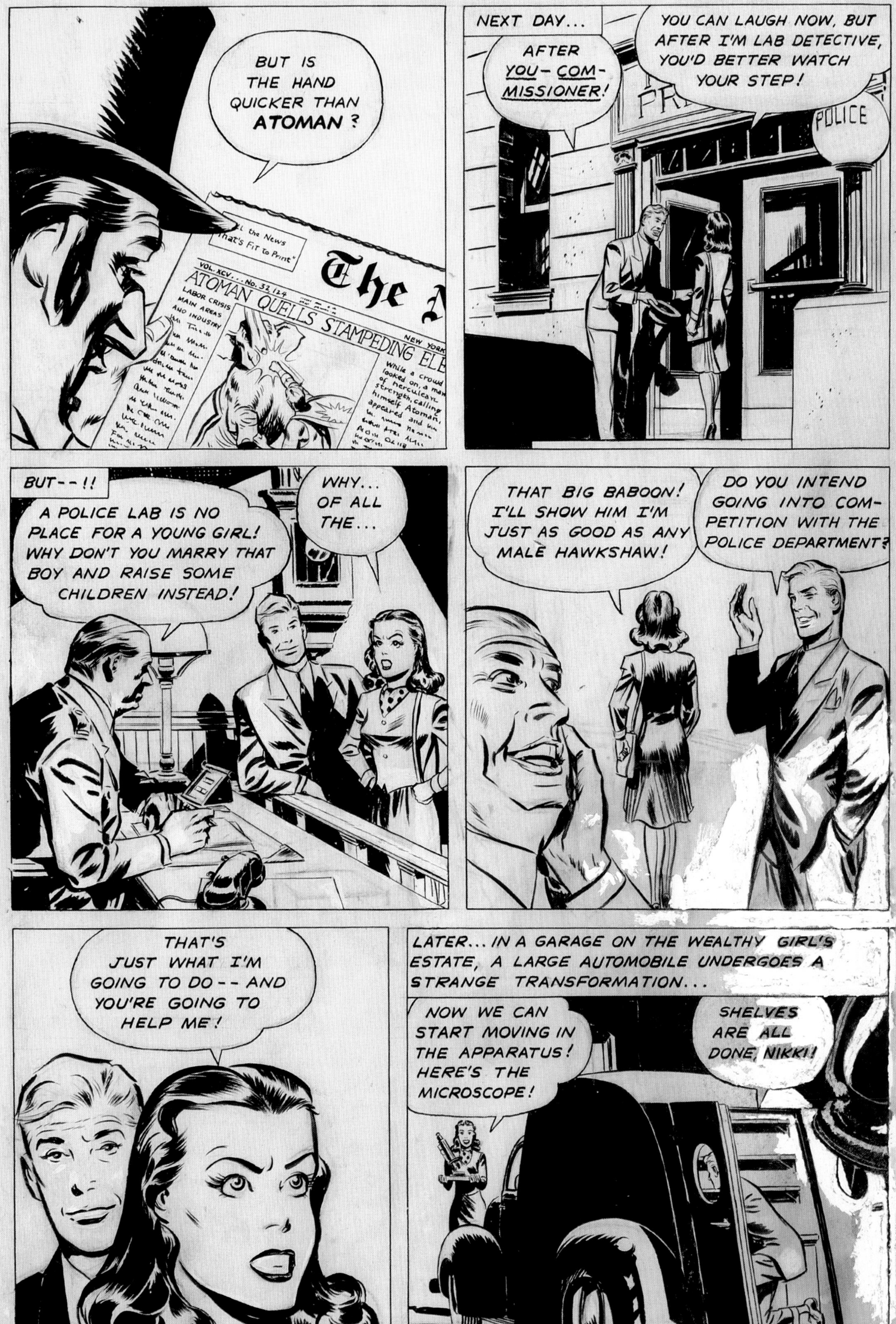
BUT IS THE HAND QUICKER THAN ATOMAN?
"All the News That's Fit to Print"
The N
VOL. XCV... No. 32,124
ATOMAN QUELLS STAMPEDING ELE
NEW YORK
LABOR CRISIS MAIN AREAS AND INDUSTRY
While a crowd looked on, a man of herculean strength, calling himself Atoman, appeared and
NEXT DAY...
AFTER YOU—COMMISSIONER!
YOU CAN LAUGH NOW, BUT AFTER I'M LAB DETECTIVE, YOU'D BETTER WATCH YOUR STEP!
POLICE
BUT--!!
A POLICE LAB IS NO PLACE FOR A YOUNG GIRL! WHY DON'T YOU MARRY THAT BOY AND RAISE SOME CHILDREN INSTEAD!
WHY... OF ALL THE...
THAT BIG BABOON! I'LL SHOW HIM I'M JUST AS GOOD AS ANY MALE HAWKSHAW!
DO YOU INTEND GOING INTO COMPETITION WITH THE POLICE DEPARTMENT?
THAT'S JUST WHAT I'M GOING TO DO -- AND YOU'RE GOING TO HELP ME!
LATER... IN A GARAGE ON THE WEALTHY GIRL'S ESTATE, A LARGE AUTOMOBILE UNDERGOES A STRANGE TRANSFORMATION...
NOW WE CAN START MOVING IN THE APPARATUS! HERE'S THE MICROSCOPE!
SHELVES ARE ALL DONE, NIKKI!

ATOMAN # 2

Cover Date ________

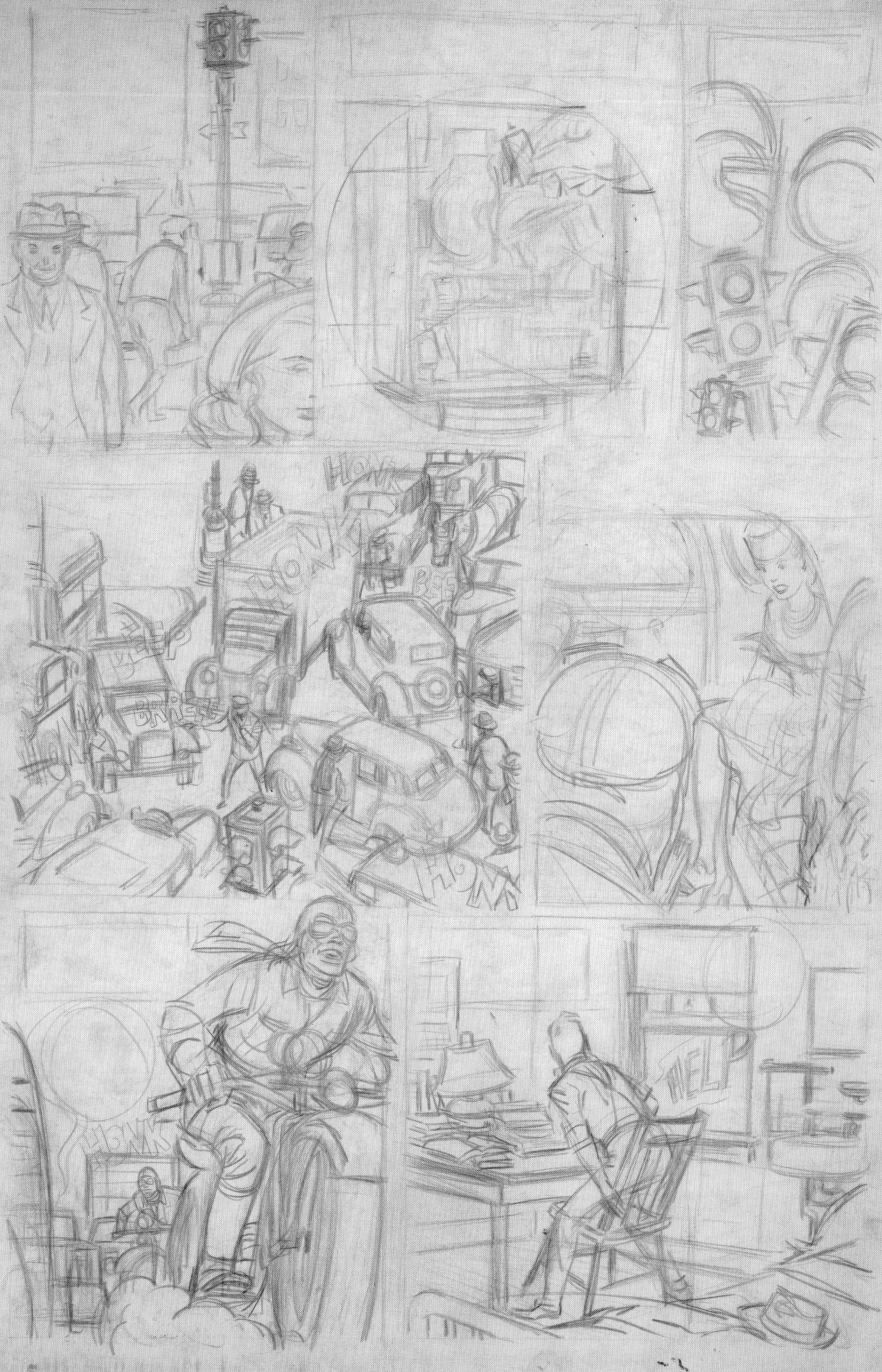
HONK
BEEP
BEEP
HONK
HONK
HELP

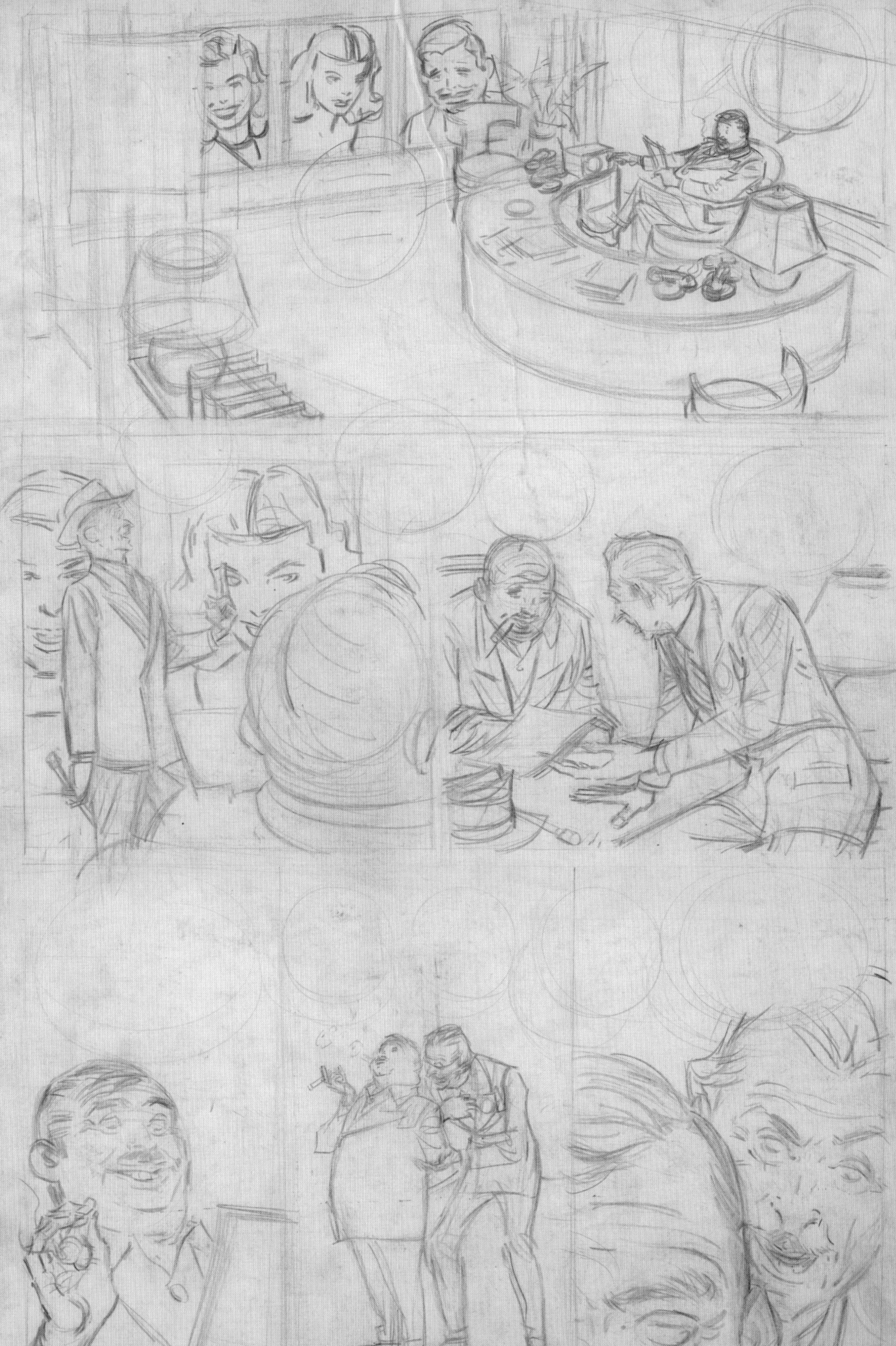

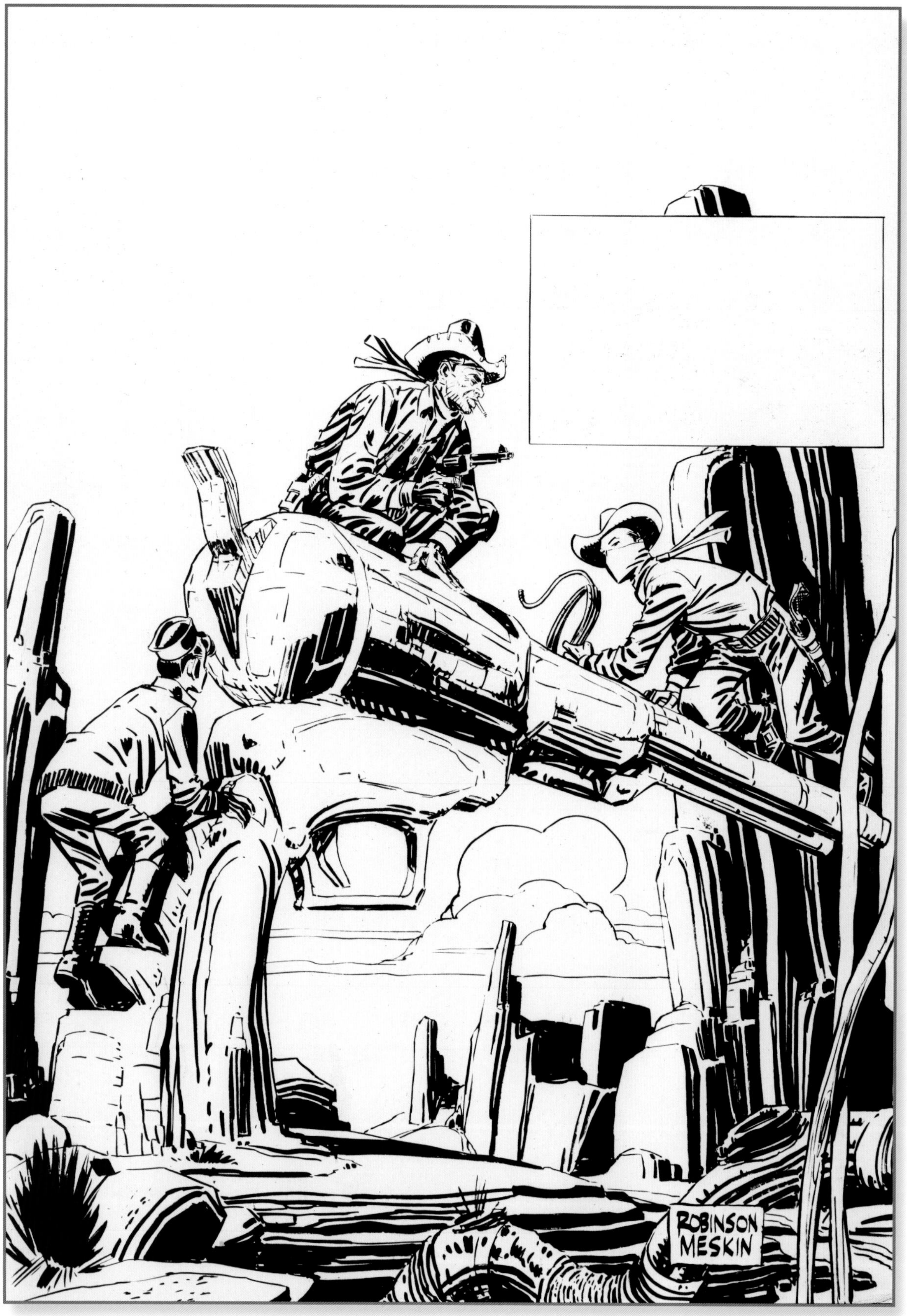
ROBINSON
MESKIN

Above
SPLASH PAGE OF "THE FOUR NOTCHES OF HATE" FROM *WESTERN COMICS* NO. 4
July – August 1948, pencils and inks by Jerry Robinson and Mort Meskin

Right and following pages
PAGES 1–2 AND 4–7 OF "THE DEATH OF DANNY LEWIS" FROM *JUSTICE* NO. 25
January 1952, pencils and inks by Jerry Robinson.

JUSTICE #25 P.1

THE DEATH OF DANNY LEWIS

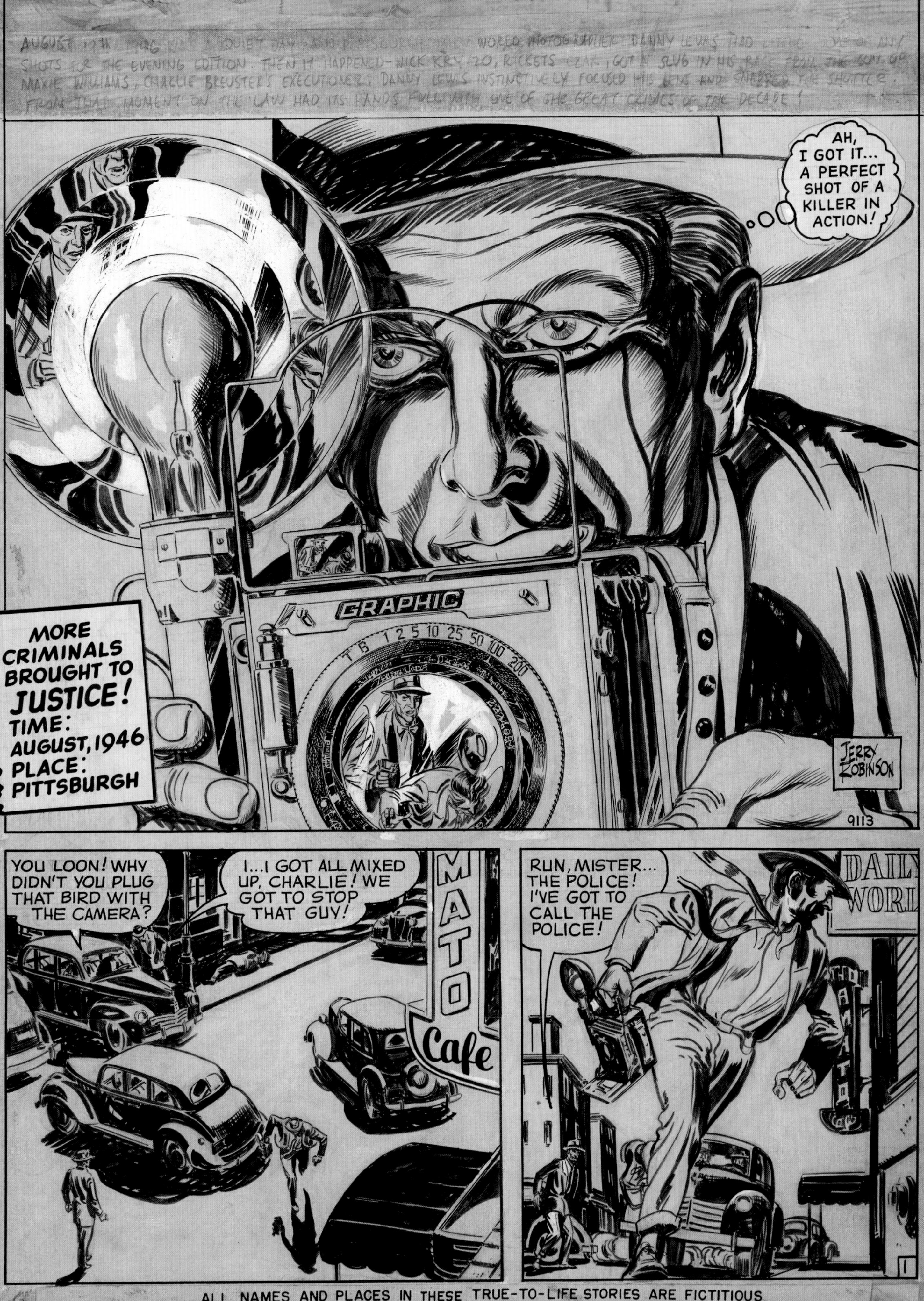

AUGUST 17TH ... WORLD PHOTOGRAPHER DANNY LEWIS HAD ...
SHOTS FOR THE EVENING EDITION. THEN IT HAPPENED—NICK KRY?ZO, RACKETS CZAR, GOT A SLUG IN HIS BACK FROM THE GUN OF
MAXIE WILLIAMS, CHARLIE BREUSTER'S EXECUTIONER. DANNY LEWIS INSTINCTIVELY FOCUSED HIS LENS AND SNAPPED THE SHUTTER.
FROM THAT MOMENT ON THE LAW HAD ITS HANDS FULL WITH ONE OF THE GREAT CRIMES OF THE DECADE!
AH, I GOT IT... A PERFECT SHOT OF A KILLER IN ACTION!
MORE CRIMINALS BROUGHT TO JUSTICE! TIME: AUGUST, 1946 PLACE: PITTSBURGH
GRAPHIC
T B 1 2 5 10 25 50 100 200
JERRY ROBINSON
9113
YOU LOON! WHY DIDN'T YOU PLUG THAT BIRD WITH THE CAMERA?
I...I GOT ALL MIXED UP, CHARLIE! WE GOT TO STOP THAT GUY!
MATO
Cafe
RUN, MISTER... THE POLICE! I'VE GOT TO CALL THE POLICE!
DAILY WORLD
1
JUSTICE

JUSTICE #25 P. 2

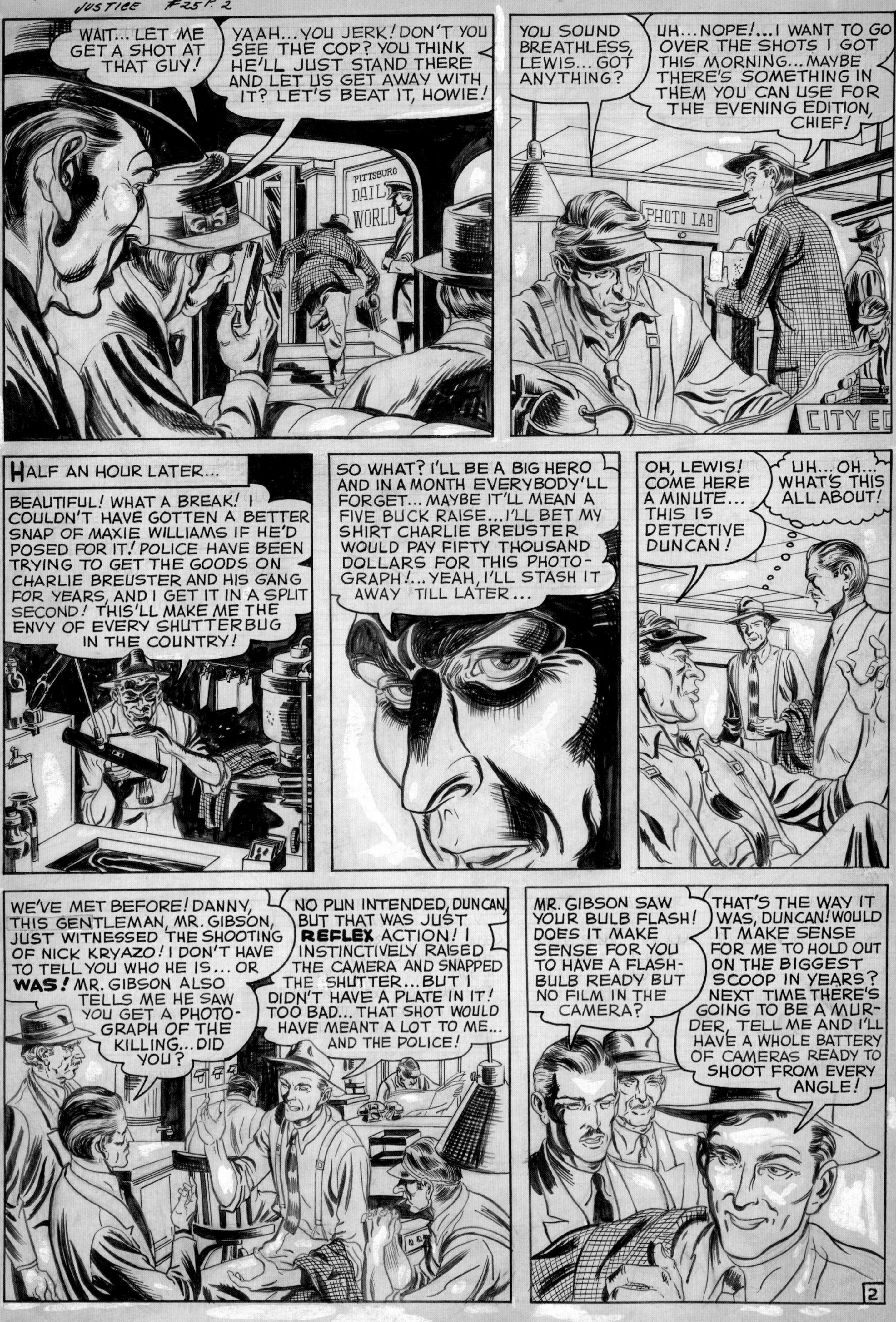
WAIT... LET ME GET A SHOT AT THAT GUY!
YAAH... YOU JERK! DON'T YOU SEE THE COP? YOU THINK HE'LL JUST STAND THERE AND LET US GET AWAY WITH IT? LET'S BEAT IT, HOWIE!
PITTSBURG DAILY WORLD
YOU SOUND BREATHLESS, LEWIS... GOT ANYTHING?
UH... NOPE!... I WANT TO GO OVER THE SHOTS I GOT THIS MORNING... MAYBE THERE'S SOMETHING IN THEM YOU CAN USE FOR THE EVENING EDITION, CHIEF!
PHOTO LAB
CITY ED
HALF AN HOUR LATER...
BEAUTIFUL! WHAT A BREAK! I COULDN'T HAVE GOTTEN A BETTER SNAP OF MAXIE WILLIAMS IF HE'D POSED FOR IT! POLICE HAVE BEEN TRYING TO GET THE GOODS ON CHARLIE BREUSTER AND HIS GANG FOR YEARS, AND I GET IT IN A SPLIT SECOND! THIS'LL MAKE ME THE ENVY OF EVERY SHUTTERBUG IN THE COUNTRY!
SO WHAT? I'LL BE A BIG HERO AND IN A MONTH EVERYBODY'LL FORGET... MAYBE IT'LL MEAN A FIVE BUCK RAISE... I'LL BET MY SHIRT CHARLIE BREUSTER WOULD PAY FIFTY THOUSAND DOLLARS FOR THIS PHOTOGRAPH!... YEAH, I'LL STASH IT AWAY TILL LATER...
OH, LEWIS! COME HERE A MINUTE... THIS IS DETECTIVE DUNCAN!
UH... OH... WHAT'S THIS ALL ABOUT!
WE'VE MET BEFORE! DANNY, THIS GENTLEMAN, MR. GIBSON, JUST WITNESSED THE SHOOTING OF NICK KRYAZO! I DON'T HAVE TO TELL YOU WHO HE IS... OR WAS! MR. GIBSON ALSO TELLS ME HE SAW YOU GET A PHOTOGRAPH OF THE KILLING... DID YOU?
NO PUN INTENDED, DUNCAN, BUT THAT WAS JUST REFLEX ACTION! I INSTINCTIVELY RAISED THE CAMERA AND SNAPPED THE SHUTTER... BUT I DIDN'T HAVE A PLATE IN IT! TOO BAD... THAT SHOT WOULD HAVE MEANT A LOT TO ME... AND THE POLICE!
MR. GIBSON SAW YOUR BULB FLASH! DOES IT MAKE SENSE FOR YOU TO HAVE A FLASH-BULB READY BUT NO FILM IN THE CAMERA?
THAT'S THE WAY IT WAS, DUNCAN! WOULD IT MAKE SENSE FOR ME TO HOLD OUT ON THE BIGGEST SCOOP IN YEARS? NEXT TIME THERE'S GOING TO BE A MURDER, TELL ME AND I'LL HAVE A WHOLE BATTERY OF CAMERAS READY TO SHOOT FROM EVERY ANGLE!
2

WAIT A SECOND! WHERE ARE YOU GOING?

RELAX! I DON'T HAVE A PHONE... I'VE GOT TO GO OUT AND CALL MY OFFICE! I'LL TELL THE NIGHT EDITOR I NEED A PACKAGE FROM MY DESK! HE DOESN'T NEED TO KNOW WHAT IT IS... HE'LL SEND IT OVER WITH AN OFFICE BOY!

DANNY LEWIS MADE A PHONE CALL, ALL RIGHT, BUT NOT TO HIS OFFICE... THEN HE RETURNED TO HIS APARTMENT... AN HOUR LATER THERE WAS A KNOCK AT THE DOOR...

WHO'S THAT?

TAKE IT EASY, WILL YOU... I'LL ANSWER IT!

KNOCK

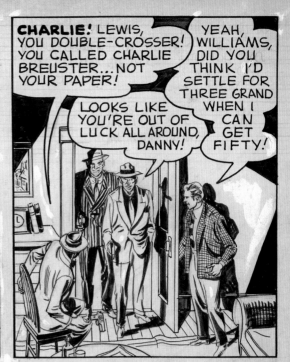

CHARLIE! LEWIS, YOU DOUBLE-CROSSER! YOU CALLED CHARLIE BREUSTER... NOT YOUR PAPER!

YEAH, WILLIAMS, DID YOU THINK I'D SETTLE FOR THREE GRAND WHEN I CAN GET FIFTY!

LOOKS LIKE YOU'RE OUT OF LUCK ALL AROUND, DANNY!

NOW, WAIT A MINUTE, BREUSTER! YOU SAID OVER THE PHONE YOU WERE WILLING TO PAY WHAT I ASKED...

SOMETIMES YOU CAN'T BELIEVE A WORD I SAY, DANNY! THAT PICTURE YOU TOOK WON'T DO THE COPS A BIT OF GOOD IF MAXIE IS DEAD... YOU GOT NO WAY OF PROVING I WAS THERE WHEN NICK KRYAZO GOT IT! YOU JUST TRIED TO BLACKMAIL THE WRONG GUY, CHISELER!

STOP HIM!

I AIN'T GOING TO BE THE PATSY FOR ALL THIS... ARGHH!

BANG

BANG

HELP, PLEASE! I'M HURT BAD... GOT TO GET TO A HOSPITAL!

GET IN, MISTER... HURRY!

MAXIE GOT AWAY! MAYBE HE'LL CROAK, MAYBE NOT! IT WON'T MATTER IF I GET THAT PHOTO... YOU HAND IT OVER OR YOU WON'T LIVE TO GIVE IT TO THE COPS! AND DON'T GIVE ME THAT BUNK ABOUT IT BEING AT YOUR OFFICE! YOU WOULDN'T RISK LEAVING IT THERE!

AND NO FIFTY THOUSAND BUCKS, BREUSTER?

4

YOU'LL BE LUCKY IF I LET YOU LIVE ANYHOW, DANNY... **HEY!**

THAT'S WHAT I WAS THINKING, BREUSTER, SO I'M NOT WAITING TO FIND OUT HOW YOU'VE MADE UP YOUR MIND!

HE TURNED OFF THE LIGHTS!

DON'T LET THAT RAT GET AWAY! HE'LL PUT US ALL IN THE HOT SEAT!

YEAH, BREUSTER, MAYBE THEY'LL EVEN LET ME PULL THE SWITCH!

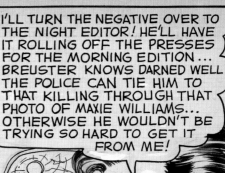

I'LL TURN THE NEGATIVE OVER TO THE NIGHT EDITOR! HE'LL HAVE IT ROLLING OFF THE PRESSES FOR THE MORNING EDITION... BREUSTER KNOWS DARNED WELL THE POLICE CAN TIE HIM TO THAT KILLING THROUGH THAT PHOTO OF MAXIE WILLIAMS... OTHERWISE HE WOULDN'T BE TRYING SO HARD TO GET IT FROM ME!

IT'LL CAUSE A SENSATION! NOT FIFTY THOUSAND WORTH MAYBE, BUT ENOUGH TO ASSURE ME A JOB ON ANY NEWSPAPER IN THE COUNTRY! THAT DETECTIVE DUNCAN WILL SAY I LIED TO HIM... I'LL JUST SAY I DIDN'T KNOW THE CAMERA WAS LOADED! ...LET HIM PROVE OTHERWISE!

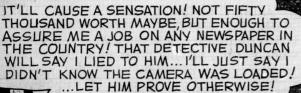

MEANWHILE, AT MEMORIAL HOSPITAL...

I GOT NOTHING TO SAY, DUNCAN! DON'T KNOW WHO PLUGGED ME...

DON'T BE A FOOL, WILLIAMS! WHEN I HEARD THEY HAD YOU HERE, IT ADDED UP TO ONE THING... YOUR BOSS, CHARLIE BREUSTER, WAS ONE OF THE MANY GUYS IN PITTSBURGH OUT GET NICK KRYAZO, AND YOU'D BE JUST THE BOY TO DO THE JOB FOR HIM... AND YOU DID! SO KRYAZO'S MOB GOT YOU...

NO, DUNCAN... IT WASN'T KRYAZO'S BOYS... LOOK, I WOULDN'T MIND TALKING... I KNOW I'M DONE FOR, ANYHOW... BUT I GOT A FAMILY... IF I SPILLED, THEY MIGHT GET HURT!

I PROMISE YOU THEY WON'T! WE'LL NAB WHOEVER GUNNED YOU, MAXIE, AND LISTEN... NICK KRYAZO'S FAMILY IS OFFERING TEN THOUSAND DOLLARS REWARD FOR THE MEN RESPONSIBLE FOR HIS MURDER... YOUR FAMILY COULD USE THAT KIND OF MONEY!

... OKAY, DUNCAN... I CAN DO ONE DECENT THING IN MY LIFE... GOT TO TALK FAST IF I'M GOING TO MAKE IT...

COME CLOSER, O'HEARN... GET THIS DOWN!

5

JUSTICE #25 P. 6

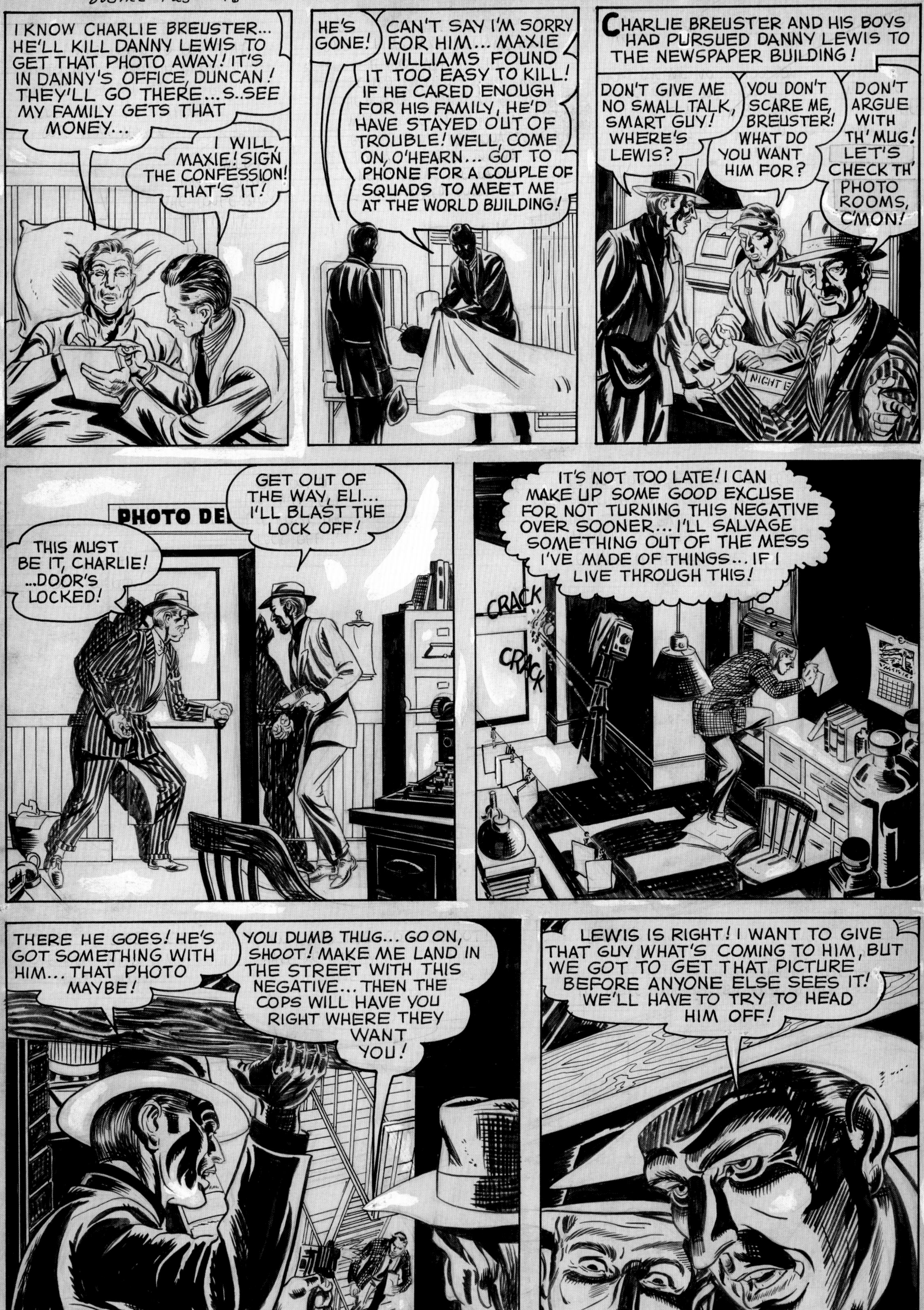
I KNOW CHARLIE BREUSTER... HE'LL KILL DANNY LEWIS TO GET THAT PHOTO AWAY! IT'S IN DANNY'S OFFICE, DUNCAN! THEY'LL GO THERE... S..SEE MY FAMILY GETS THAT MONEY...
I WILL, MAXIE! SIGN THE CONFESSION! THAT'S IT!
HE'S GONE!
CAN'T SAY I'M SORRY FOR HIM... MAXIE WILLIAMS FOUND IT TOO EASY TO KILL! IF HE CARED ENOUGH FOR HIS FAMILY, HE'D HAVE STAYED OUT OF TROUBLE! WELL, COME ON, O'HEARN... GOT TO PHONE FOR A COUPLE OF SQUADS TO MEET ME AT THE WORLD BUILDING!
CHARLIE BREUSTER AND HIS BOYS HAD PURSUED DANNY LEWIS TO THE NEWSPAPER BUILDING!
DON'T GIVE ME NO SMALL TALK, SMART GUY! WHERE'S LEWIS?
YOU DON'T SCARE ME, BREUSTER! WHAT DO YOU WANT HIM FOR?
DON'T ARGUE WITH TH' MUG! LET'S CHECK TH' PHOTO ROOMS, C'MON!
NIGHT E
PHOTO DE
THIS MUST BE IT, CHARLIE! ...DOOR'S LOCKED!
GET OUT OF THE WAY, ELI... I'LL BLAST THE LOCK OFF!
IT'S NOT TOO LATE! I CAN MAKE UP SOME GOOD EXCUSE FOR NOT TURNING THIS NEGATIVE OVER SOONER... I'LL SALVAGE SOMETHING OUT OF THE MESS I'VE MADE OF THINGS... IF I LIVE THROUGH THIS!
CRACK
CRACK
THERE HE GOES! HE'S GOT SOMETHING WITH HIM... THAT PHOTO MAYBE!
YOU DUMB THUG... GO ON, SHOOT! MAKE ME LAND IN THE STREET WITH THIS NEGATIVE... THEN THE COPS WILL HAVE YOU RIGHT WHERE THEY WANT YOU!
LEWIS IS RIGHT! I WANT TO GIVE THAT GUY WHAT'S COMING TO HIM, BUT WE GOT TO GET THAT PICTURE BEFORE ANYONE ELSE SEES IT! WE'LL HAVE TO TRY TO HEAD HIM OFF!
6

JUSTICE #25 P. 7

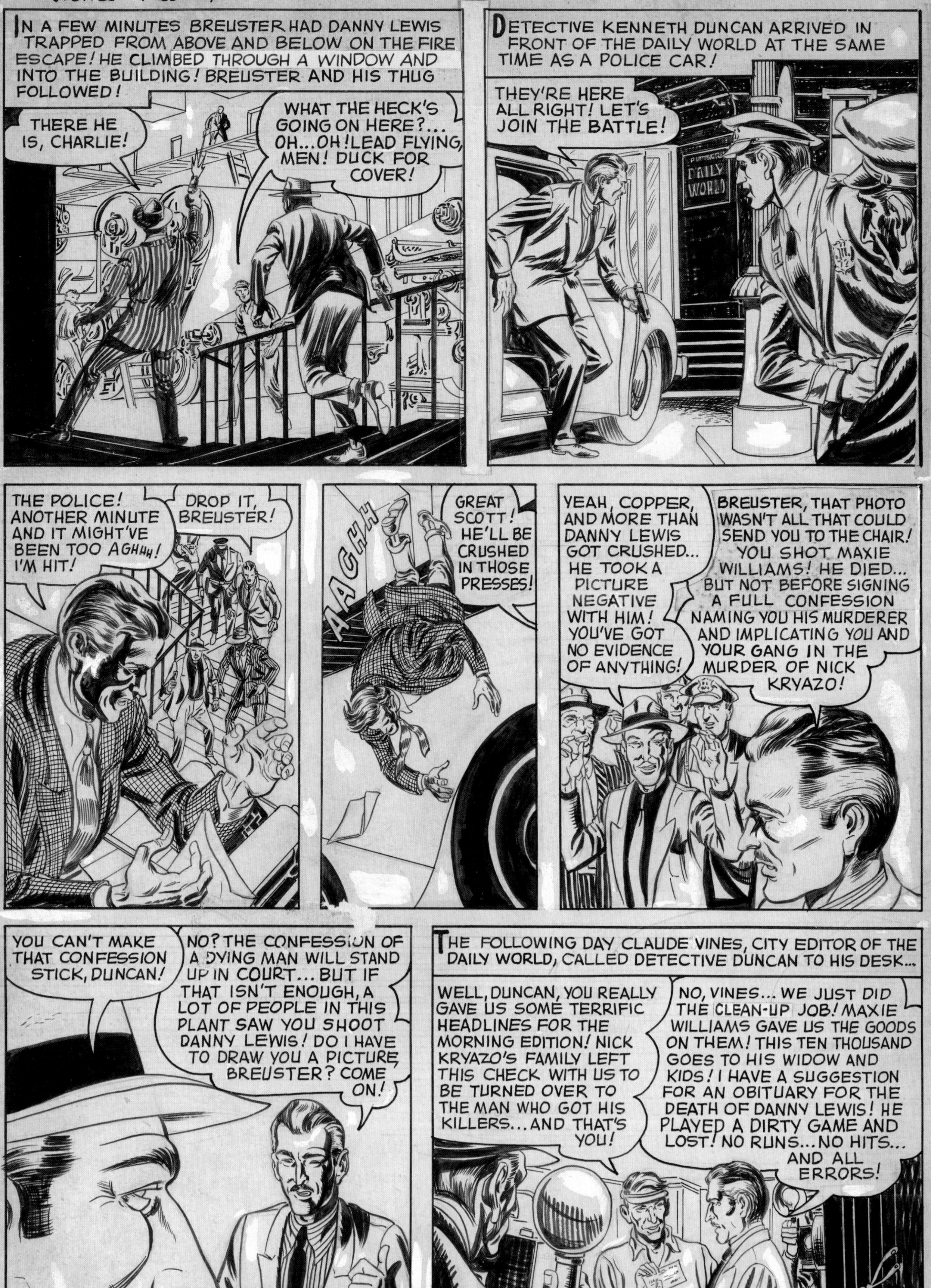
IN A FEW MINUTES BREUSTER HAD DANNY LEWIS TRAPPED FROM ABOVE AND BELOW ON THE FIRE ESCAPE! HE CLIMBED THROUGH A WINDOW AND INTO THE BUILDING! BREUSTER AND HIS THUG FOLLOWED!
THERE HE IS, CHARLIE!
WHAT THE HECK'S GOING ON HERE?... OH...OH! LEAD FLYING, MEN! DUCK FOR COVER!
DETECTIVE KENNETH DUNCAN ARRIVED IN FRONT OF THE DAILY WORLD AT THE SAME TIME AS A POLICE CAR!
THEY'RE HERE ALL RIGHT! LET'S JOIN THE BATTLE!
DAILY WORLD
THE POLICE! ANOTHER MINUTE AND IT MIGHT'VE BEEN TOO AGHHH! I'M HIT!
DROP IT, BREUSTER!
AAGHH
GREAT SCOTT! HE'LL BE CRUSHED IN THOSE PRESSES!
YEAH, COPPER, AND MORE THAN DANNY LEWIS GOT CRUSHED... HE TOOK A PICTURE NEGATIVE WITH HIM! YOU'VE GOT NO EVIDENCE OF ANYTHING!
BREUSTER, THAT PHOTO WASN'T ALL THAT COULD SEND YOU TO THE CHAIR! YOU SHOT MAXIE WILLIAMS! HE DIED... BUT NOT BEFORE SIGNING A FULL CONFESSION NAMING YOU HIS MURDERER AND IMPLICATING YOU AND YOUR GANG IN THE MURDER OF NICK KRYAZO!
YOU CAN'T MAKE THAT CONFESSION STICK, DUNCAN!
NO? THE CONFESSION OF A DYING MAN WILL STAND UP IN COURT... BUT IF THAT ISN'T ENOUGH, A LOT OF PEOPLE IN THIS PLANT SAW YOU SHOOT DANNY LEWIS! DO I HAVE TO DRAW YOU A PICTURE, BREUSTER? COME ON!
7
THE FOLLOWING DAY CLAUDE VINES, CITY EDITOR OF THE DAILY WORLD, CALLED DETECTIVE DUNCAN TO HIS DESK...
WELL, DUNCAN, YOU REALLY GAVE US SOME TERRIFIC HEADLINES FOR THE MORNING EDITION! NICK KRYAZO'S FAMILY LEFT THIS CHECK WITH US TO BE TURNED OVER TO THE MAN WHO GOT HIS KILLERS... AND THAT'S YOU!
NO, VINES... WE JUST DID THE CLEAN-UP JOB! MAXIE WILLIAMS GAVE US THE GOODS ON THEM! THIS TEN THOUSAND GOES TO HIS WIDOW AND KIDS! I HAVE A SUGGESTION FOR AN OBITUARY FOR THE DEATH OF DANNY LEWIS! HE PLAYED A DIRTY GAME AND LOST! NO RUNS... NO HITS... AND ALL ERRORS!
THE END

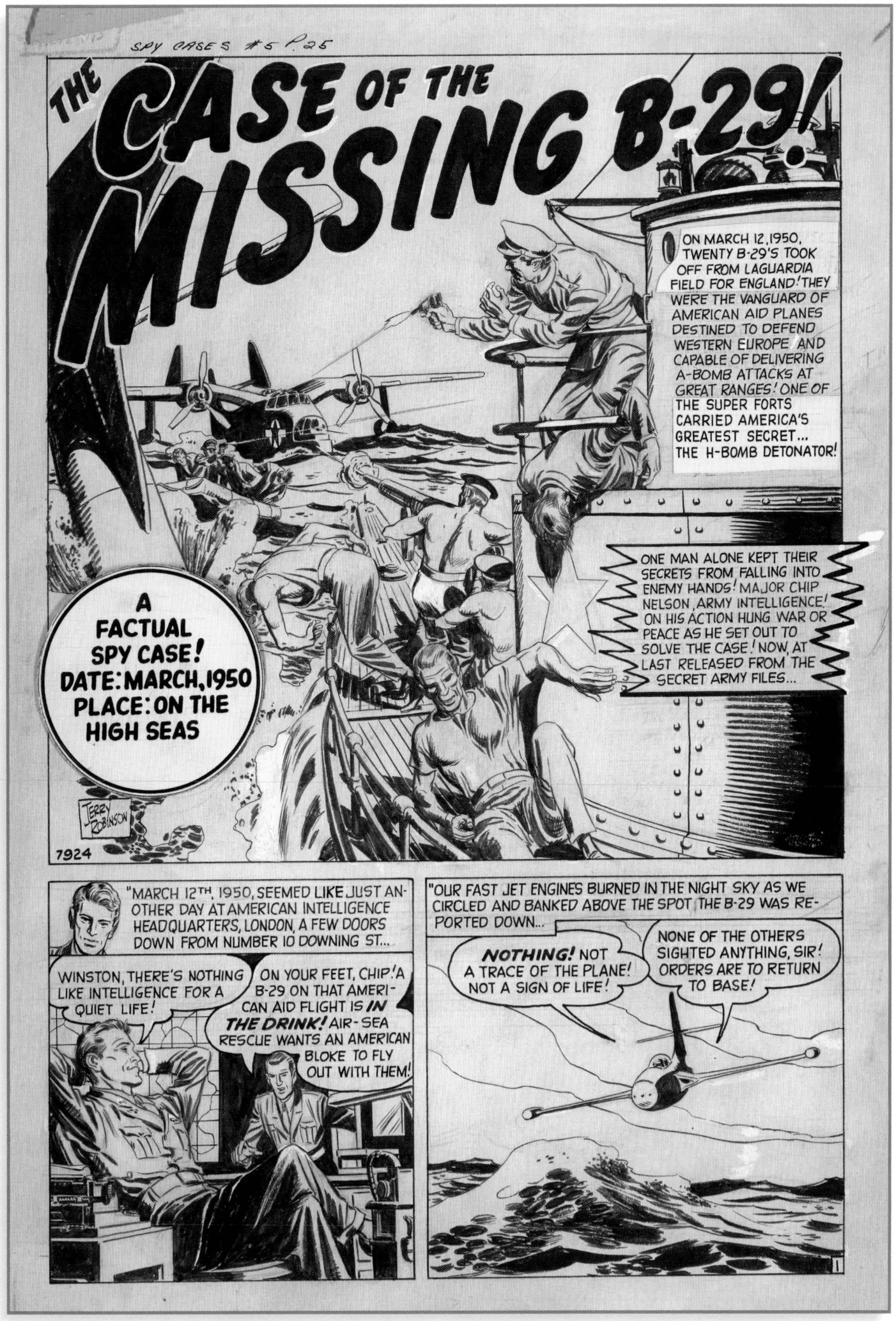
SPY CASES #5 P.25
THE CASE OF THE MISSING B-29!
ON MARCH 12,1950, TWENTY B-29'S TOOK OFF FROM LAGUARDIA FIELD FOR ENGLAND! THEY WERE THE VANGUARD OF AMERICAN AID PLANES DESTINED TO DEFEND WESTERN EUROPE AND CAPABLE OF DELIVERING A-BOMB ATTACKS AT GREAT RANGES! ONE OF THE SUPER FORTS CARRIED AMERICA'S GREATEST SECRET... THE H-BOMB DETONATOR!
ONE MAN ALONE KEPT THEIR SECRETS FROM FALLING INTO ENEMY HANDS! MAJOR CHIP NELSON, ARMY INTELLIGENCE! ON HIS ACTION HUNG WAR OR PEACE AS HE SET OUT TO SOLVE THE CASE! NOW, AT LAST RELEASED FROM THE SECRET ARMY FILES...
A FACTUAL SPY CASE! DATE: MARCH, 1950 PLACE: ON THE HIGH SEAS
JERRY ROBINSON
7924
"MARCH 12TH, 1950, SEEMED LIKE JUST ANOTHER DAY AT AMERICAN INTELLIGENCE HEADQUARTERS, LONDON, A FEW DOORS DOWN FROM NUMBER 10 DOWNING ST...
WINSTON, THERE'S NOTHING LIKE INTELLIGENCE FOR A QUIET LIFE!
ON YOUR FEET, CHIP! A B-29 ON THAT AMERICAN AID FLIGHT IS IN THE DRINK! AIR-SEA RESCUE WANTS AN AMERICAN BLOKE TO FLY OUT WITH THEM!
"OUR FAST JET ENGINES BURNED IN THE NIGHT SKY AS WE CIRCLED AND BANKED ABOVE THE SPOT THE B-29 WAS REPORTED DOWN...
NOTHING! NOT A TRACE OF THE PLANE! NOT A SIGN OF LIFE!
NONE OF THE OTHERS SIGHTED ANYTHING, SIR! ORDERS ARE TO RETURN TO BASE!
1

Above
SPLASH PAGE 1 OF "THE CASE OF THE MISSING B-29!" FROM *SPY CASES* NO. 5
June 1951, pencils and inks by Jerry Robinson.

Above and following pages
ORIGINAL ART FOR PAGES 20 AND 22–30 OF "SHOWDOWN IN DODGE CITY" FROM *BAT MASTERSON* NO. 6
February – April 1961, pencils and inks by Jerry Robinson.

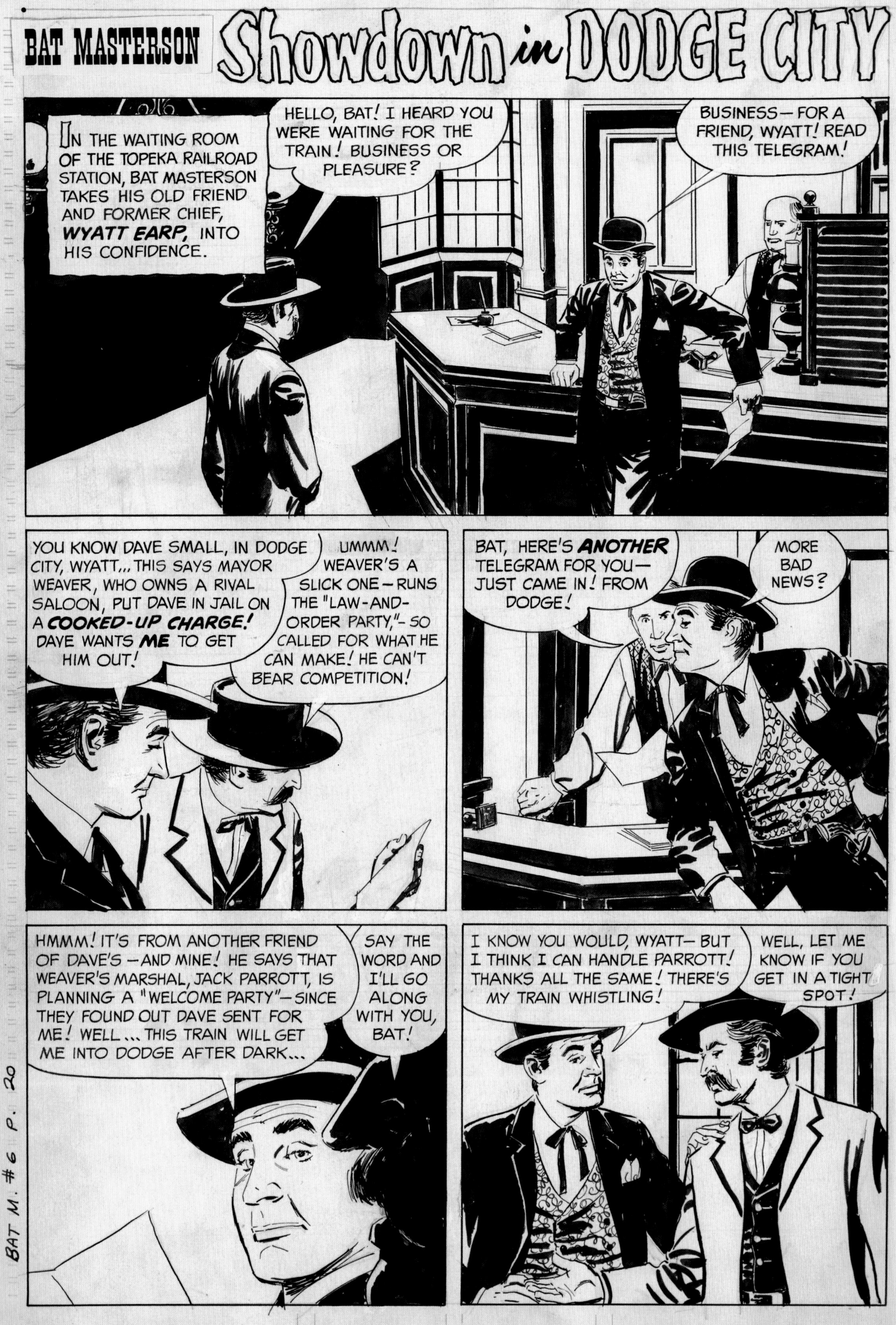
BAT MASTERSON
Showdown in DODGE CITY
IN THE WAITING ROOM OF THE TOPEKA RAILROAD STATION, BAT MASTERSON TAKES HIS OLD FRIEND AND FORMER CHIEF, WYATT EARP, INTO HIS CONFIDENCE.
HELLO, BAT! I HEARD YOU WERE WAITING FOR THE TRAIN! BUSINESS OR PLEASURE?
BUSINESS — FOR A FRIEND, WYATT! READ THIS TELEGRAM!
YOU KNOW DAVE SMALL, IN DODGE CITY, WYATT... THIS SAYS MAYOR WEAVER, WHO OWNS A RIVAL SALOON, PUT DAVE IN JAIL ON A COOKED-UP CHARGE! DAVE WANTS ME TO GET HIM OUT!
UMMM! WEAVER'S A SLICK ONE — RUNS THE "LAW-AND-ORDER PARTY," - SO CALLED FOR WHAT HE CAN MAKE! HE CAN'T BEAR COMPETITION!
BAT, HERE'S ANOTHER TELEGRAM FOR YOU — JUST CAME IN! FROM DODGE!
MORE BAD NEWS?
HMMM! IT'S FROM ANOTHER FRIEND OF DAVE'S — AND MINE! HE SAYS THAT WEAVER'S MARSHAL, JACK PARROTT, IS PLANNING A "WELCOME PARTY" — SINCE THEY FOUND OUT DAVE SENT FOR ME! WELL ... THIS TRAIN WILL GET ME INTO DODGE AFTER DARK...
SAY THE WORD AND I'LL GO ALONG WITH YOU, BAT!
I KNOW YOU WOULD, WYATT — BUT I THINK I CAN HANDLE PARROTT! THANKS ALL THE SAME! THERE'S MY TRAIN WHISTLING!
WELL, LET ME KNOW IF YOU GET IN A TIGHT SPOT!
BAT M. #6 P. 20

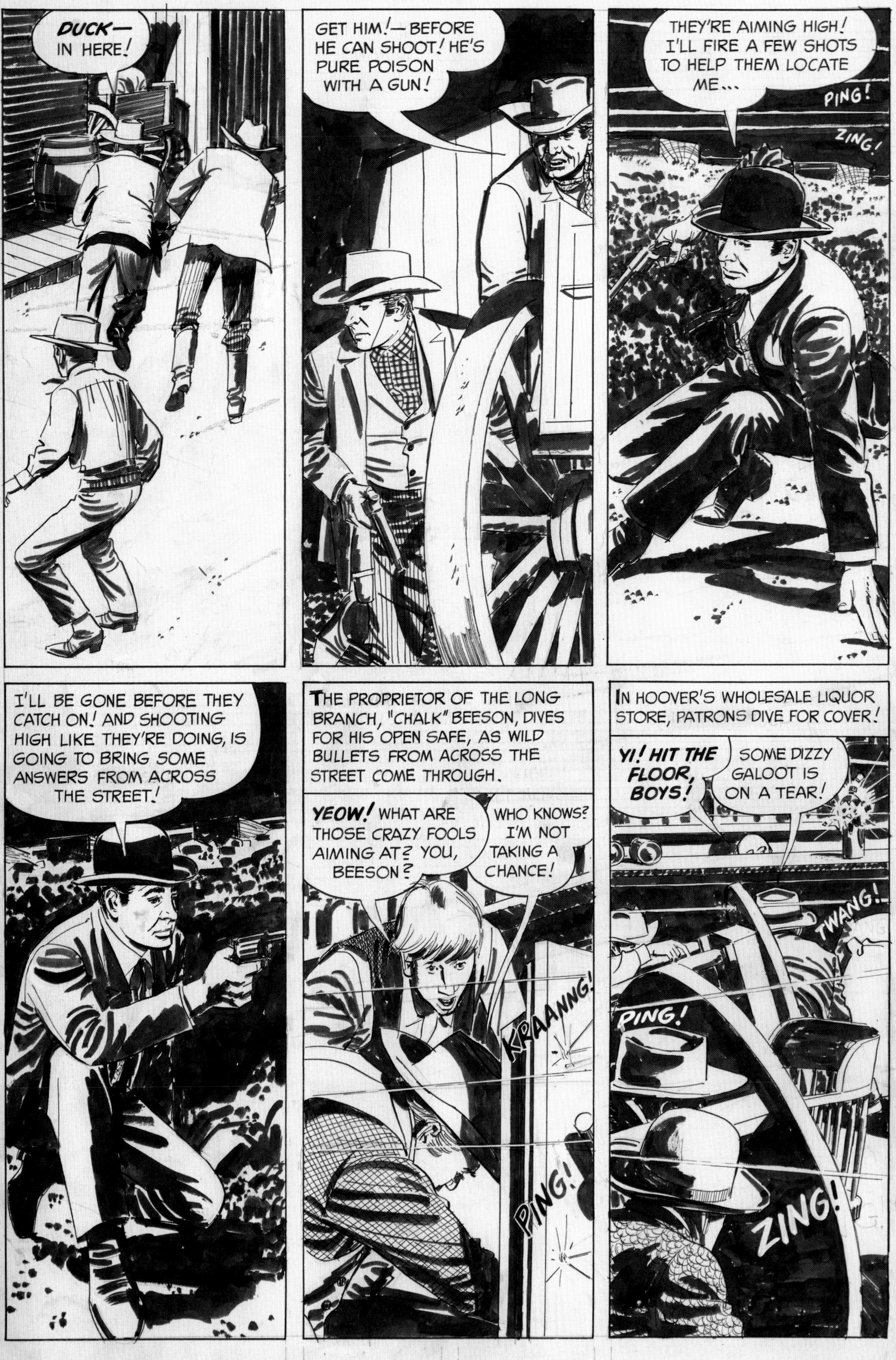
DUCK— IN HERE!
GET HIM!— BEFORE HE CAN SHOOT! HE'S PURE POISON WITH A GUN!
THEY'RE AIMING HIGH! I'LL FIRE A FEW SHOTS TO HELP THEM LOCATE ME...
PING!
ZING!
I'LL BE GONE BEFORE THEY CATCH ON! AND SHOOTING HIGH LIKE THEY'RE DOING, IS GOING TO BRING SOME ANSWERS FROM ACROSS THE STREET!
THE PROPRIETOR OF THE LONG BRANCH, "CHALK" BEESON, DIVES FOR HIS OPEN SAFE, AS WILD BULLETS FROM ACROSS THE STREET COME THROUGH.
YEOW! WHAT ARE THOSE CRAZY FOOLS AIMING AT? YOU, BEESON?
WHO KNOWS? I'M NOT TAKING A CHANCE!
KRAANNG!
PING!
IN HOOVER'S WHOLESALE LIQUOR STORE, PATRONS DIVE FOR COVER!
YI! HIT THE FLOOR, BOYS!
SOME DIZZY GALOOT IS ON A TEAR!
TWANG!
PING!
ZING!

BAT M. #6 P. 22

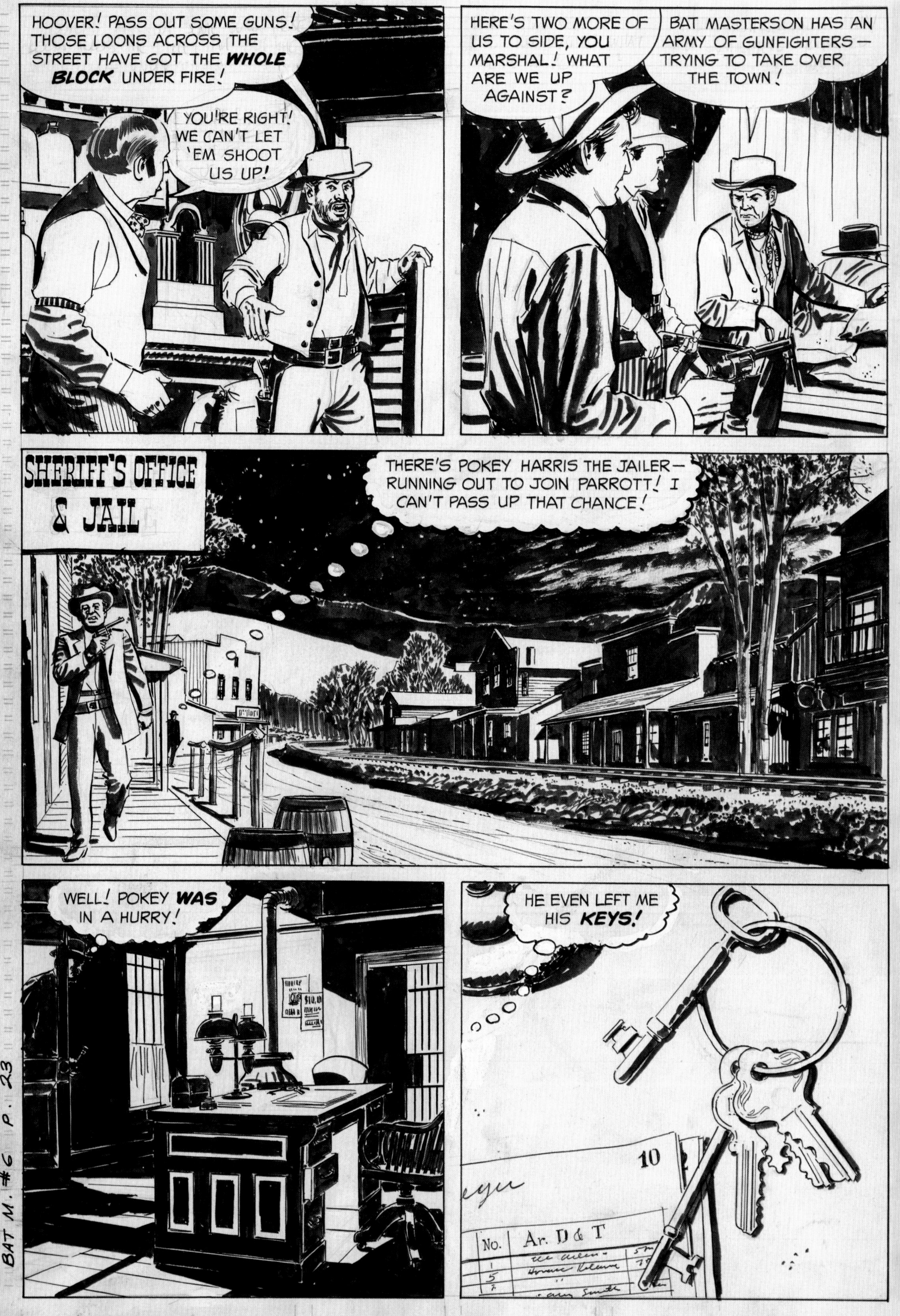
HOOVER! PASS OUT SOME GUNS! THOSE LOONS ACROSS THE STREET HAVE GOT THE WHOLE BLOCK UNDER FIRE!
YOU'RE RIGHT! WE CAN'T LET 'EM SHOOT US UP!
HERE'S TWO MORE OF US TO SIDE, YOU MARSHAL! WHAT ARE WE UP AGAINST?
BAT MASTERSON HAS AN ARMY OF GUNFIGHTERS — TRYING TO TAKE OVER THE TOWN!
SHERIFF'S OFFICE & JAIL
THERE'S POKEY HARRIS THE JAILER — RUNNING OUT TO JOIN PARROTT! I CAN'T PASS UP THAT CHANCE!
WELL! POKEY WAS IN A HURRY!
HE EVEN LEFT ME HIS KEYS!
10
No. Ar. D & T
BAT M. #6 P. 23

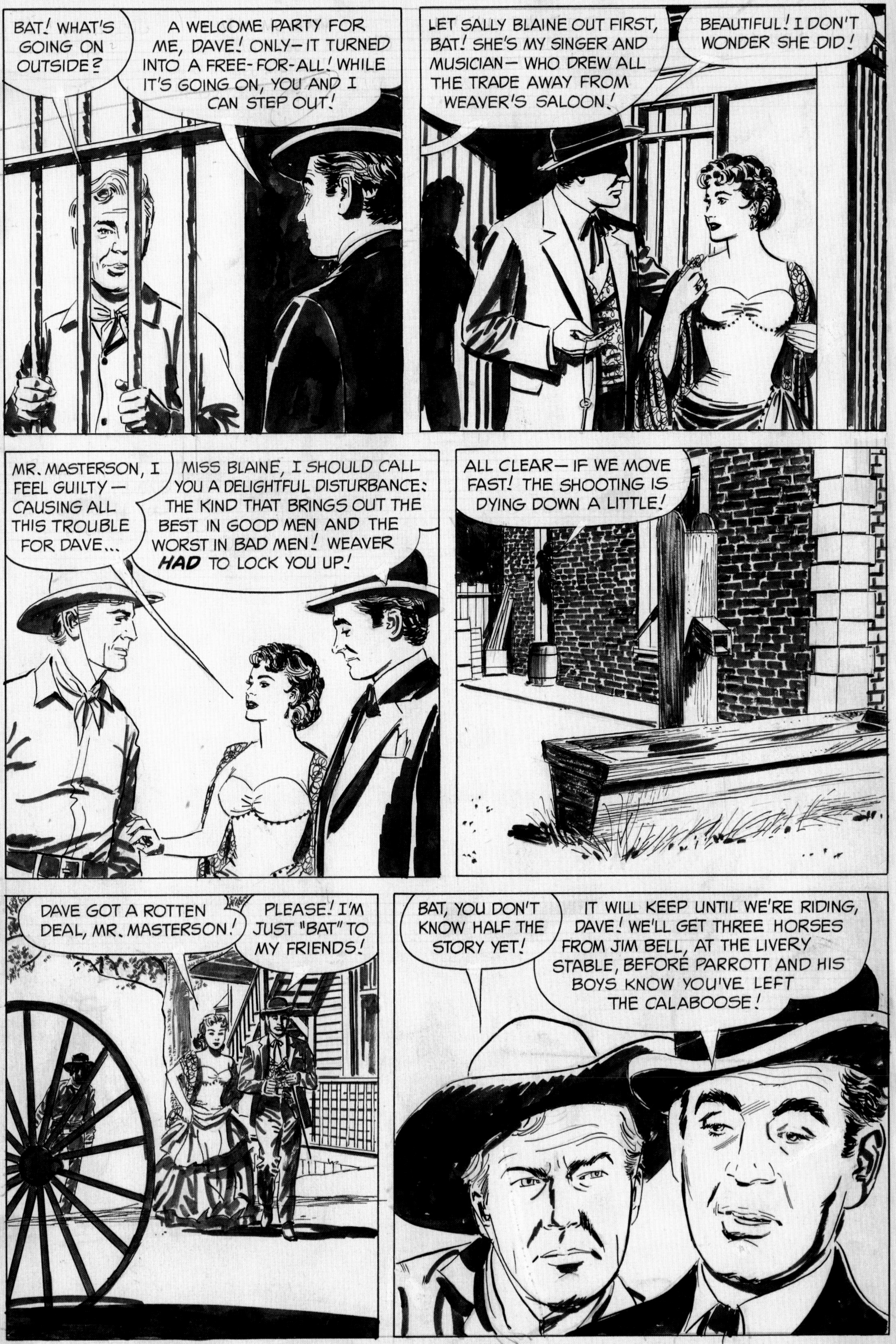
BAT! WHAT'S GOING ON OUTSIDE?
A WELCOME PARTY FOR ME, DAVE! ONLY– IT TURNED INTO A FREE-FOR-ALL! WHILE IT'S GOING ON, YOU AND I CAN STEP OUT!
LET SALLY BLAINE OUT FIRST, BAT! SHE'S MY SINGER AND MUSICIAN– WHO DREW ALL THE TRADE AWAY FROM WEAVER'S SALOON!
BEAUTIFUL! I DON'T WONDER SHE DID!
MR. MASTERSON, I FEEL GUILTY– CAUSING ALL THIS TROUBLE FOR DAVE...
MISS BLAINE, I SHOULD CALL YOU A DELIGHTFUL DISTURBANCE: THE KIND THAT BRINGS OUT THE BEST IN GOOD MEN AND THE WORST IN BAD MEN! WEAVER HAD TO LOCK YOU UP!
ALL CLEAR– IF WE MOVE FAST! THE SHOOTING IS DYING DOWN A LITTLE!
DAVE GOT A ROTTEN DEAL, MR. MASTERSON!
PLEASE! I'M JUST "BAT" TO MY FRIENDS!
BAT, YOU DON'T KNOW HALF THE STORY YET!
IT WILL KEEP UNTIL WE'RE RIDING, DAVE! WE'LL GET THREE HORSES FROM JIM BELL, AT THE LIVERY STABLE, BEFORE PARROTT AND HIS BOYS KNOW YOU'VE LEFT THE CALABOOSE!

BAT M. #6 P. 24

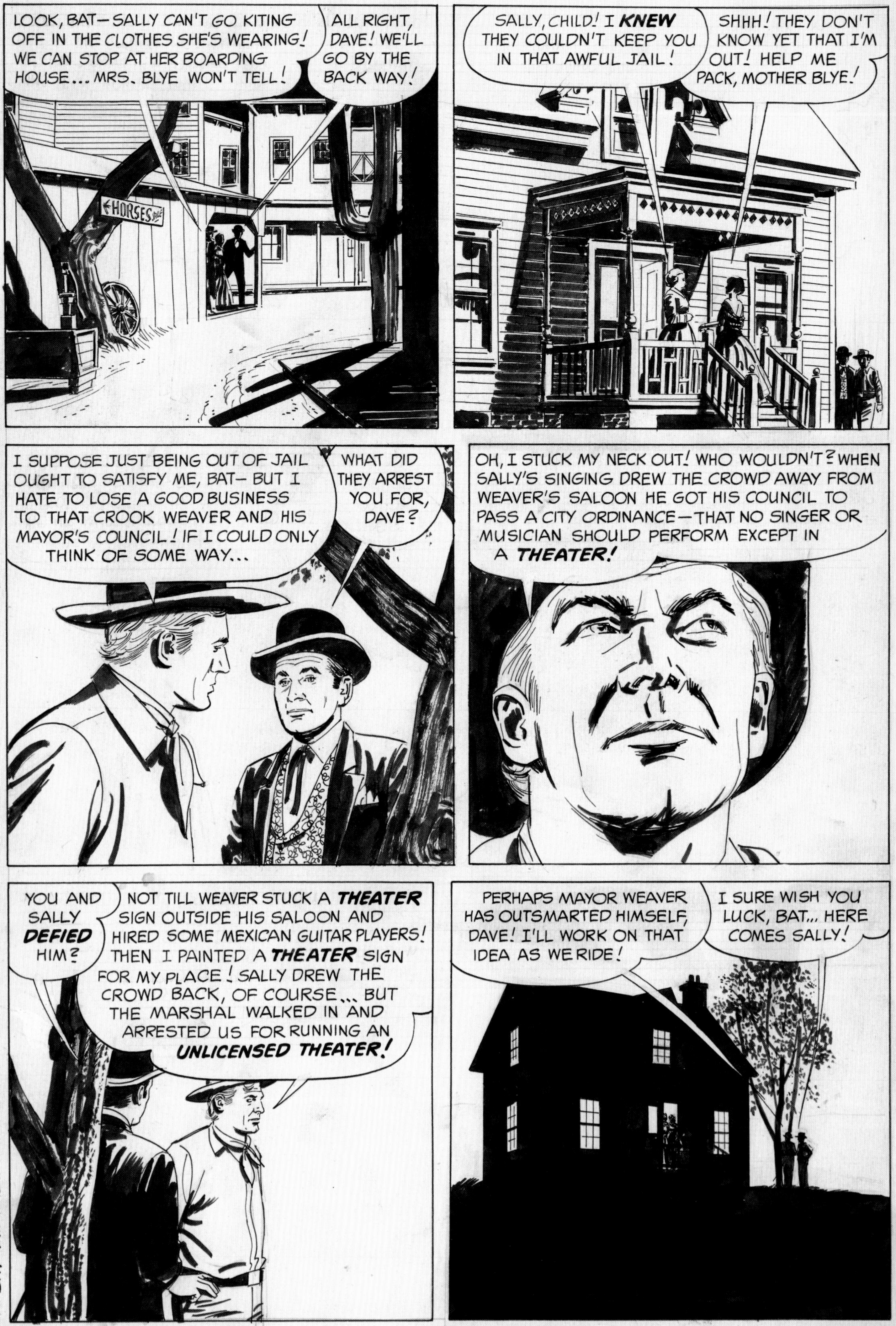
LOOK, BAT—SALLY CAN'T GO KITING OFF IN THE CLOTHES SHE'S WEARING! WE CAN STOP AT HER BOARDING HOUSE... MRS. BLYE WON'T TELL!
ALL RIGHT, DAVE! WE'LL GO BY THE BACK WAY!
HORSES
SALLY, CHILD! I KNEW THEY COULDN'T KEEP YOU IN THAT AWFUL JAIL!
SHHH! THEY DON'T KNOW YET THAT I'M OUT! HELP ME PACK, MOTHER BLYE!
I SUPPOSE JUST BEING OUT OF JAIL OUGHT TO SATISFY ME, BAT—BUT I HATE TO LOSE A GOOD BUSINESS TO THAT CROOK WEAVER AND HIS MAYOR'S COUNCIL! IF I COULD ONLY THINK OF SOME WAY...
WHAT DID THEY ARREST YOU FOR, DAVE?
OH, I STUCK MY NECK OUT! WHO WOULDN'T? WHEN SALLY'S SINGING DREW THE CROWD AWAY FROM WEAVER'S SALOON HE GOT HIS COUNCIL TO PASS A CITY ORDINANCE—THAT NO SINGER OR MUSICIAN SHOULD PERFORM EXCEPT IN A THEATER!
YOU AND SALLY DEFIED HIM?
NOT TILL WEAVER STUCK A THEATER SIGN OUTSIDE HIS SALOON AND HIRED SOME MEXICAN GUITAR PLAYERS! THEN I PAINTED A THEATER SIGN FOR MY PLACE! SALLY DREW THE CROWD BACK, OF COURSE... BUT THE MARSHAL WALKED IN AND ARRESTED US FOR RUNNING AN UNLICENSED THEATER!
PERHAPS MAYOR WEAVER HAS OUTSMARTED HIMSELF, DAVE! I'LL WORK ON THAT IDEA AS WE RIDE!
I SURE WISH YOU LUCK, BAT... HERE COMES SALLY!

BAT M. #6 P. 25

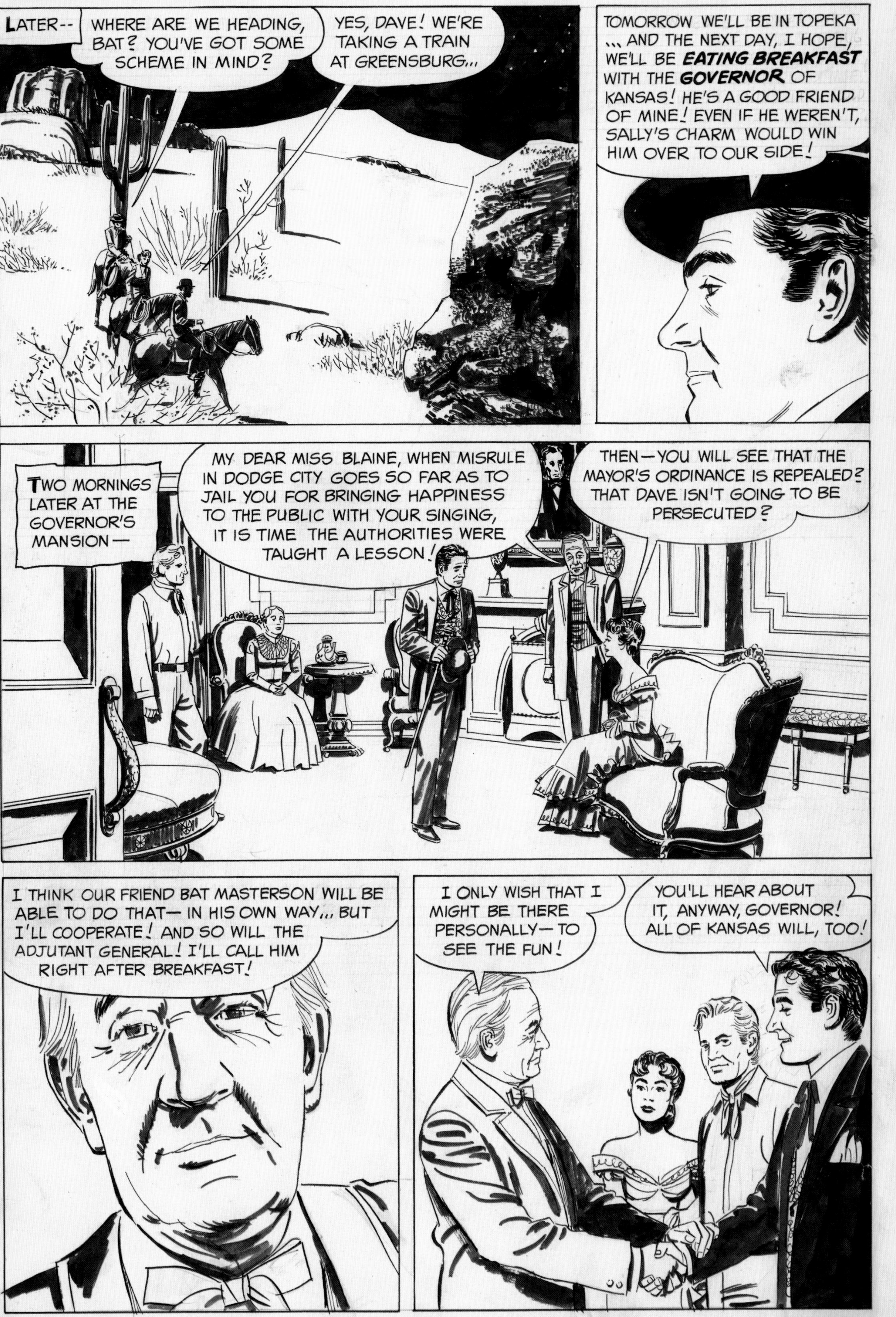
LATER--
WHERE ARE WE HEADING, BAT? YOU'VE GOT SOME SCHEME IN MIND?
YES, DAVE! WE'RE TAKING A TRAIN AT GREENSBURG...
TOMORROW WE'LL BE IN TOPEKA ... AND THE NEXT DAY, I HOPE, WE'LL BE EATING BREAKFAST WITH THE GOVERNOR OF KANSAS! HE'S A GOOD FRIEND OF MINE! EVEN IF HE WEREN'T, SALLY'S CHARM WOULD WIN HIM OVER TO OUR SIDE!
TWO MORNINGS LATER AT THE GOVERNOR'S MANSION—
MY DEAR MISS BLAINE, WHEN MISRULE IN DODGE CITY GOES SO FAR AS TO JAIL YOU FOR BRINGING HAPPINESS TO THE PUBLIC WITH YOUR SINGING, IT IS TIME THE AUTHORITIES WERE TAUGHT A LESSON!
THEN—YOU WILL SEE THAT THE MAYOR'S ORDINANCE IS REPEALED? THAT DAVE ISN'T GOING TO BE PERSECUTED?
I THINK OUR FRIEND BAT MASTERSON WILL BE ABLE TO DO THAT— IN HIS OWN WAY... BUT I'LL COOPERATE! AND SO WILL THE ADJUTANT GENERAL! I'LL CALL HIM RIGHT AFTER BREAKFAST!
I ONLY WISH THAT I MIGHT BE THERE PERSONALLY— TO SEE THE FUN!
YOU'LL HEAR ABOUT IT, ANYWAY, GOVERNOR! ALL OF KANSAS WILL, TOO!

BAT M. #6 P. 26

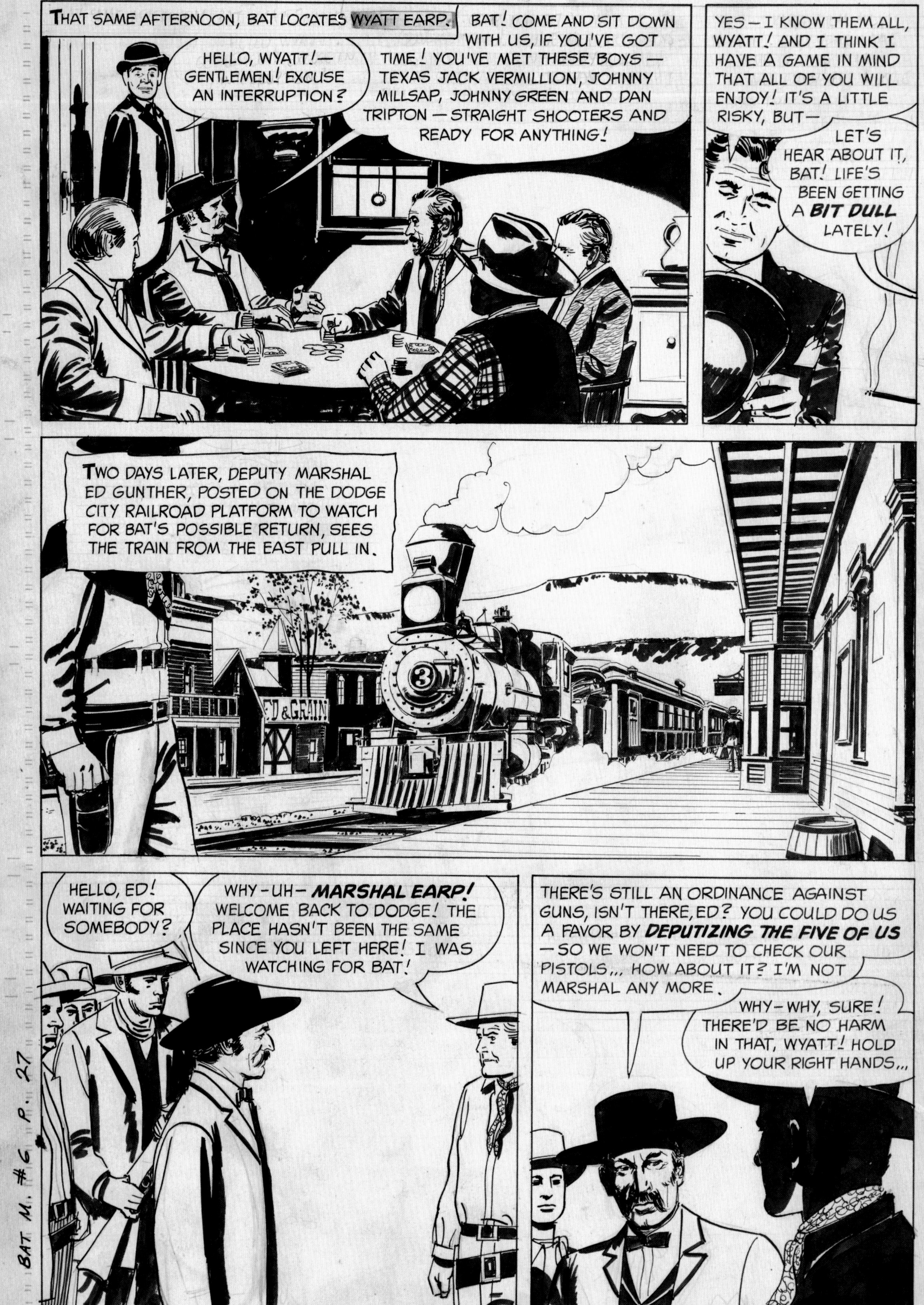

THAT SAME AFTERNOON, BAT LOCATES WYATT EARP.
HELLO, WYATT!— GENTLEMEN! EXCUSE AN INTERRUPTION?
BAT! COME AND SIT DOWN WITH US, IF YOU'VE GOT TIME! YOU'VE MET THESE BOYS — TEXAS JACK VERMILLION, JOHNNY MILLSAP, JOHNNY GREEN AND DAN TRIPTON — STRAIGHT SHOOTERS AND READY FOR ANYTHING!
YES — I KNOW THEM ALL, WYATT! AND I THINK I HAVE A GAME IN MIND THAT ALL OF YOU WILL ENJOY! IT'S A LITTLE RISKY, BUT—
LET'S HEAR ABOUT IT, BAT! LIFE'S BEEN GETTING A BIT DULL LATELY!
TWO DAYS LATER, DEPUTY MARSHAL ED GUNTHER, POSTED ON THE DODGE CITY RAILROAD PLATFORM TO WATCH FOR BAT'S POSSIBLE RETURN, SEES THE TRAIN FROM THE EAST PULL IN.
HELLO, ED! WAITING FOR SOMEBODY?
WHY-UH- MARSHAL EARP! WELCOME BACK TO DODGE! THE PLACE HASN'T BEEN THE SAME SINCE YOU LEFT HERE! I WAS WATCHING FOR BAT!
THERE'S STILL AN ORDINANCE AGAINST GUNS, ISN'T THERE, ED? YOU COULD DO US A FAVOR BY DEPUTIZING THE FIVE OF US —SO WE WON'T NEED TO CHECK OUR PISTOLS... HOW ABOUT IT? I'M NOT MARSHAL ANY MORE.
WHY-WHY, SURE! THERE'D BE NO HARM IN THAT, WYATT! HOLD UP YOUR RIGHT HANDS...
BAT. M. #6 P. 27

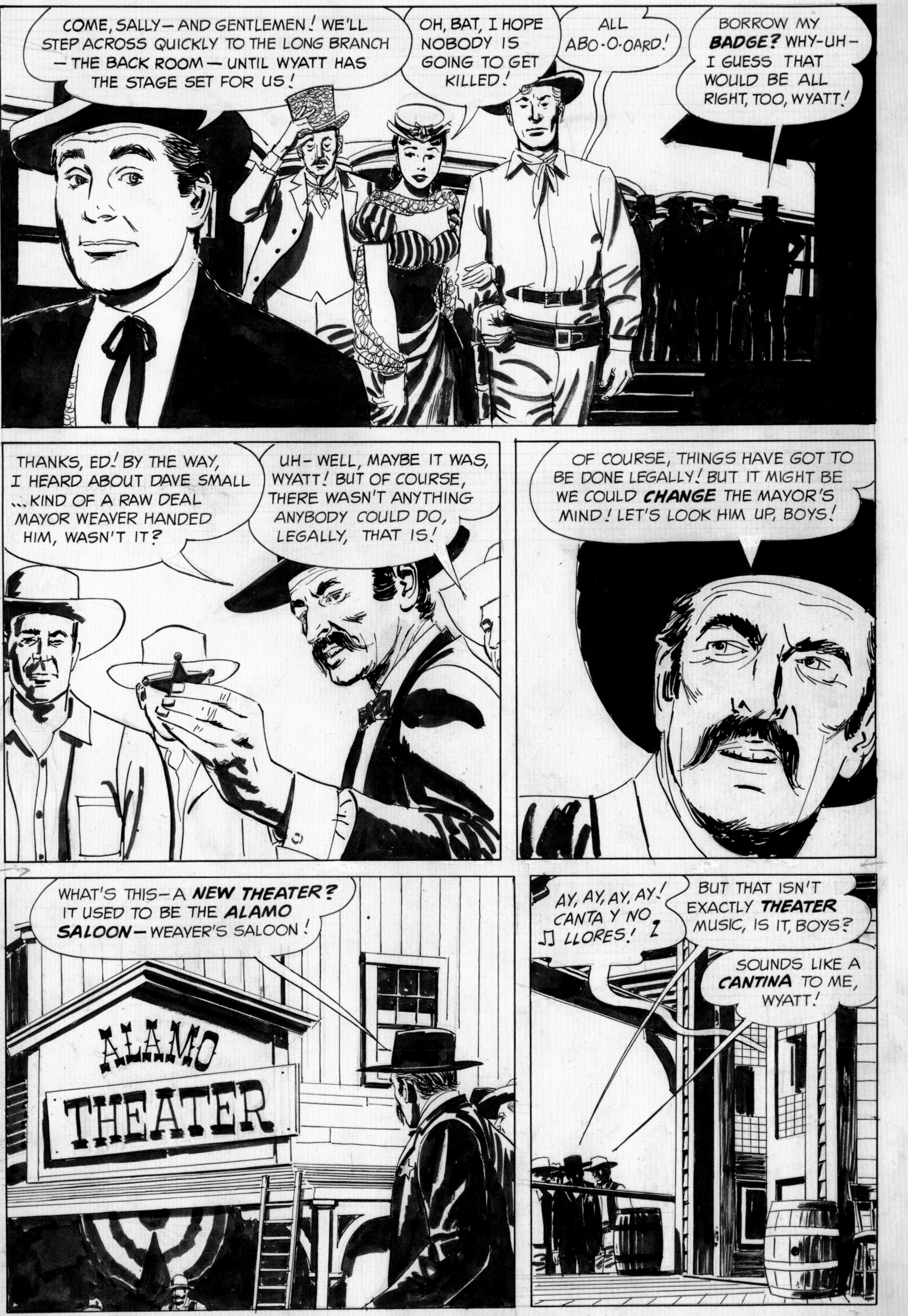
COME, SALLY— AND GENTLEMEN! WE'LL STEP ACROSS QUICKLY TO THE LONG BRANCH — THE BACK ROOM — UNTIL WYATT HAS THE STAGE SET FOR US!
OH, BAT, I HOPE NOBODY IS GOING TO GET KILLED!
ALL ABO-O-OARD!
BORROW MY BADGE? WHY-UH- I GUESS THAT WOULD BE ALL RIGHT, TOO, WYATT!
THANKS, ED! BY THE WAY, I HEARD ABOUT DAVE SMALL ...KIND OF A RAW DEAL MAYOR WEAVER HANDED HIM, WASN'T IT?
UH- WELL, MAYBE IT WAS, WYATT! BUT OF COURSE, THERE WASN'T ANYTHING ANYBODY COULD DO, LEGALLY, THAT IS!
OF COURSE, THINGS HAVE GOT TO BE DONE LEGALLY! BUT IT MIGHT BE WE COULD CHANGE THE MAYOR'S MIND! LET'S LOOK HIM UP, BOYS!
WHAT'S THIS— A NEW THEATER? IT USED TO BE THE ALAMO SALOON— WEAVER'S SALOON!
ALAMO
THEATER
AY, AY, AY, AY! CANTA Y NO ♫ LLORES!
BUT THAT ISN'T EXACTLY THEATER MUSIC, IS IT, BOYS?
SOUNDS LIKE A CANTINA TO ME, WYATT!

BAT M. #6 P. 28

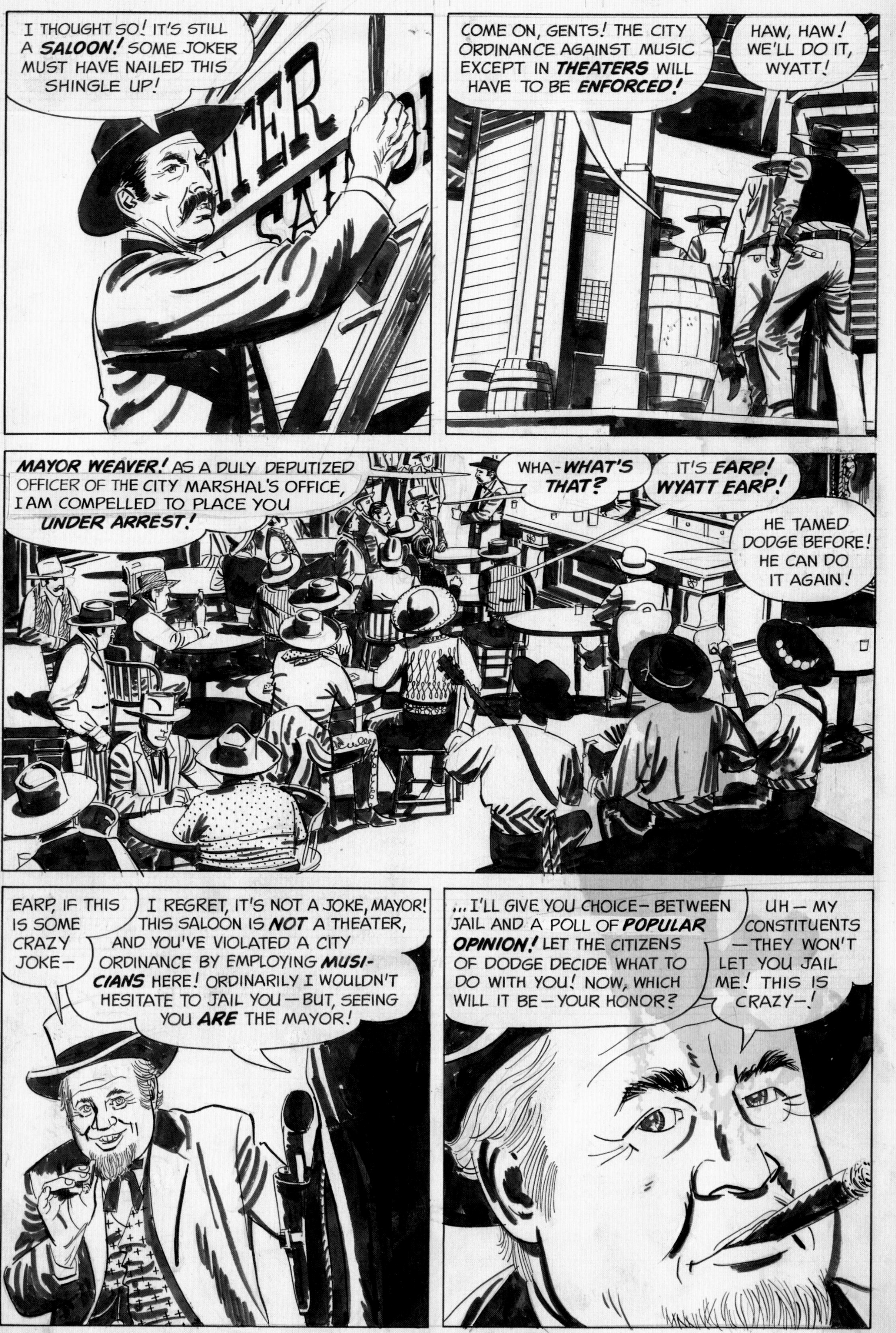
I THOUGHT SO! IT'S STILL A SALOON! SOME JOKER MUST HAVE NAILED THIS SHINGLE UP!
COME ON, GENTS! THE CITY ORDINANCE AGAINST MUSIC EXCEPT IN THEATERS WILL HAVE TO BE ENFORCED!
HAW, HAW! WE'LL DO IT, WYATT!
MAYOR WEAVER! AS A DULY DEPUTIZED OFFICER OF THE CITY MARSHAL'S OFFICE, I AM COMPELLED TO PLACE YOU UNDER ARREST!
OFFICER
WHA-WHAT'S THAT?
IT'S EARP! WYATT EARP!
HE TAMED DODGE BEFORE! HE CAN DO IT AGAIN!
EARP, IF THIS IS SOME CRAZY JOKE—
I REGRET, IT'S NOT A JOKE, MAYOR! THIS SALOON IS NOT A THEATER, AND YOU'VE VIOLATED A CITY ORDINANCE BY EMPLOYING MUSI-CIANS HERE! ORDINARILY I WOULDN'T HESITATE TO JAIL YOU—BUT, SEEING YOU ARE THE MAYOR!
...I'LL GIVE YOU CHOICE—BETWEEN JAIL AND A POLL OF POPULAR OPINION! LET THE CITIZENS OF DODGE DECIDE WHAT TO DO WITH YOU! NOW, WHICH WILL IT BE—YOUR HONOR?
UH—MY CONSTITUENTS—THEY WON'T LET YOU JAIL ME! THIS IS CRAZY—!

BAT M. #6 P. 29

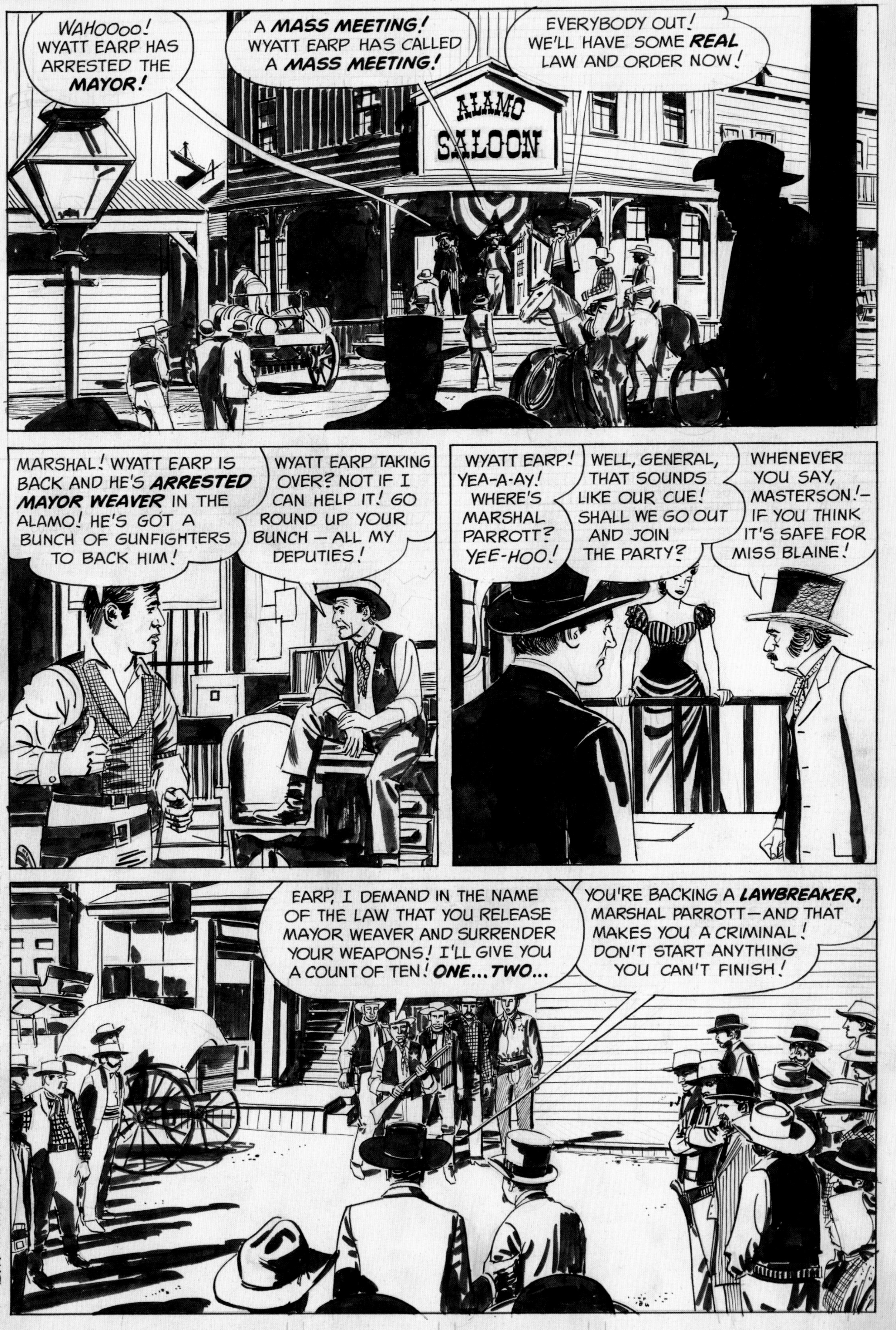
WAHOOOOO! WYATT EARP HAS ARRESTED THE MAYOR!
A MASS MEETING! WYATT EARP HAS CALLED A MASS MEETING!
EVERYBODY OUT! WE'LL HAVE SOME REAL LAW AND ORDER NOW!
ALAMO SALOON
MARSHAL! WYATT EARP IS BACK AND HE'S ARRESTED MAYOR WEAVER IN THE ALAMO! HE'S GOT A BUNCH OF GUNFIGHTERS TO BACK HIM!
WYATT EARP TAKING OVER? NOT IF I CAN HELP IT! GO ROUND UP YOUR BUNCH — ALL MY DEPUTIES!
WYATT EARP! YEA-A-AY! WHERE'S MARSHAL PARROTT? YEE-HOO!
WELL, GENERAL, THAT SOUNDS LIKE OUR CUE! SHALL WE GO OUT AND JOIN THE PARTY?
WHENEVER YOU SAY, MASTERSON! — IF YOU THINK IT'S SAFE FOR MISS BLAINE!
EARP, I DEMAND IN THE NAME OF THE LAW THAT YOU RELEASE MAYOR WEAVER AND SURRENDER YOUR WEAPONS! I'LL GIVE YOU A COUNT OF TEN! ONE... TWO...
YOU'RE BACKING A LAWBREAKER, MARSHAL PARROTT — AND THAT MAKES YOU A CRIMINAL! DON'T START ANYTHING YOU CAN'T FINISH!
BAT M. #6 P. 30

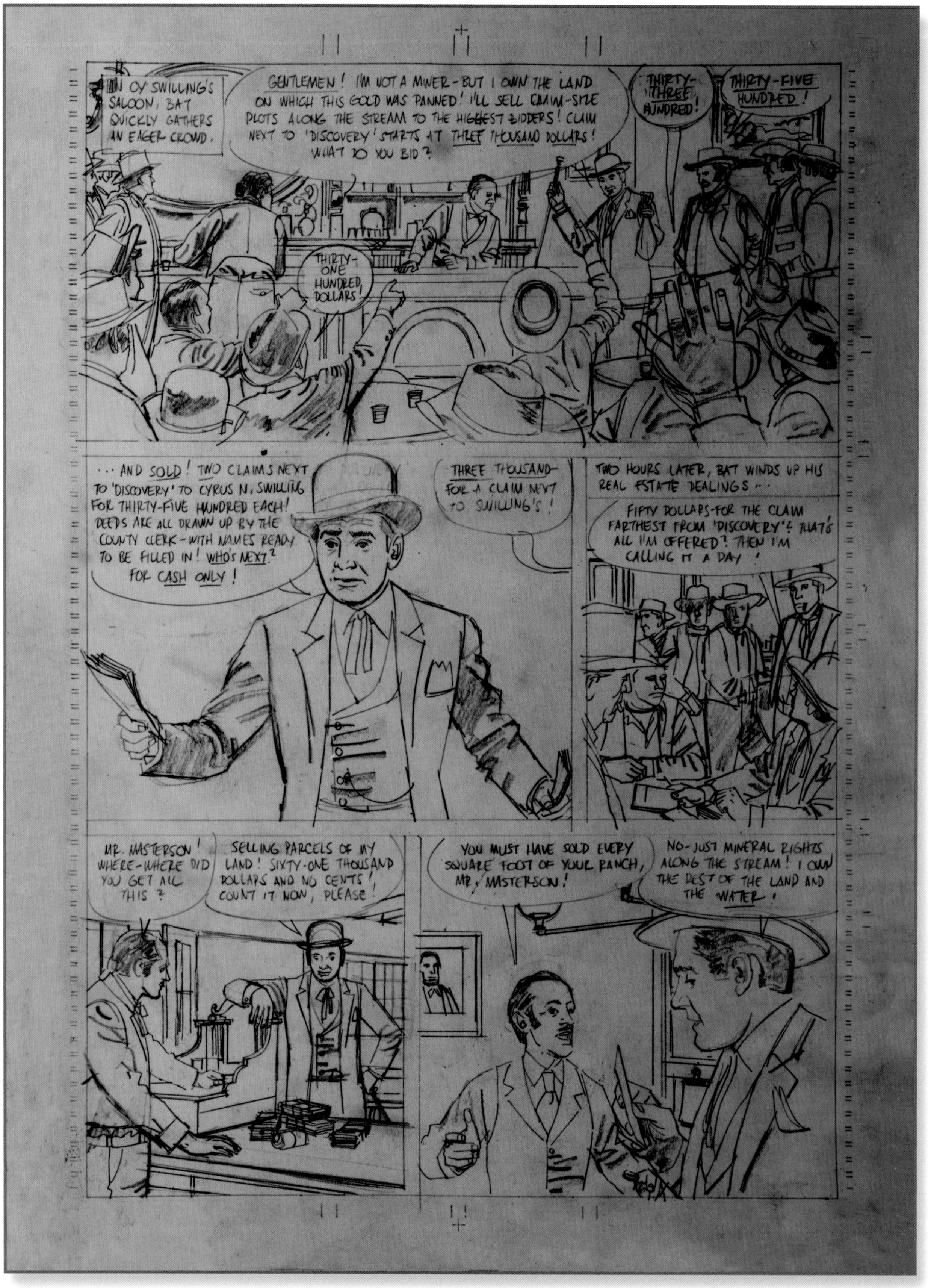
IN CY SWILLING'S SALOON, BAT QUICKLY GATHERS AN EAGER CROWD.
GENTLEMEN! I'M NOT A MINER—BUT I OWN THE LAND ON WHICH THIS GOLD WAS PANNED! I'LL SELL CLAIM-SIZE PLOTS ALONG THE STREAM TO THE HIGHEST BIDDERS! CLAIM NEXT TO 'DISCOVERY' STARTS AT THREE THOUSAND DOLLARS! WHAT DO YOU BID?
THIRTY-ONE HUNDRED DOLLARS!
THIRTY-THREE HUNDRED!
THIRTY-FIVE HUNDRED!
... AND SOLD! TWO CLAIMS NEXT TO 'DISCOVERY' TO CYRUS N. SWILLING FOR THIRTY-FIVE HUNDRED EACH! DEEDS ARE ALL DRAWN UP BY THE COUNTY CLERK—WITH NAMES READY TO BE FILLED IN! WHO'S NEXT? FOR CASH ONLY!
THREE THOUSAND FOR A CLAIM NEXT TO SWILLING'S!
TWO HOURS LATER, BAT WINDS UP HIS REAL ESTATE DEALINGS...
FIFTY DOLLARS FOR THE CLAIM FARTHEST FROM 'DISCOVERY'? THAT'S ALL I'M OFFERED? THEN I'M CALLING IT A DAY!
MR. MASTERSON! WHERE—WHERE DID YOU GET ALL THIS?
SELLING PARCELS OF MY LAND! SIXTY-ONE THOUSAND DOLLARS AND NO CENTS! COUNT IT NOW, PLEASE!
YOU MUST HAVE SOLD EVERY SQUARE FOOT OF YOUR RANCH, MR. MASTERSON!
NO—JUST MINERAL RIGHTS ALONG THE STREAM! I OWN THE REST OF THE LAND AND THE WATER!

Above and right
ROUGH PAGES FROM "GOLD FEVER" FROM *BAT MASTERSON* NO. 6
February – April 1961, pencils by Jerry Robinson.

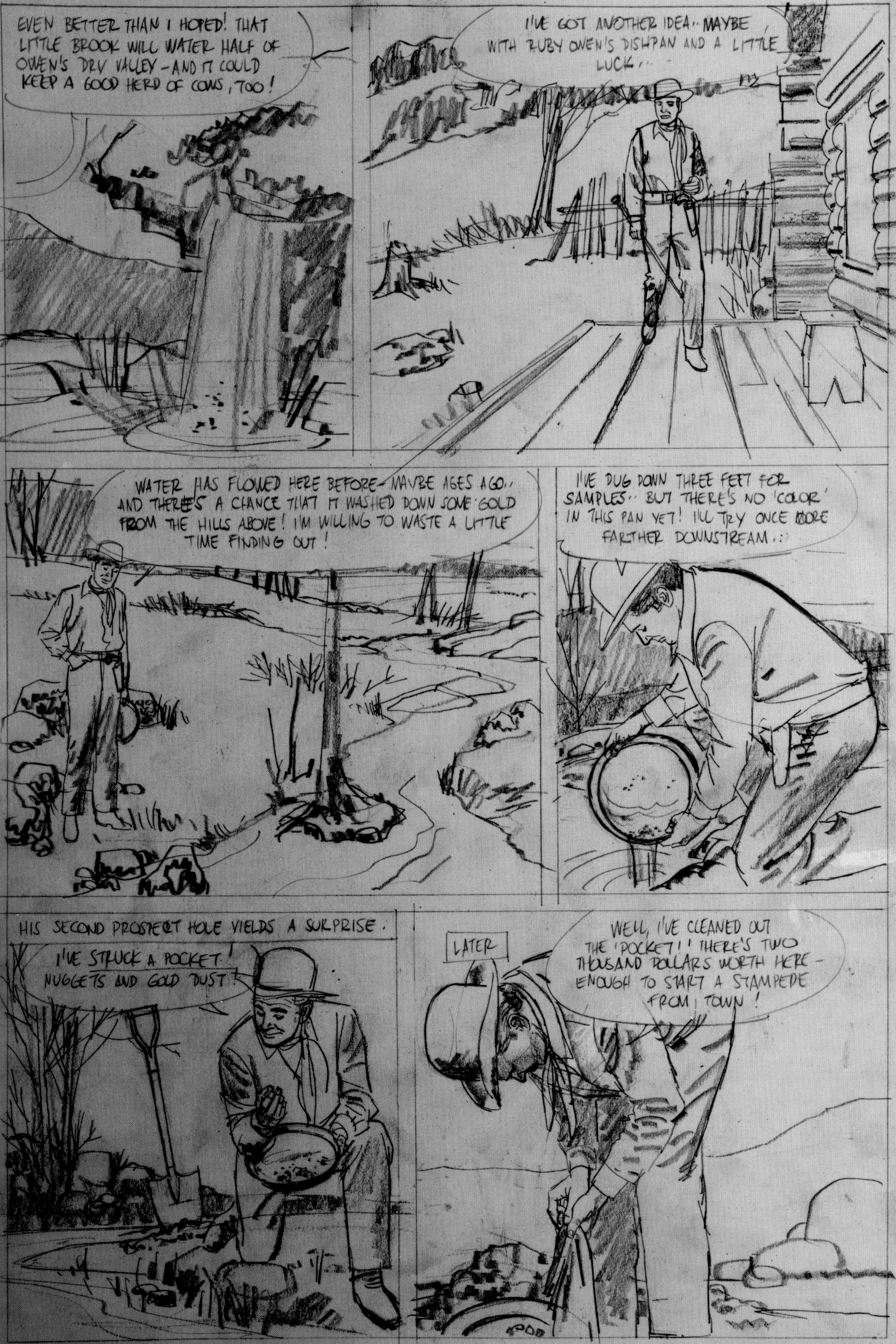
EVEN BETTER THAN I HOPED! THAT LITTLE BROOK WILL WATER HALF OF OWEN'S DRY VALLEY - AND IT COULD KEEP A GOOD HERD OF COWS, TOO!
I'VE GOT ANOTHER IDEA.. MAYBE WITH RUBY OWEN'S DISHPAN AND A LITTLE LUCK..
WATER HAS FLOWED HERE BEFORE- MAYBE AGES AGO.. AND THERE'S A CHANCE THAT IT WASHED DOWN SOME GOLD FROM THE HILLS ABOVE! I'M WILLING TO WASTE A LITTLE TIME FINDING OUT!
I'VE DUG DOWN THREE FEET FOR SAMPLES.. BUT THERE'S NO 'COLOR' IN THIS PAN YET! I'LL TRY ONCE MORE FARTHER DOWNSTREAM..
HIS SECOND PROSPECT HOLE YIELDS A SURPRISE.
I'VE STRUCK A POCKET! NUGGETS AND GOLD DUST!
LATER
WELL, I'VE CLEANED OUT THE 'POCKET'! THERE'S TWO THOUSAND DOLLARS WORTH HERE - ENOUGH TO START A STAMPEDE FROM TOWN!

4 PAGES MYST. TALES 7 P.15
RUDOLF'S
REVENGE!
TIE
GETCHA NECKTIES HERE... ONLY A QUARTER... ALMOST BRAND NEW!
TIES 25¢
JERRY ROBINSON
B637
RUDOLF NUBBS HAD ONLY ONE DREAM...ONE AMBITION! FOR YEARS HE HAD TRIED TO SELL ENOUGH NECKTIES TO SAVE UP $20!
I'LL GIVE YA 15¢ FER THIS TIE! TAKE IT, OR LEAVE IT!
I'LL TAKE IT! WHERE'S YER 15¢? I AIN'T GOT NO CHARGE ACCOUNTS!
TIES 25¢
BECAUSE HE ALWAYS HAD WANTED TO BUY ONE OF THE SUITS THAT CHARLIE FILFOOL HAD IN THE WINDOW OF "CHARLIE'S CLOTHING STORE!"
ALL I NEED IS ANOTHER 25¢! MAYBE I'LL BE ABLE TO BUY ME THE SUIT TODAY!
CHARLIE'S CLOTHING STORE
CHARLIE'S
SALE $20
HAVE POST. RETURN

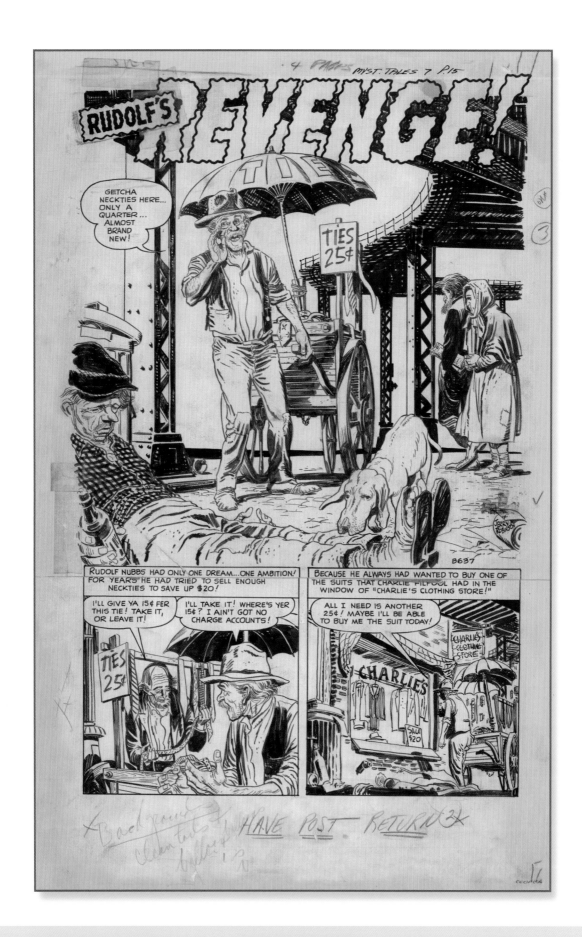

Above
SPLASH PAGE OF "RUDOLF'S REVENGE!" FROM *MYSTERY TALES* NO. 7
January 1953, pencils and inks by Jerry Robinson.

Right and following spread
ORIGINAL ART FOR PAGES 2–4 OF "RUDOLF'S REVENGE!" FROM *MYSTERY TALES* NO. 7
January 1953, pencils and inks by Jerry Robinson.

MYST. TALES 7 P.16

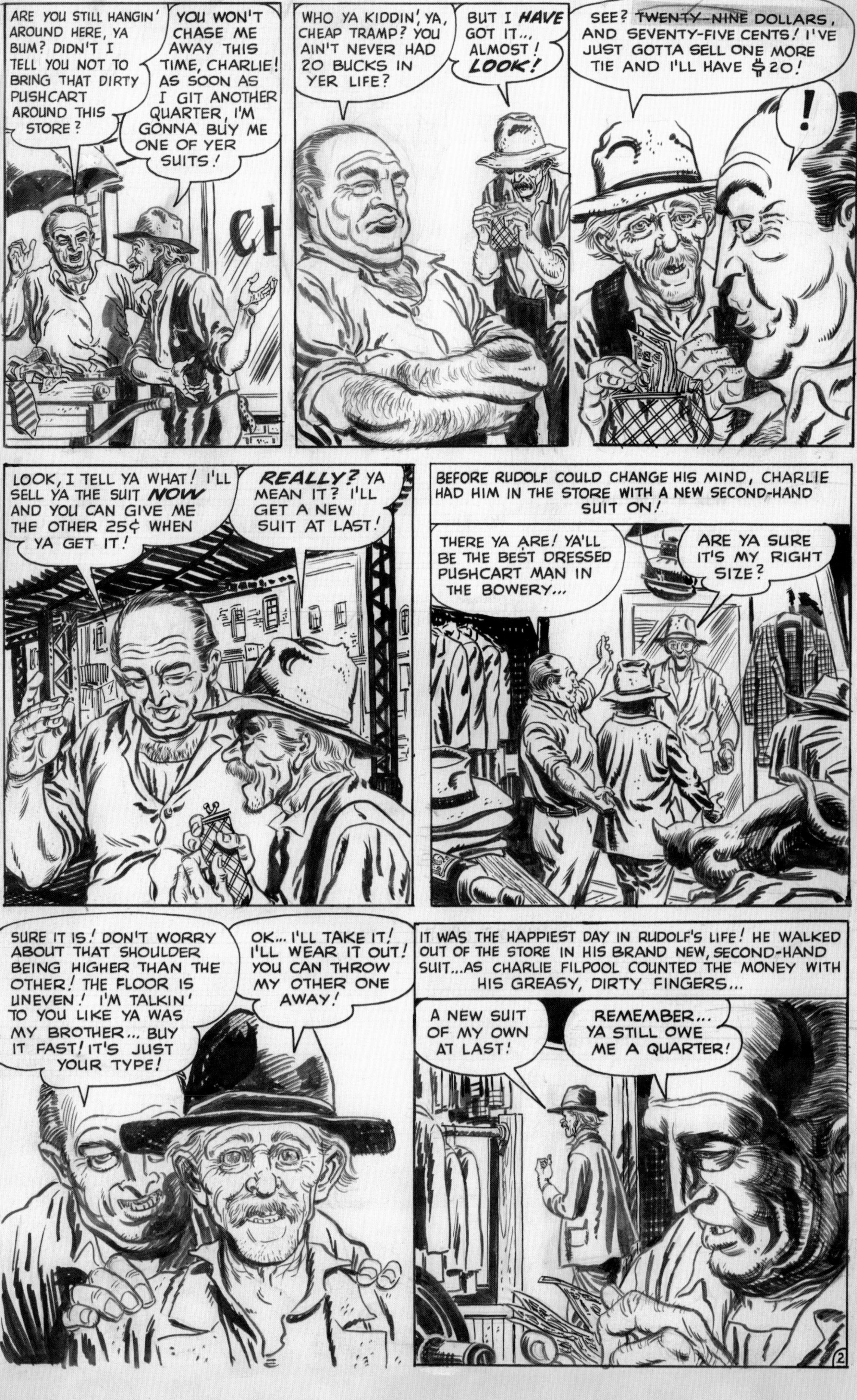

ARE YOU STILL HANGIN' AROUND HERE, YA BUM? DIDN'T I TELL YOU NOT TO BRING THAT DIRTY PUSHCART AROUND THIS STORE?
YOU WON'T CHASE ME AWAY THIS TIME, CHARLIE! AS SOON AS I GIT ANOTHER QUARTER, I'M GONNA BUY ME ONE OF YER SUITS!
CH
WHO YA KIDDIN', YA, CHEAP TRAMP? YOU AIN'T NEVER HAD 20 BUCKS IN YER LIFE?
BUT I HAVE GOT IT... ALMOST! LOOK!
SEE? TWENTY-NINE DOLLARS, AND SEVENTY-FIVE CENTS! I'VE JUST GOTTA SELL ONE MORE TIE AND I'LL HAVE $20!
!
LOOK, I TELL YA WHAT! I'LL SELL YA THE SUIT NOW AND YOU CAN GIVE ME THE OTHER 25¢ WHEN YA GET IT!
REALLY? YA MEAN IT? I'LL GET A NEW SUIT AT LAST!
BEFORE RUDOLF COULD CHANGE HIS MIND, CHARLIE HAD HIM IN THE STORE WITH A NEW SECOND-HAND SUIT ON!
THERE YA ARE! YA'LL BE THE BEST DRESSED PUSHCART MAN IN THE BOWERY...
ARE YA SURE IT'S MY RIGHT SIZE?
SURE IT IS! DON'T WORRY ABOUT THAT SHOULDER BEING HIGHER THAN THE OTHER! THE FLOOR IS UNEVEN! I'M TALKIN' TO YOU LIKE YA WAS MY BROTHER... BUY IT FAST! IT'S JUST YOUR TYPE!
OK... I'LL TAKE IT! I'LL WEAR IT OUT! YOU CAN THROW MY OTHER ONE AWAY!
IT WAS THE HAPPIEST DAY IN RUDOLF'S LIFE! HE WALKED OUT OF THE STORE IN HIS BRAND NEW, SECOND-HAND SUIT... AS CHARLIE FILPOOL COUNTED THE MONEY WITH HIS GREASY, DIRTY FINGERS...
A NEW SUIT OF MY OWN AT LAST!
REMEMBER... YA STILL OWE ME A QUARTER!
2

MYST. TALES 7 P.17

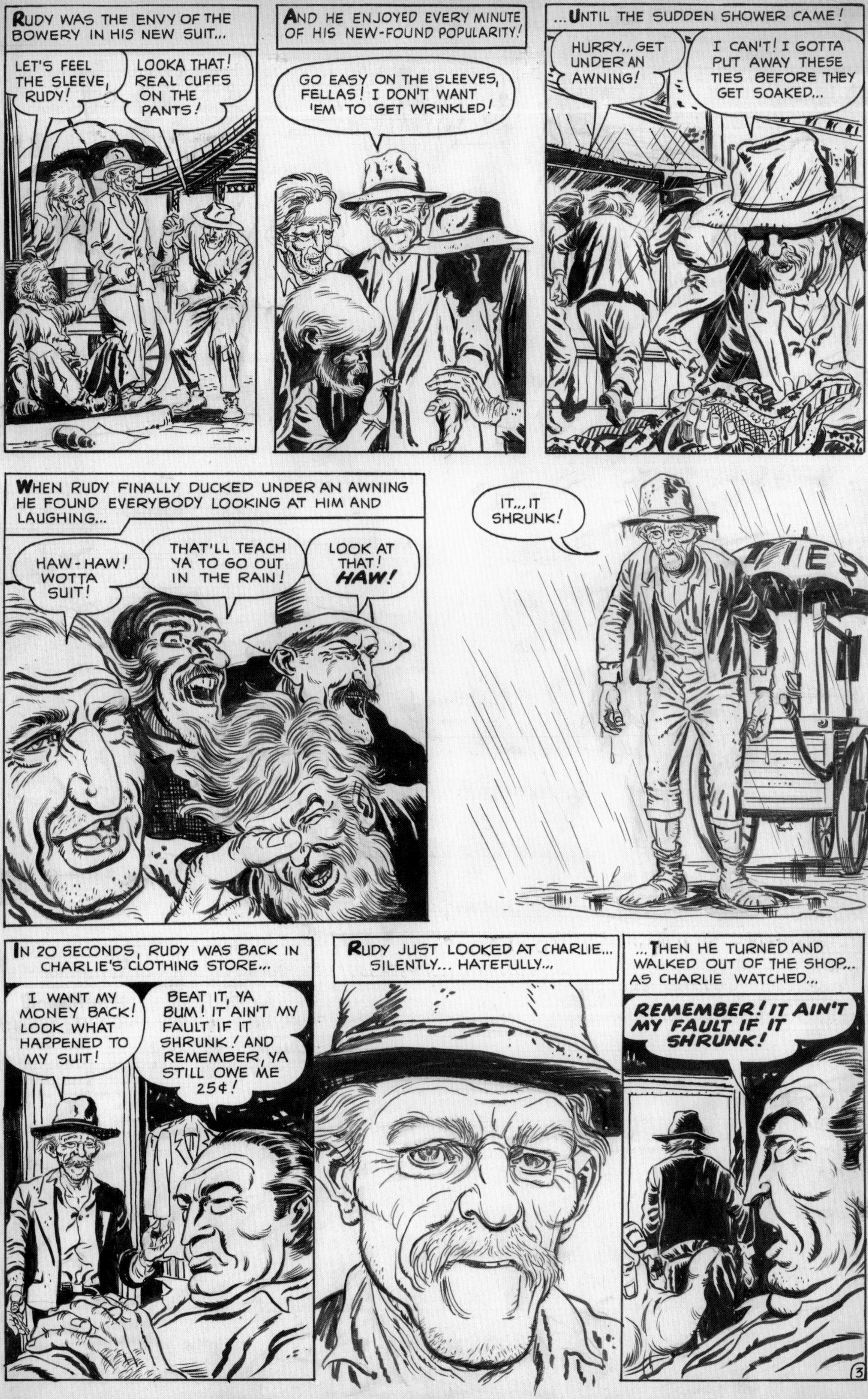
RUDY WAS THE ENVY OF THE BOWERY IN HIS NEW SUIT...
LET'S FEEL THE SLEEVE, RUDY!
LOOKA THAT! REAL CUFFS ON THE PANTS!
AND HE ENJOYED EVERY MINUTE OF HIS NEW-FOUND POPULARITY!
GO EASY ON THE SLEEVES, FELLAS! I DON'T WANT 'EM TO GET WRINKLED!
...UNTIL THE SUDDEN SHOWER CAME!
HURRY... GET UNDER AN AWNING!
I CAN'T! I GOTTA PUT AWAY THESE TIES BEFORE THEY GET SOAKED...
WHEN RUDY FINALLY DUCKED UNDER AN AWNING HE FOUND EVERYBODY LOOKING AT HIM AND LAUGHING...
HAW-HAW! WOTTA SUIT!
THAT'LL TEACH YA TO GO OUT IN THE RAIN!
LOOK AT THAT! HAW!
IT... IT SHRUNK!
TIES
IN 20 SECONDS, RUDY WAS BACK IN CHARLIE'S CLOTHING STORE...
I WANT MY MONEY BACK! LOOK WHAT HAPPENED TO MY SUIT!
BEAT IT, YA BUM! IT AIN'T MY FAULT IF IT SHRUNK! AND REMEMBER, YA STILL OWE ME 25¢!
RUDY JUST LOOKED AT CHARLIE... SILENTLY... HATEFULLY...
...THEN HE TURNED AND WALKED OUT OF THE SHOP... AS CHARLIE WATCHED...
REMEMBER! IT AIN'T MY FAULT IF IT SHRUNK!
3

486

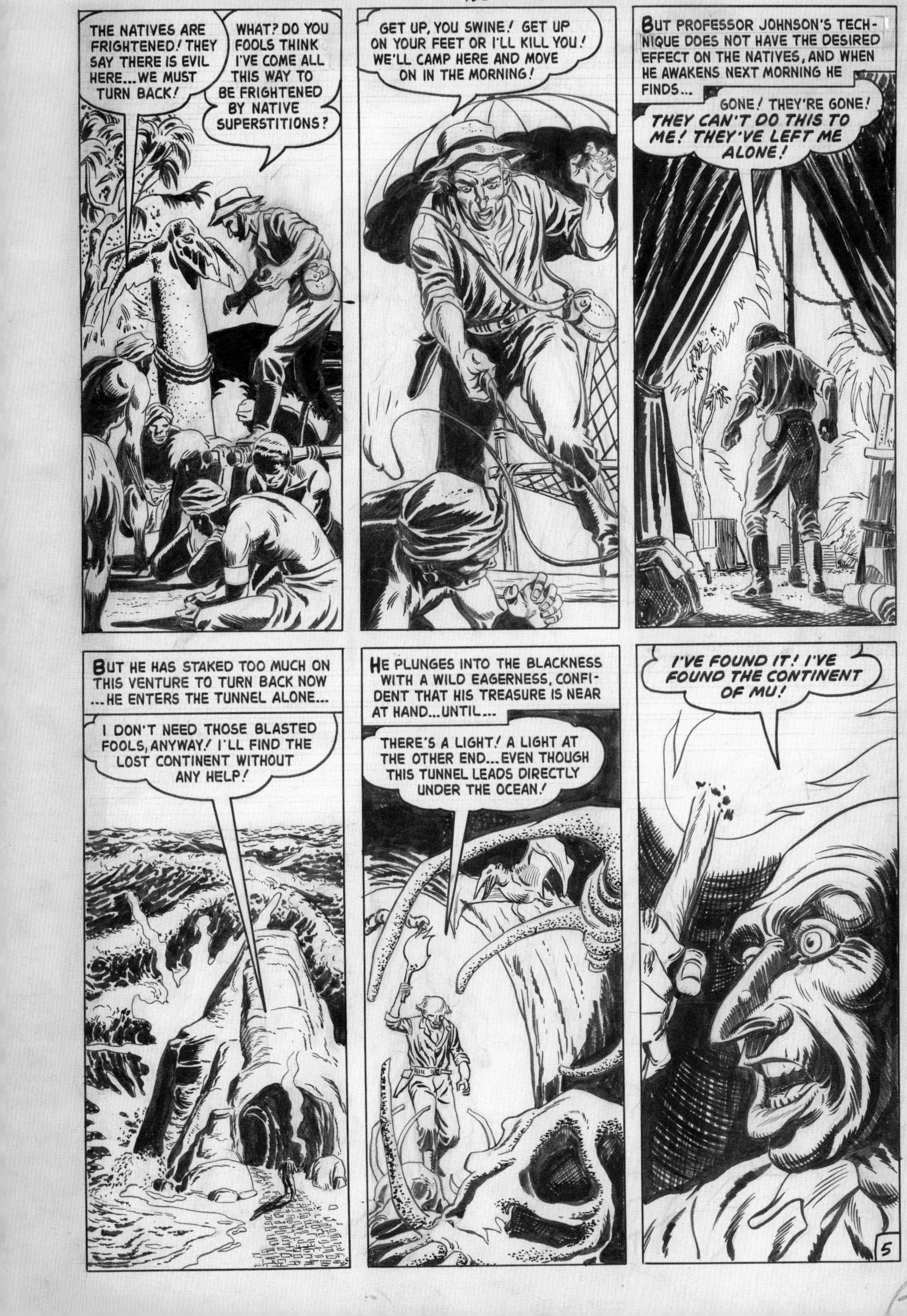
THE NATIVES ARE FRIGHTENED! THEY SAY THERE IS EVIL HERE... WE MUST TURN BACK!
WHAT? DO YOU FOOLS THINK I'VE COME ALL THIS WAY TO BE FRIGHTENED BY NATIVE SUPERSTITIONS?
GET UP, YOU SWINE! GET UP ON YOUR FEET OR I'LL KILL YOU! WE'LL CAMP HERE AND MOVE ON IN THE MORNING!
BUT PROFESSOR JOHNSON'S TECHNIQUE DOES NOT HAVE THE DESIRED EFFECT ON THE NATIVES, AND WHEN HE AWAKENS NEXT MORNING HE FINDS...
GONE! THEY'RE GONE! THEY CAN'T DO THIS TO ME! THEY'VE LEFT ME ALONE!
BUT HE HAS STAKED TOO MUCH ON THIS VENTURE TO TURN BACK NOW ... HE ENTERS THE TUNNEL ALONE...
I DON'T NEED THOSE BLASTED FOOLS, ANYWAY! I'LL FIND THE LOST CONTINENT WITHOUT ANY HELP!
HE PLUNGES INTO THE BLACKNESS WITH A WILD EAGERNESS, CONFIDENT THAT HIS TREASURE IS NEAR AT HAND... UNTIL...
THERE'S A LIGHT! A LIGHT AT THE OTHER END... EVEN THOUGH THIS TUNNEL LEADS DIRECTLY UNDER THE OCEAN!
I'VE FOUND IT! I'VE FOUND THE CONTINENT OF MU!
5

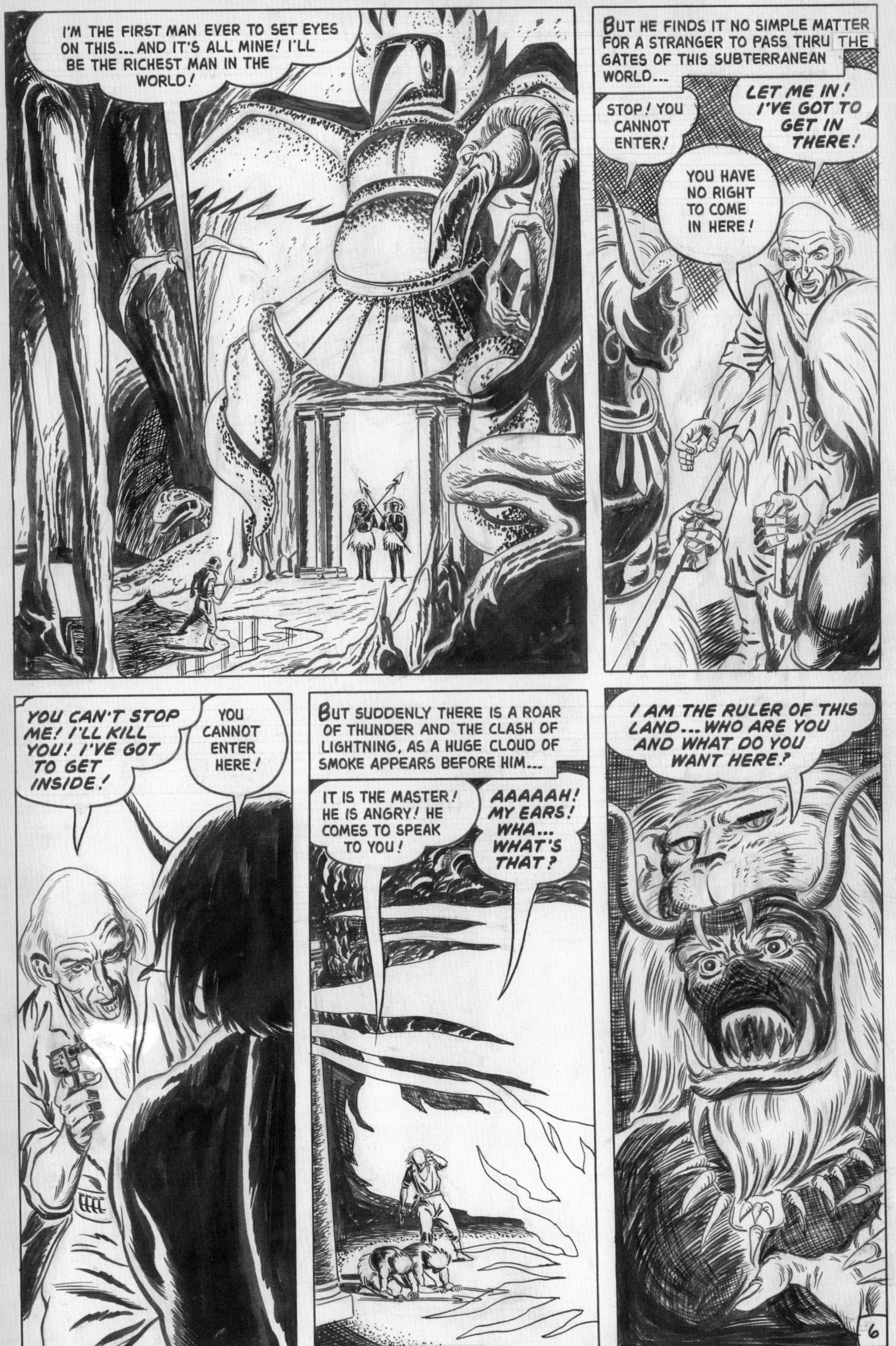
I'M THE FIRST MAN EVER TO SET EYES ON THIS... AND IT'S ALL MINE! I'LL BE THE RICHEST MAN IN THE WORLD!
BUT HE FINDS IT NO SIMPLE MATTER FOR A STRANGER TO PASS THRU THE GATES OF THIS SUBTERRANEAN WORLD...
STOP! YOU CANNOT ENTER!
LET ME IN! I'VE GOT TO GET IN THERE!
YOU HAVE NO RIGHT TO COME IN HERE!
YOU CAN'T STOP ME! I'LL KILL YOU! I'VE GOT TO GET INSIDE!
YOU CANNOT ENTER HERE!
BUT SUDDENLY THERE IS A ROAR OF THUNDER AND THE CLASH OF LIGHTNING, AS A HUGE CLOUD OF SMOKE APPEARS BEFORE HIM...
IT IS THE MASTER! HE IS ANGRY! HE COMES TO SPEAK TO YOU!
AAAAAH! MY EARS! WHA... WHAT'S THAT?
I AM THE RULER OF THIS LAND... WHO ARE YOU AND WHAT DO YOU WANT HERE?

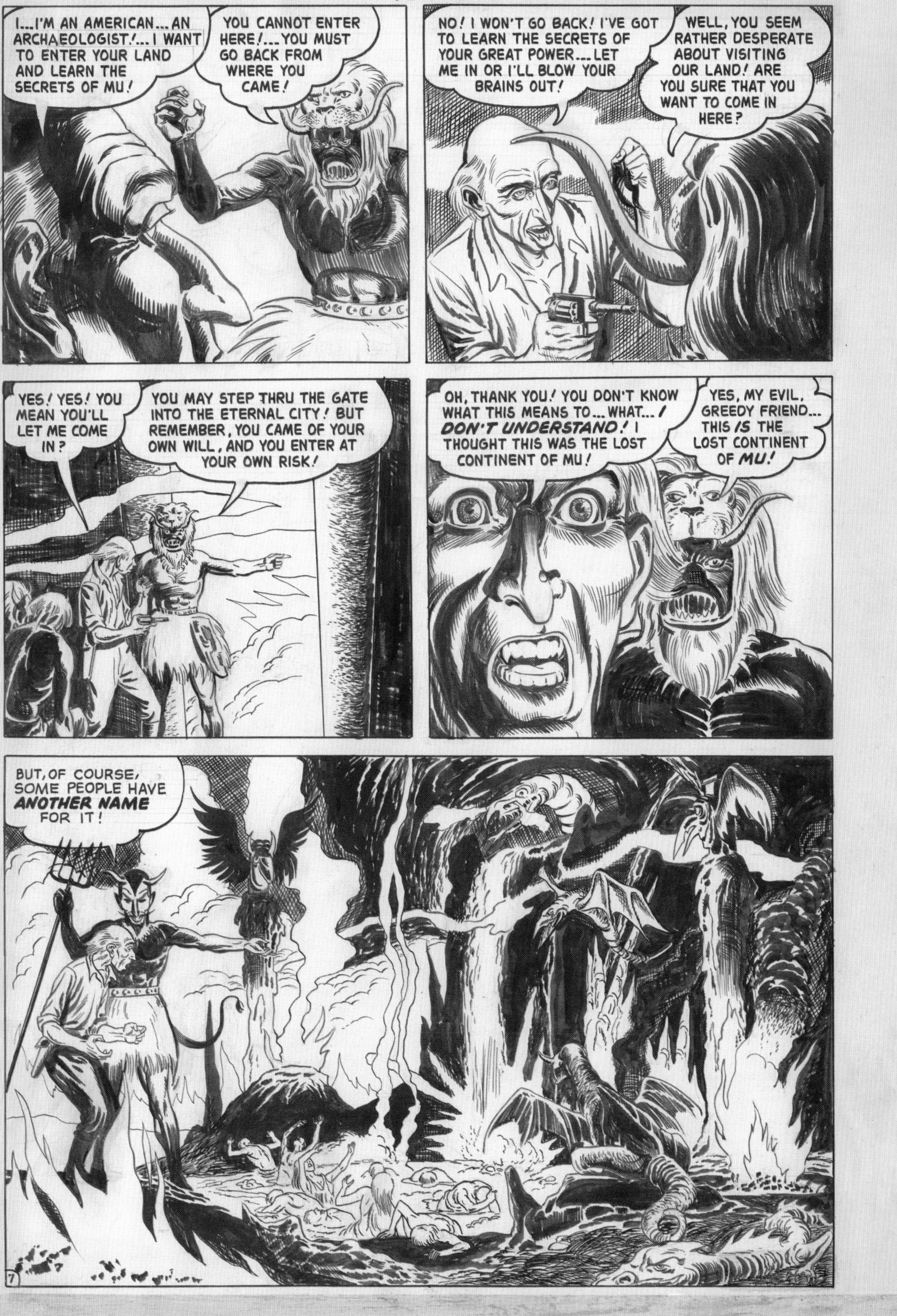

I...I'M AN AMERICAN... AN ARCHAEOLOGIST!... I WANT TO ENTER YOUR LAND AND LEARN THE SECRETS OF MU!
YOU CANNOT ENTER HERE!... YOU MUST GO BACK FROM WHERE YOU CAME!
NO! I WON'T GO BACK! I'VE GOT TO LEARN THE SECRETS OF YOUR GREAT POWER.... LET ME IN OR I'LL BLOW YOUR BRAINS OUT!
WELL, YOU SEEM RATHER DESPERATE ABOUT VISITING OUR LAND! ARE YOU SURE THAT YOU WANT TO COME IN HERE?
YES! YES! YOU MEAN YOU'LL LET ME COME IN?
YOU MAY STEP THRU THE GATE INTO THE ETERNAL CITY! BUT REMEMBER, YOU CAME OF YOUR OWN WILL, AND YOU ENTER AT YOUR OWN RISK!
OH, THANK YOU! YOU DON'T KNOW WHAT THIS MEANS TO... WHAT... I DON'T UNDERSTAND! I THOUGHT THIS WAS THE LOST CONTINENT OF MU!
YES, MY EVIL, GREEDY FRIEND... THIS IS THE LOST CONTINENT OF MU!
BUT, OF COURSE, SOME PEOPLE HAVE ANOTHER NAME FOR IT!
7

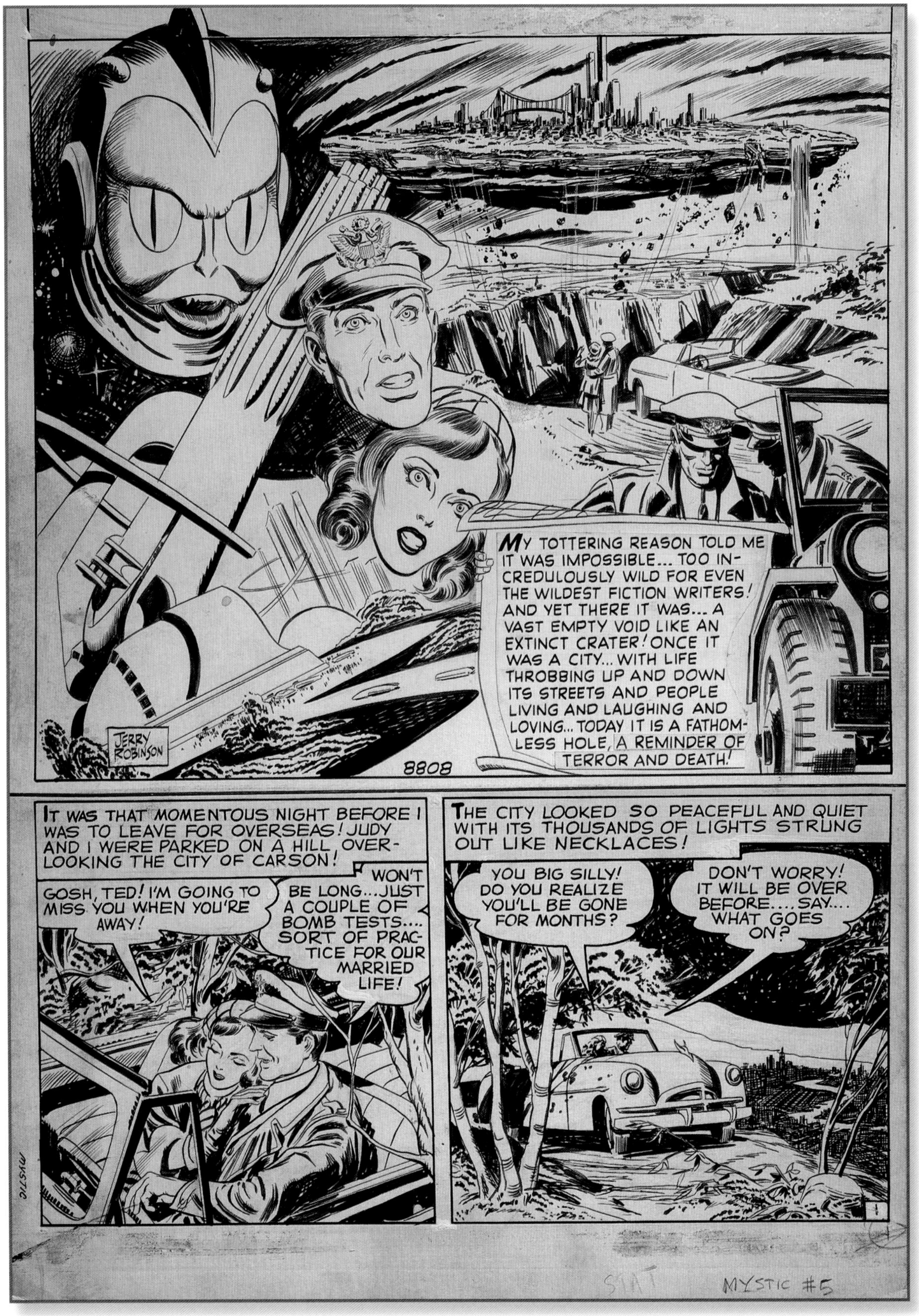
MY TOTTERING REASON TOLD ME IT WAS IMPOSSIBLE... TOO INCREDULOUSLY WILD FOR EVEN THE WILDEST FICTION WRITERS! AND YET THERE IT WAS... A VAST EMPTY VOID LIKE AN EXTINCT CRATER! ONCE IT WAS A CITY... WITH LIFE THROBBING UP AND DOWN ITS STREETS AND PEOPLE LIVING AND LAUGHING AND LOVING... TODAY IT IS A FATHOMLESS HOLE, A REMINDER OF TERROR AND DEATH!
JERRY ROBINSON
8808
IT WAS THAT MOMENTOUS NIGHT BEFORE I WAS TO LEAVE FOR OVERSEAS! JUDY AND I WERE PARKED ON A HILL OVERLOOKING THE CITY OF CARSON!
GOSH, TED! I'M GOING TO MISS YOU WHEN YOU'RE AWAY!
WON'T BE LONG... JUST A COUPLE OF BOMB TESTS.... SORT OF PRACTICE FOR OUR MARRIED LIFE!
THE CITY LOOKED SO PEACEFUL AND QUIET WITH ITS THOUSANDS OF LIGHTS STRUNG OUT LIKE NECKLACES!
YOU BIG SILLY! DO YOU REALIZE YOU'LL BE GONE FOR MONTHS?
DON'T WORRY! IT WILL BE OVER BEFORE.... SAY... WHAT GOES ON?
MYSTIC
MYSTIC #5

Above
SPLASH PAGE FOR "CITY THAT VANISHED" FROM *MYSTIC* NO.5
Pencils and inks by Jerry Robinson.

Right and following pages
ORIGINAL ART FOR PAGES 2–3 AND 5 OF "THE CITY THAT VANISHED" FROM *MYSTIC* NO.5
November 1951, pencils and inks by Jerry Robinson.

MYSTIC #5 P.2

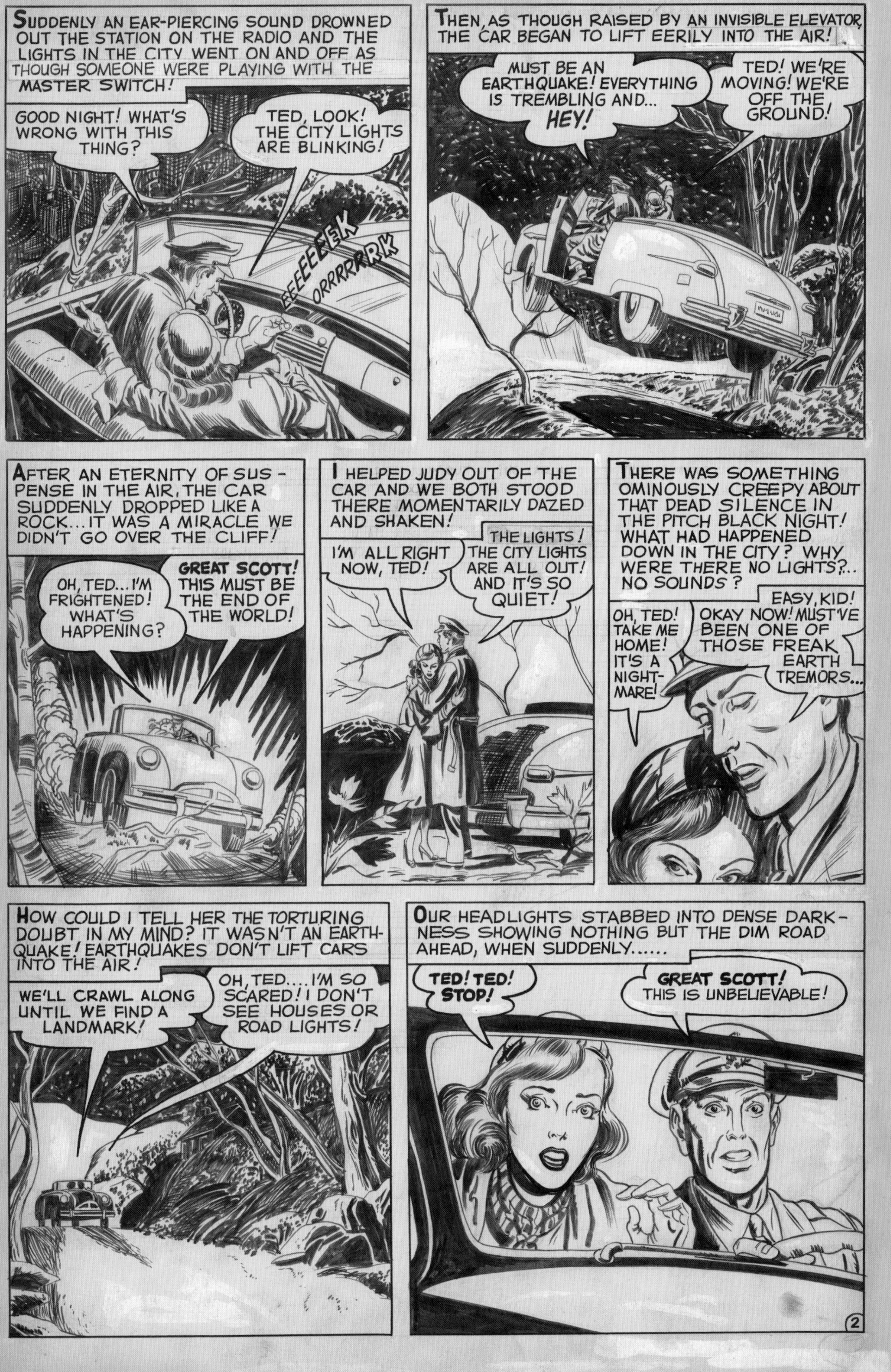

SUDDENLY AN EAR-PIERCING SOUND DROWNED OUT THE STATION ON THE RADIO AND THE LIGHTS IN THE CITY WENT ON AND OFF AS THOUGH SOMEONE WERE PLAYING WITH THE MASTER SWITCH!
GOOD NIGHT! WHAT'S WRONG WITH THIS THING?
TED, LOOK! THE CITY LIGHTS ARE BLINKING!
EEEEEEEK
ORRRRRRK
THEN, AS THOUGH RAISED BY AN INVISIBLE ELEVATOR, THE CAR BEGAN TO LIFT EERILY INTO THE AIR!
MUST BE AN EARTHQUAKE! EVERYTHING IS TREMBLING AND... HEY!
TED! WE'RE MOVING! WE'RE OFF THE GROUND!
AFTER AN ETERNITY OF SUSPENSE IN THE AIR, THE CAR SUDDENLY DROPPED LIKE A ROCK... IT WAS A MIRACLE WE DIDN'T GO OVER THE CLIFF!
OH, TED... I'M FRIGHTENED! WHAT'S HAPPENING?
GREAT SCOTT! THIS MUST BE THE END OF THE WORLD!
I HELPED JUDY OUT OF THE CAR AND WE BOTH STOOD THERE MOMENTARILY DAZED AND SHAKEN!
I'M ALL RIGHT NOW, TED!
THE LIGHTS! THE CITY LIGHTS ARE ALL OUT! AND IT'S SO QUIET!
THERE WAS SOMETHING OMINOUSLY CREEPY ABOUT THAT DEAD SILENCE IN THE PITCH BLACK NIGHT! WHAT HAD HAPPENED DOWN IN THE CITY? WHY WERE THERE NO LIGHTS?.. NO SOUNDS?
OH, TED! TAKE ME HOME! IT'S A NIGHTMARE!
EASY, KID! OKAY NOW! MUST'VE BEEN ONE OF THOSE FREAK EARTH TREMORS...
HOW COULD I TELL HER THE TORTURING DOUBT IN MY MIND? IT WASN'T AN EARTHQUAKE! EARTHQUAKES DON'T LIFT CARS INTO THE AIR!
WE'LL CRAWL ALONG UNTIL WE FIND A LANDMARK!
OH, TED.... I'M SO SCARED! I DON'T SEE HOUSES OR ROAD LIGHTS!
OUR HEADLIGHTS STABBED INTO DENSE DARKNESS SHOWING NOTHING BUT THE DIM ROAD AHEAD, WHEN SUDDENLY......
TED! TED! STOP!
GREAT SCOTT! THIS IS UNBELIEVABLE!
2

MYSTIC #5 P.3

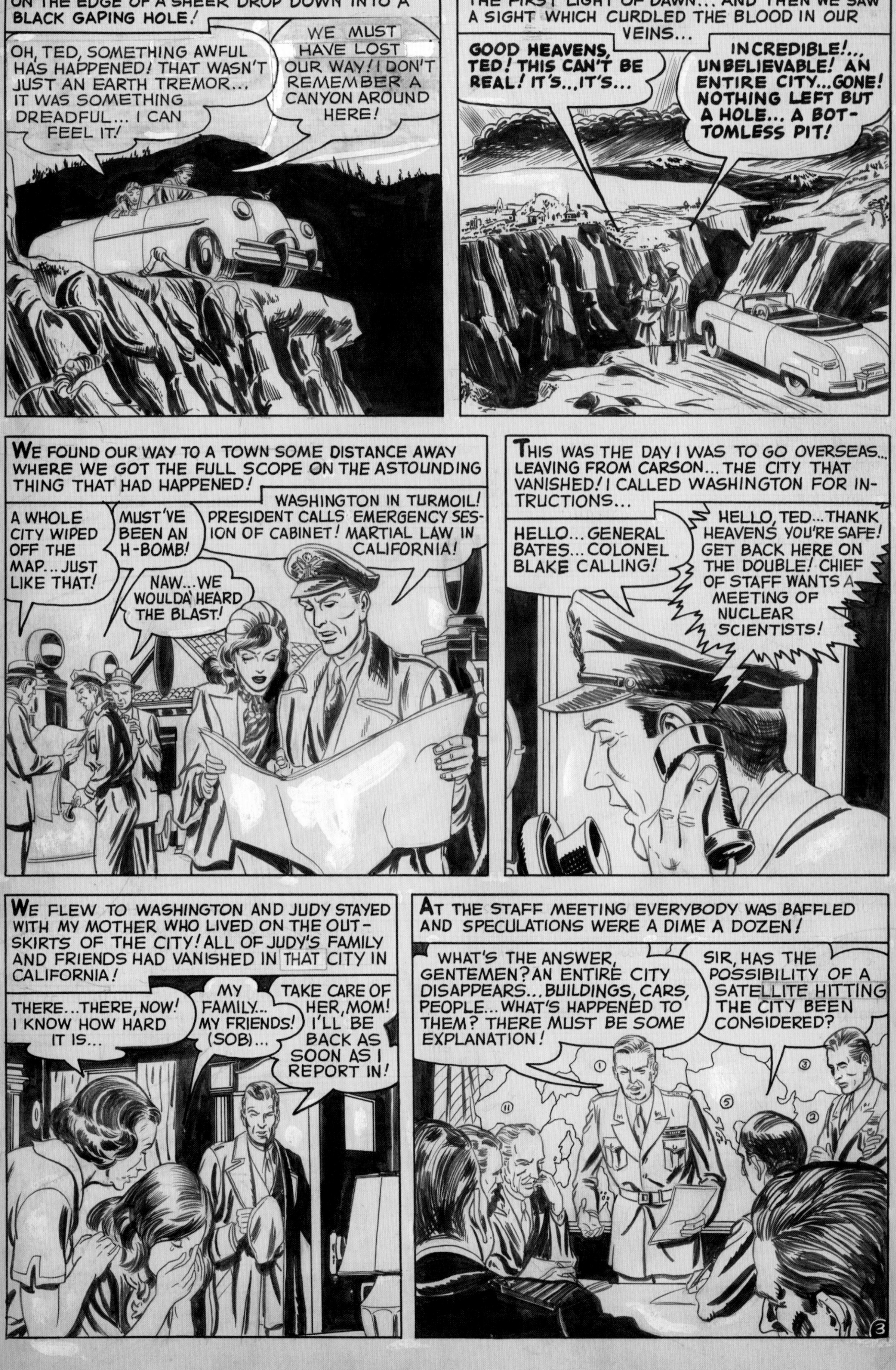
MY FOOT JAMMED THE BRAKES AND WE STOPPED ON THE EDGE OF A SHEER DROP DOWN INTO A BLACK GAPING HOLE!
OH, TED, SOMETHING AWFUL HAS HAPPENED! THAT WASN'T JUST AN EARTH TREMOR... IT WAS SOMETHING DREADFUL... I CAN FEEL IT!
WE MUST HAVE LOST OUR WAY! I DON'T REMEMBER A CANYON AROUND HERE!
HAGGARD AND TENSE, WE STRAINED THROUGH THE FIRST LIGHT OF DAWN... AND THEN WE SAW A SIGHT WHICH CURDLED THE BLOOD IN OUR VEINS...
GOOD HEAVENS, TED! THIS CAN'T BE REAL! IT'S... IT'S...
INCREDIBLE!... UNBELIEVABLE! AN ENTIRE CITY... GONE! NOTHING LEFT BUT A HOLE... A BOTTOMLESS PIT!
WE FOUND OUR WAY TO A TOWN SOME DISTANCE AWAY WHERE WE GOT THE FULL SCOPE ON THE ASTOUNDING THING THAT HAD HAPPENED!
A WHOLE CITY WIPED OFF THE MAP... JUST LIKE THAT!
MUST'VE BEEN AN H-BOMB!
NAW... WE WOULDA' HEARD THE BLAST!
WASHINGTON IN TURMOIL! PRESIDENT CALLS EMERGENCY SESSION OF CABINET! MARTIAL LAW IN CALIFORNIA!
THIS WAS THE DAY I WAS TO GO OVERSEAS... LEAVING FROM CARSON... THE CITY THAT VANISHED! I CALLED WASHINGTON FOR INTRUCTIONS...
HELLO... GENERAL BATES... COLONEL BLAKE CALLING!
HELLO, TED... THANK HEAVENS YOU'RE SAFE! GET BACK HERE ON THE DOUBLE! CHIEF OF STAFF WANTS A MEETING OF NUCLEAR SCIENTISTS!
WE FLEW TO WASHINGTON AND JUDY STAYED WITH MY MOTHER WHO LIVED ON THE OUTSKIRTS OF THE CITY! ALL OF JUDY'S FAMILY AND FRIENDS HAD VANISHED IN THAT CITY IN CALIFORNIA!
THERE... THERE, NOW! I KNOW HOW HARD IT IS...
MY FAMILY... MY FRIENDS! (SOB)...
TAKE CARE OF HER, MOM! I'LL BE BACK AS SOON AS I REPORT IN!
AT THE STAFF MEETING EVERYBODY WAS BAFFLED AND SPECULATIONS WERE A DIME A DOZEN!
WHAT'S THE ANSWER, GENTEMEN? AN ENTIRE CITY DISAPPEARS... BUILDINGS, CARS, PEOPLE... WHAT'S HAPPENED TO THEM? THERE MUST BE SOME EXPLANATION!
SIR, HAS THE POSSIBILITY OF A SATELLITE HITTING THE CITY BEEN CONSIDERED?
3

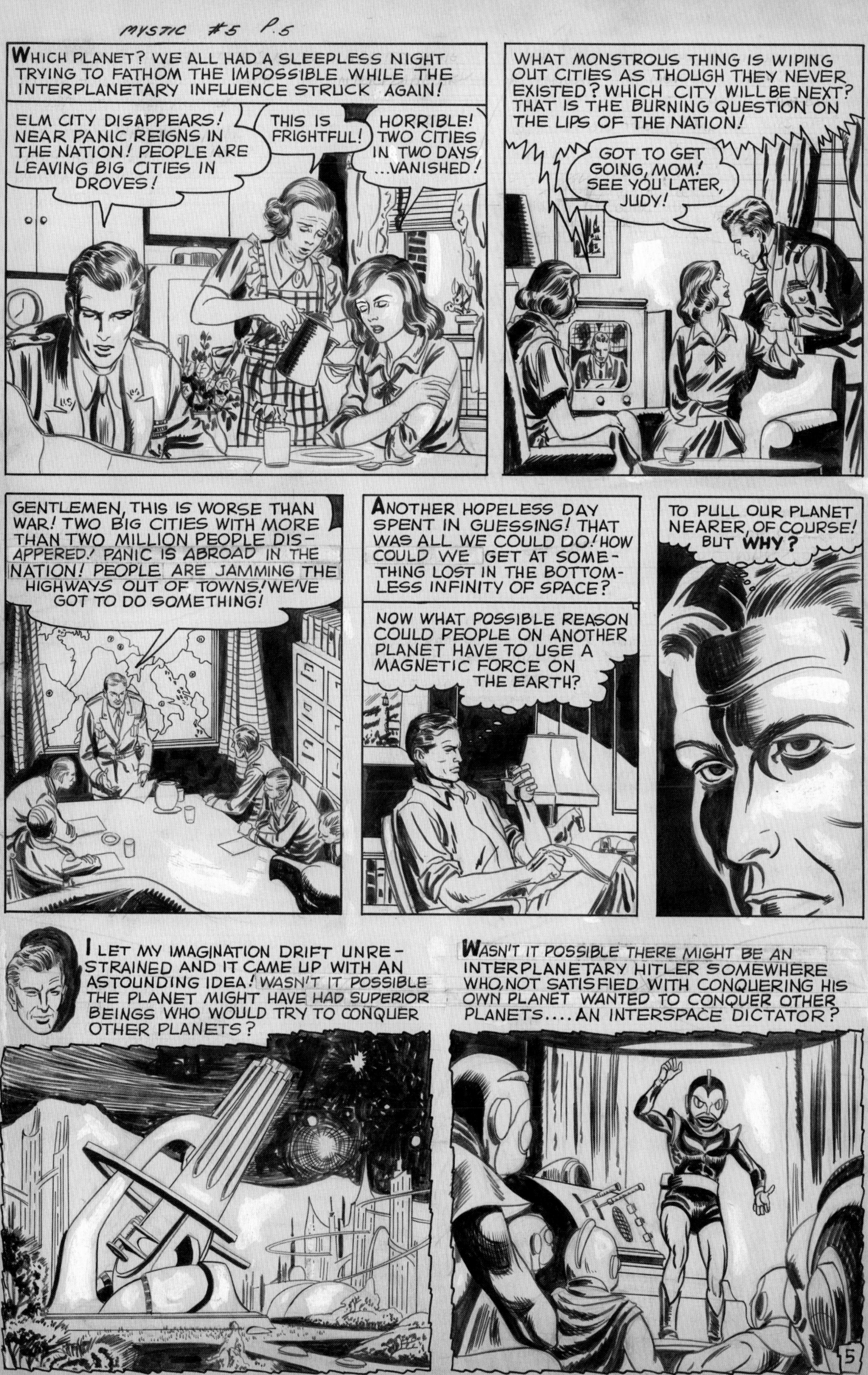
MYSTIC #5 P.5
WHICH PLANET? WE ALL HAD A SLEEPLESS NIGHT TRYING TO FATHOM THE IMPOSSIBLE WHILE THE INTERPLANETARY INFLUENCE STRUCK AGAIN!
ELM CITY DISAPPEARS! NEAR PANIC REIGNS IN THE NATION! PEOPLE ARE LEAVING BIG CITIES IN DROVES!
THIS IS FRIGHTFUL!
HORRIBLE! TWO CITIES IN TWO DAYS ...VANISHED!
WHAT MONSTROUS THING IS WIPING OUT CITIES AS THOUGH THEY NEVER EXISTED? WHICH CITY WILL BE NEXT? THAT IS THE BURNING QUESTION ON THE LIPS OF THE NATION!
GOT TO GET GOING, MOM! SEE YOU LATER, JUDY!
GENTLEMEN, THIS IS WORSE THAN WAR! TWO BIG CITIES WITH MORE THAN TWO MILLION PEOPLE DIS-APPERED! PANIC IS ABROAD IN THE NATION! PEOPLE ARE JAMMING THE HIGHWAYS OUT OF TOWNS! WE'VE GOT TO DO SOMETHING!
ANOTHER HOPELESS DAY SPENT IN GUESSING! THAT WAS ALL WE COULD DO! HOW COULD WE GET AT SOME-THING LOST IN THE BOTTOM-LESS INFINITY OF SPACE?
NOW WHAT POSSIBLE REASON COULD PEOPLE ON ANOTHER PLANET HAVE TO USE A MAGNETIC FORCE ON THE EARTH?
TO PULL OUR PLANET NEARER, OF COURSE! BUT WHY?
I LET MY IMAGINATION DRIFT UNRE-STRAINED AND IT CAME UP WITH AN ASTOUNDING IDEA! WASN'T IT POSSIBLE THE PLANET MIGHT HAVE HAD SUPERIOR BEINGS WHO WOULD TRY TO CONQUER OTHER PLANETS?
WASN'T IT POSSIBLE THERE MIGHT BE AN INTERPLANETARY HITLER SOMEWHERE WHO, NOT SATISFIED WITH CONQUERING HIS OWN PLANET WANTED TO CONQUER OTHER PLANETS.... AN INTERSPACE DICTATOR?
5

DAREDEVIL NOV 1941
53
LONDON
BY JERRY ROBINSON
FROM THE SMASHING SPIRES AND WRECKED WALLS OF THE CITY WHICH IS BRITAIN'S CITADEL, FROM THE FLAMING CHAOS WHICH IS LONDON NOW---HAS RISEN UP A FIGURE-SPLENDID, COURAGEOUS! WHO IS THIS MAN? HOW SHALL WE CALL HIM? WE WILL CALL HIM, SIMPLY - LONDON - FOR IN VERY TRUTH, HE IS LONDON - A LIVING BREATHING REALITY TO PROVE--- LONDON CAN TAKE IT!!! BUT LOOK!!... WHO IS THIS FIGURE, MYSTERIOUSLY MASKED, WHO---YES, LOOKS LIKE LONDON - CRACKING LIGHTNING PACED HAMMER-BLOWS TO THE JAW OF A MAN WHO LOOKS---YES, WHO LOOKS SUSPICIOUSLY LIKE ADOLPH HITLER-- HOW COULD THIS POSSIBLY BE TRUE? HOW COULD THIS ACTUALLY TAKE PLACE? LOOK CLOSER, READ THIS STORY---AND DISCOVER HOW LONDON CAN ACTUALLY FIGHT HITLER-FACE TO FACE---AND PROVE, ALSO, THAT-- LONDON STRIKES BACK!
A TERRIFIC BLOW...
FLOORS THE SCREAMING "HITLER"
from the collection of jerry robinson

Above

ORIGINAL ART FOR SPLASH PAGE OF *DAREDEVIL COMICS* NO. 5

November 1941, pencils, inks, and colors by Jerry Robinson.

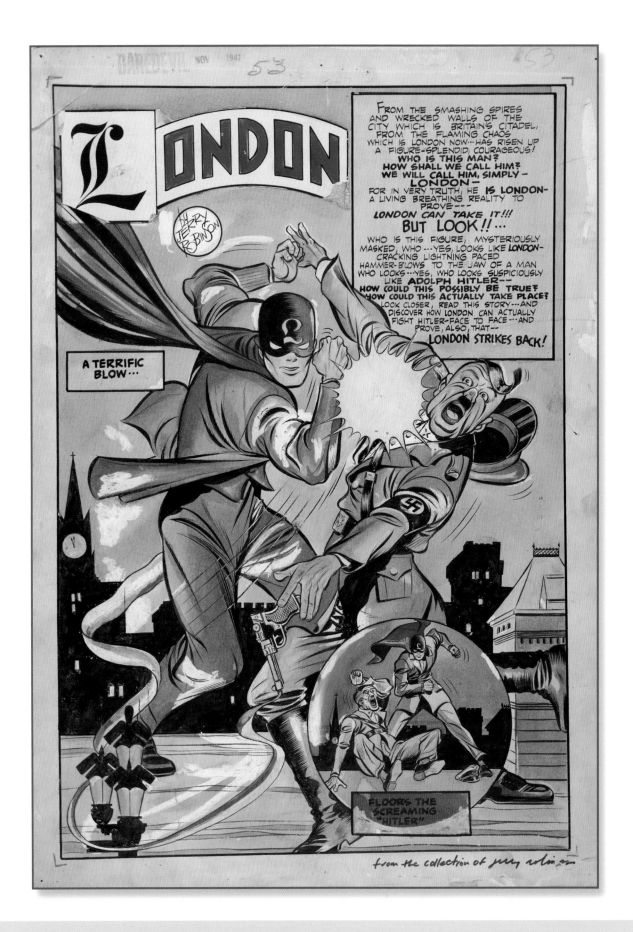

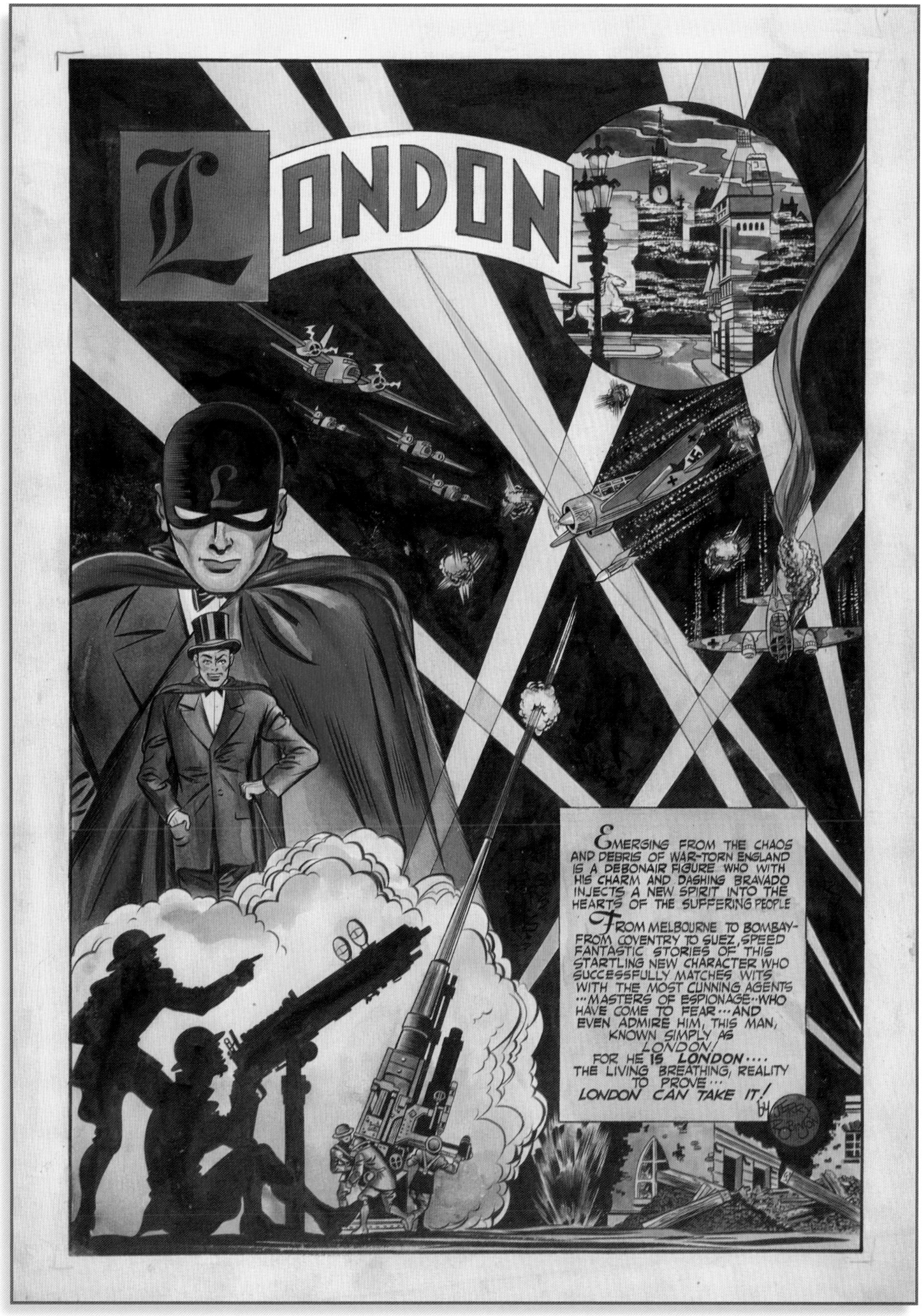
LONDON
EMERGING FROM THE CHAOS AND DEBRIS OF WAR-TORN ENGLAND IS A DEBONAIR FIGURE WHO WITH HIS CHARM AND DASHING BRAVADO INJECTS A NEW SPIRIT INTO THE HEARTS OF THE SUFFERING PEOPLE
FROM MELBOURNE TO BOMBAY- FROM COVENTRY TO SUEZ, SPEED FANTASTIC STORIES OF THIS STARTLING NEW CHARACTER WHO SUCCESSFULLY MATCHES WITS WITH THE MOST CUNNING AGENTS ...MASTERS OF ESPIONAGE..WHO HAVE COME TO FEAR...AND EVEN ADMIRE HIM, THIS MAN, KNOWN SIMPLY AS LONDON!
FOR HE IS LONDON.... THE LIVING BREATHING, REALITY TO PROVE... LONDON CAN TAKE IT!

Above

ORIGINAL ART FOR SPLASH PAGE OF *DAREDEVIL COMICS* NO. 2

November 1941, pencils, inks, and colors by Jerry Robinson.

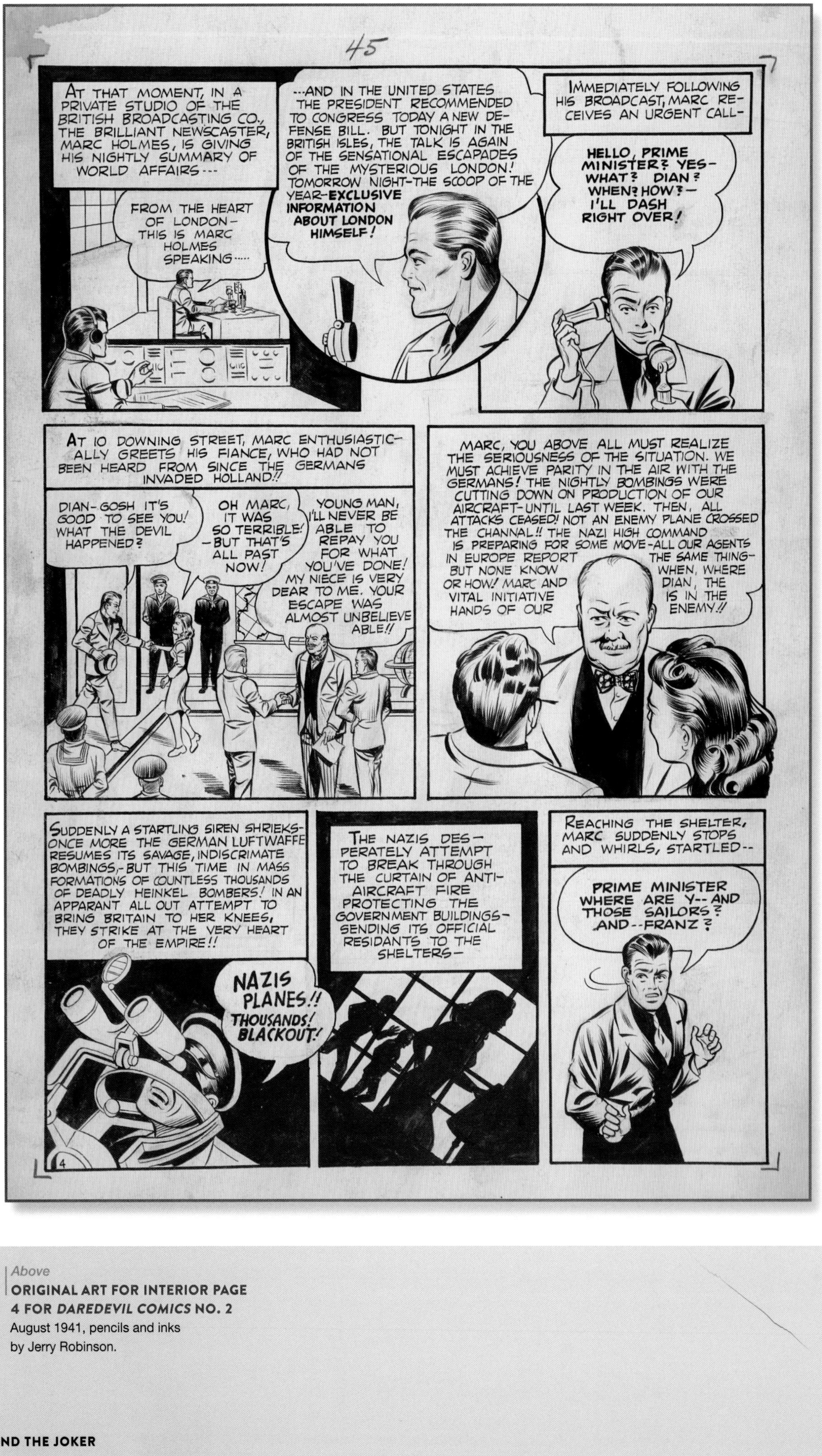
45
AT THAT MOMENT, IN A PRIVATE STUDIO OF THE BRITISH BROADCASTING CO., THE BRILLIANT NEWSCASTER, MARC HOLMES, IS GIVING HIS NIGHTLY SUMMARY OF WORLD AFFAIRS---
FROM THE HEART OF LONDON- THIS IS MARC HOLMES SPEAKING.....
--AND IN THE UNITED STATES THE PRESIDENT RECOMMENDED TO CONGRESS TODAY A NEW DEFENSE BILL. BUT TONIGHT IN THE BRITISH ISLES, THE TALK IS AGAIN OF THE SENSATIONAL ESCAPADES OF THE MYSTERIOUS LONDON! TOMORROW NIGHT-THE SCOOP OF THE YEAR-EXCLUSIVE INFORMATION ABOUT LONDON HIMSELF!
IMMEDIATELY FOLLOWING HIS BROADCAST, MARC RECEIVES AN URGENT CALL-
HELLO, PRIME MINISTER? YES- WHAT? DIAN? WHEN? HOW?- I'LL DASH RIGHT OVER!
AT 10 DOWNING STREET, MARC ENTHUSIASTICALLY GREETS HIS FIANCE, WHO HAD NOT BEEN HEARD FROM SINCE THE GERMANS INVADED HOLLAND!!
DIAN- GOSH IT'S GOOD TO SEE YOU! WHAT THE DEVIL HAPPENED?
OH MARC, IT WAS SO TERRIBLE! -BUT THAT'S ALL PAST NOW!
YOUNG MAN, I'LL NEVER BE ABLE TO REPAY YOU FOR WHAT YOU'VE DONE! MY NIECE IS VERY DEAR TO ME. YOUR ESCAPE WAS ALMOST UNBELIEVEABLE!!
MARC, YOU ABOVE ALL MUST REALIZE THE SERIOUSNESS OF THE SITUATION. WE MUST ACHIEVE PARITY IN THE AIR WITH THE GERMANS! THE NIGHTLY BOMBINGS WERE CUTTING DOWN ON PRODUCTION OF OUR AIRCRAFT-UNTIL LAST WEEK. THEN, ALL ATTACKS CEASED! NOT AN ENEMY PLANE CROSSED THE CHANNAL!! THE NAZI HIGH COMMAND IS PREPARING FOR SOME MOVE-ALL OUR AGENTS IN EUROPE REPORT THE SAME THING- BUT NONE KNOW WHEN, WHERE OR HOW! MARC AND DIAN, THE VITAL INITIATIVE IS IN THE HANDS OF OUR ENEMY!!
SUDDENLY A STARTLING SIREN SHRIEKS-ONCE MORE THE GERMAN LUFTWAFFE RESUMES ITS SAVAGE, INDISCRIMATE BOMBINGS,-BUT THIS TIME IN MASS FORMATIONS OF COUNTLESS THOUSANDS OF DEADLY HEINKEL BOMBERS! IN AN APPARANT ALL OUT ATTEMPT TO BRING BRITAIN TO HER KNEES, THEY STRIKE AT THE VERY HEART OF THE EMPIRE!!
NAZIS PLANES!! THOUSANDS! BLACKOUT!
THE NAZIS DESPERATELY ATTEMPT TO BREAK THROUGH THE CURTAIN OF ANTI-AIRCRAFT FIRE PROTECTING THE GOVERNMENT BUILDINGS-SENDING ITS OFFICIAL RESIDANTS TO THE SHELTERS-
REACHING THE SHELTER, MARC SUDDENLY STOPS AND WHIRLS, STARTLED--
PRIME MINISTER WHERE ARE Y-- AND THOSE SAILORS? AND--FRANZ?
4

Above

ORIGINAL ART FOR INTERIOR PAGE 4 FOR *DAREDEVIL COMICS* NO. 2

August 1941, pencils and inks by Jerry Robinson.

And one man in his time plays many parts...*
*Shakespeare "As You Like It"
December 31, 1980

To Jerry Robinson, whose "Still Life" frequently brings smiles into my life
With best wishes,

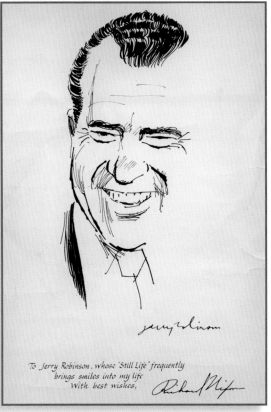

Top
CARICATURES OF WORLD LEADERS
Pencils and inks by Jerry Robinson.

Bottom left
ABRAHAM LINCOLN
Pencils and inks by Jerry Robinson.

Bottom right
RICHARD NIXON
Pencils and inks by Jerry Robinson.

robert heinlein
STARSHIP
SOLDIER

STARSHIP SOLDIER
ROBERT HEINLEIN

STARSHIP SOLDIER

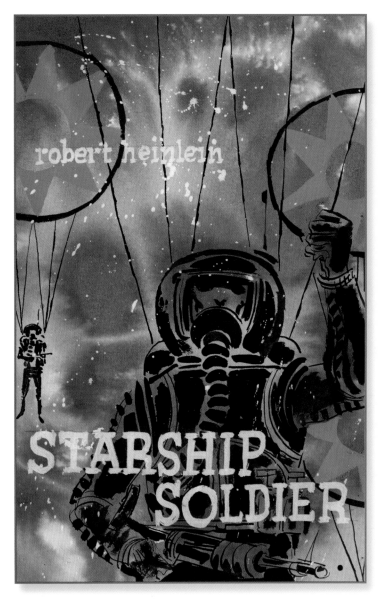

Above

"STARSHIP SOLDIER" BOOK COVER

Preliminary designs by Jerry Robinson.

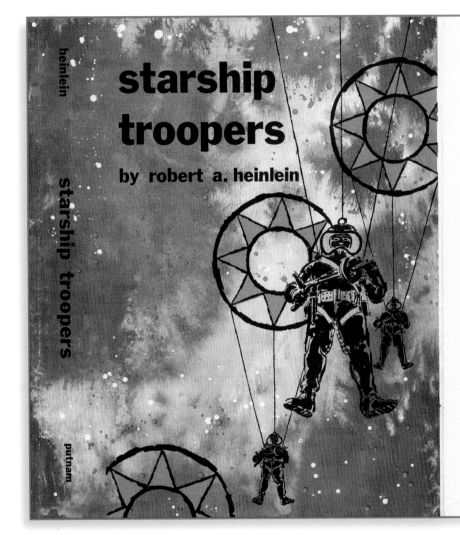

heinlein
starship troopers
putnam
starship
troopers
by robert a. heinlein
ST
$3.95

starship troopers

By ROBERT A. HEINLEIN

"I always get the shakes before a drop. I've had the injections, of course, the hypnotic preparation, and it stands to reason that I can't really be afraid."

From the battle of Marathon to Korea's Porkchop Hill a certain breed of men have come forth to shoulder the burdens and beliefs of their particular world. For the Mobile Infantryman (MI) of this hard-hitting story of combat 5,000 years in the future, the passage of time has not made the job any easier.

"The ship's psychiatrist checked my brain waves and asked me silly questions while I was asleep. He tells me it isn't fear..."

Starships tick away light years on a drop mission, MI armored suits are jet-equipped and weapons are technical masterpieces, but the act of dying

(Continued on back flap)

Jacket design by Jerry Robinson
YA

Above
***STARSHIP TROOPERS* FINAL PUBLISHED BOOK COVER (WITH FINAL TITLE)**
Designed by Jerry Robinson.

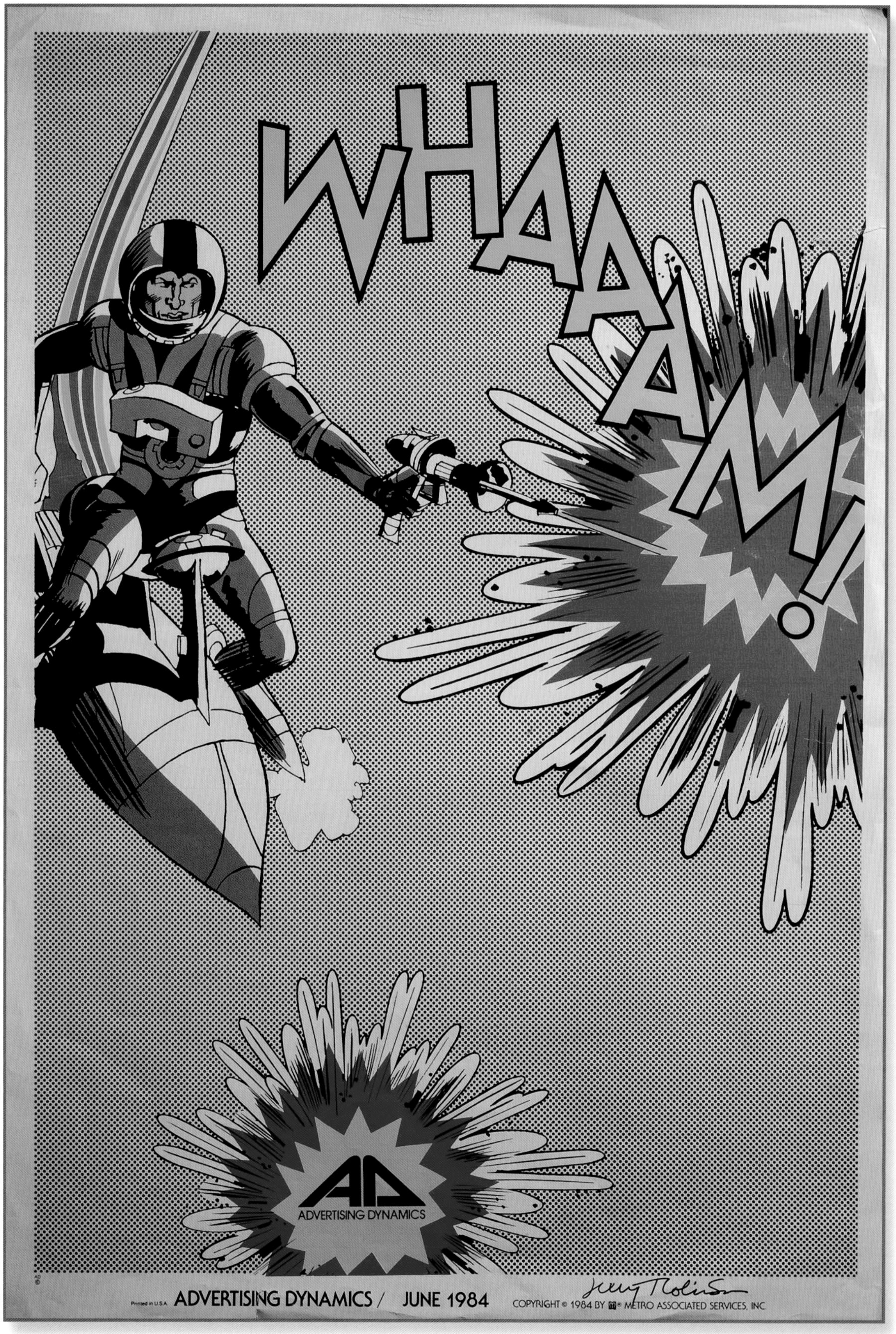
WHAAAM!
ADVERTISING DYNAMICS
Printed in U.S.A.
ADVERTISING DYNAMICS / JUNE 1984
COPYRIGHT © 1984 BY METRO ASSOCIATED SERVICES, INC
Jerry Robinson

Above
POP-ART INFLUENCED COMMERCIAL ART FOR *ADVERTISING DYNAMICS*
1984, Jerry Robinson.

Above

ORIGINAL ANIMATION CEL FROM
***STEREOTYPES,* AN HOUR-LONG**
FILM CO-ART DIRECTED BY JERRY
ROBINSON IN MOSCOW
1991, Jerry Robinson.

CHAPTER 7: **ADDITIONAL COMICS, BOOKS, AND MAGAZINE ART**   **147**

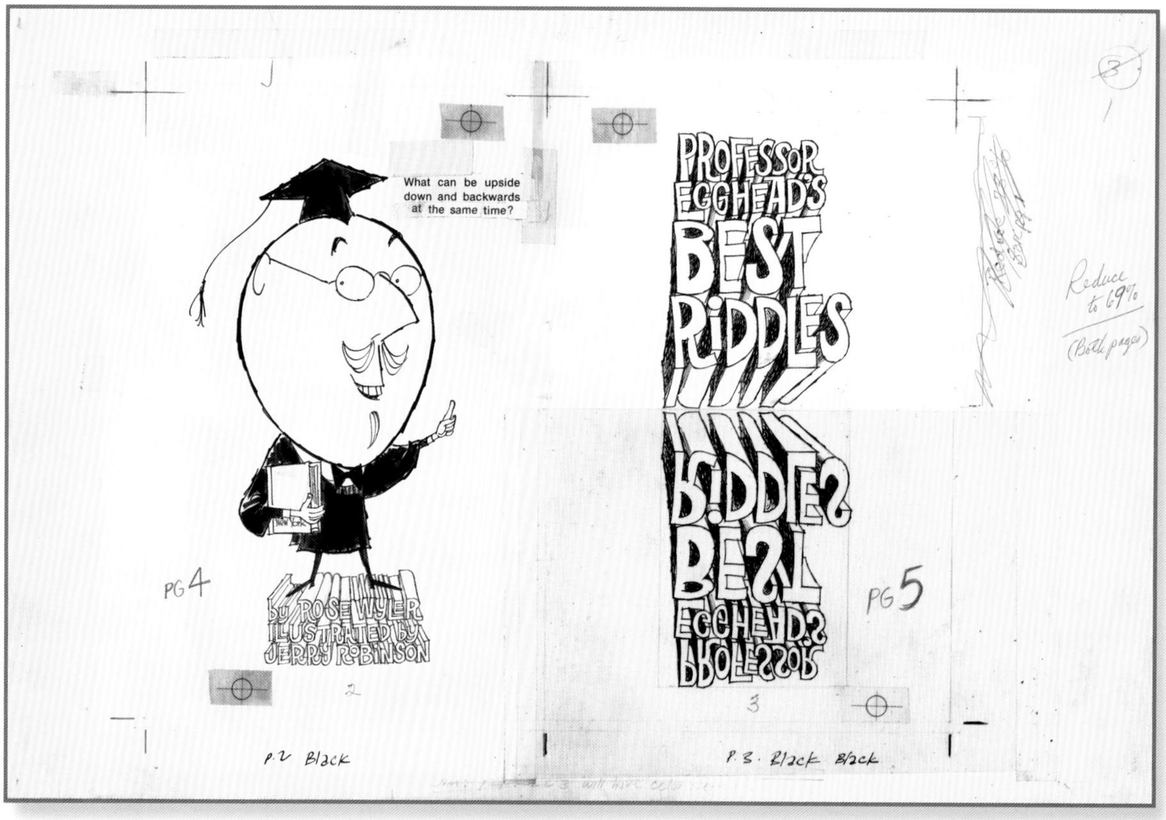
What can be upside down and backwards at the same time?
PROFESSOR EGGHEAD'S BEST RIDDLES
by ROSE WYLER
ILLUSTRATED by JERRY ROBINSON
PG 4
PG 5
Reduce to 69% (Both pages)
P.2 Black
P.3. Black Black

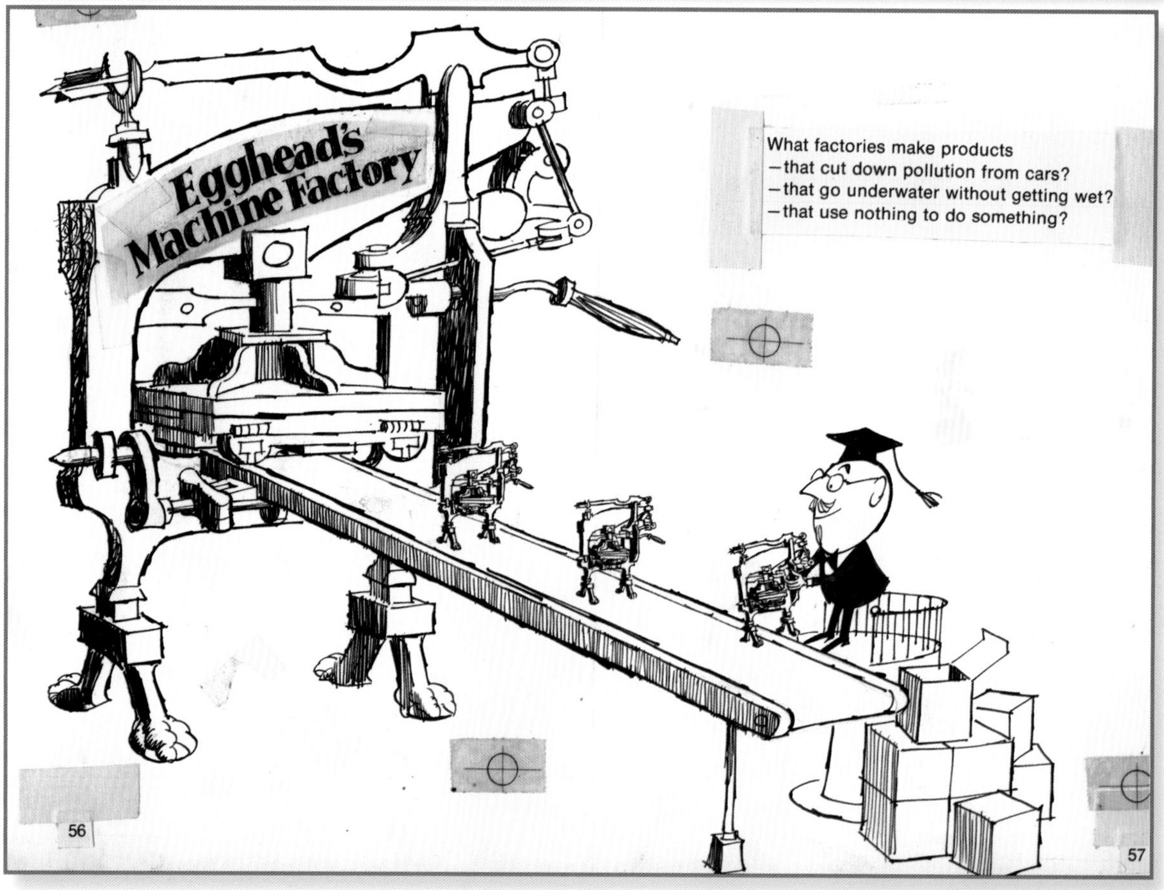
Egghead's Machine Factory
What factories make products
–that cut down pollution from cars?
–that go underwater without getting wet?
–that use nothing to do something?
56
57

Top
INTERIOR ART FOR PAGES 4–5 FROM *PROFESSOR EGGHEAD'S BEST RIDDLES*
By Jerry Robinson.

Bottom
INTERIOR ART FOR PAGES 56–57 FROM *PROFESSOR EGGHEAD'S BEST RIDDLES*
By Jerry Robinson.

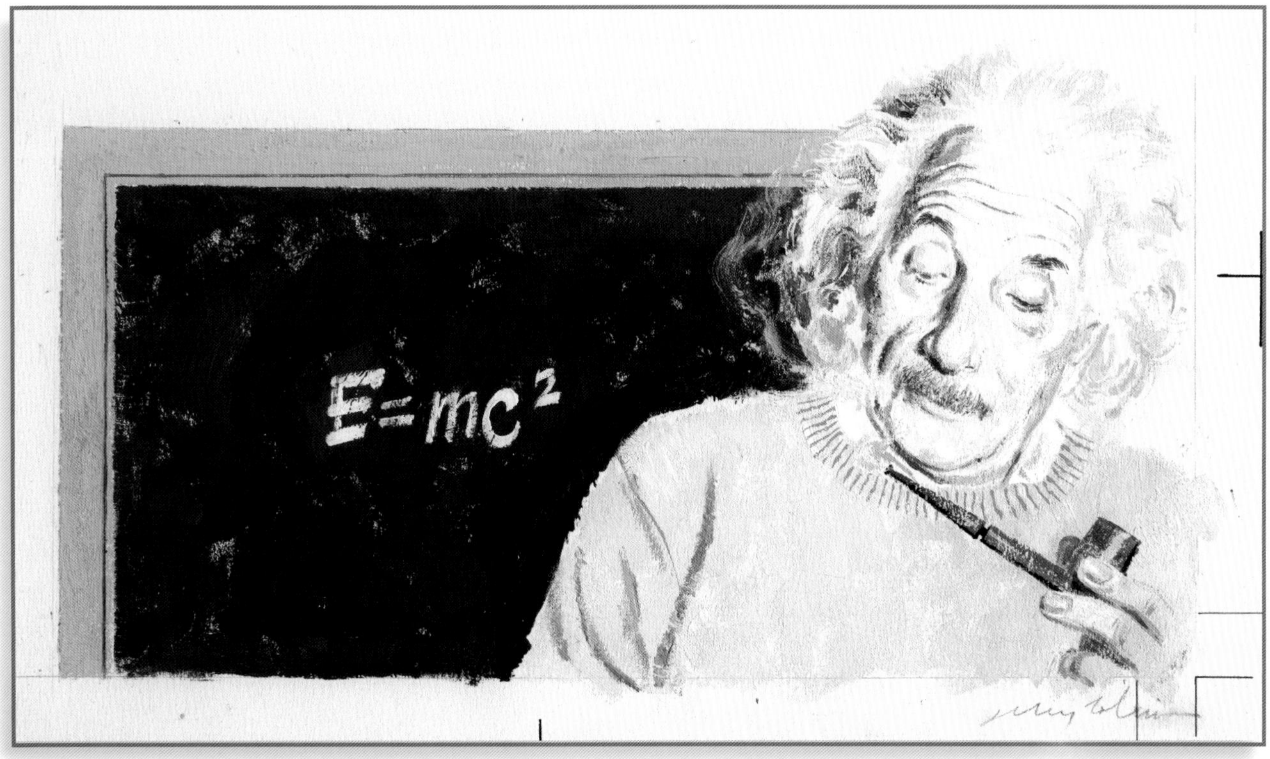
E=mc²

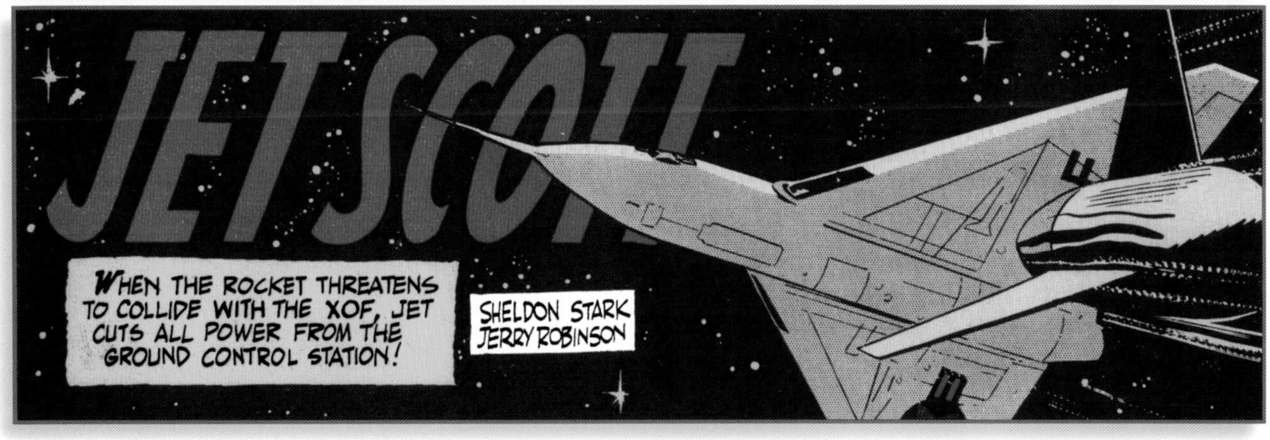
JET SCOTT
WHEN THE ROCKET THREATENS TO COLLIDE WITH THE XOF, JET CUTS ALL POWER FROM THE GROUND CONTROL STATION!
SHELDON STARK
JERRY ROBINSON

Top
ALBERT EINSTEIN
1959, illustration for *A Maxton Book About Atomic Energy*.

Bottom
JET SCOTT
June 1955, pencils, inks, and colors by Jerry Robinson.

ABOUT JERRY ROBINSON

Jerry Robinson (1922–2011) was an accomplished artist, writer, historian, and curator. He served as president and editorial director of CartoonArts International and Cartoonists & Writers Syndicate (CWS), affiliated with the New York Times Syndicate, which syndicate and exhibit the work of 350 leading cartoonists and graphic artists from fifty countries. He also negotiated the first regular use of foreign cartoons in the Russian, and Chinese-language presses.

In 1939, as a seventeen-year-old journalism student at Columbia University, Robinson began his cartooning career on the original Batman comic book, for which he created the Joker, comics' first supervillain. He named Batman's protégé, Robin, and designed his costume. He later served as a creative consultant to DC Comics.

Among Robinson's thirty published works is *The Comics: An Illustrated History of Comic Strip Art* (Putnam), which first appeared in 1974 and was acclaimed as the definitive study of the genre. In 2011, Dark Horse published a 400-page revised edition. His other books include the biography *Skippy and Percy Crosby* (Holt) and *The 1970s: Best Political Cartoons of the Decade* (McGraw-Hill). In 2010 appeared a two-volume set of his 1950s sci-fi strip *Jet Scott* (Dark Horse).

Robinson served as president of both the Association of American Editorial Cartoonists (AAEC) and the National Cartoonists Society (NCS), the only person so honored by his peers. He traveled to over forty countries on behalf of CWS, served on international art juries, and entertained US servicemen on several tours of Europe, North Africa, Japan, and Korea.

His award-winning features of social and political satire, *Still Life* and *Life with Robinson*, were internationally syndicated daily for thirty-two years. Robinson's drawings appeared regularly in the Broadway theater magazine *Playbill*. He was the co–art director of the hourlong animation *Stereotypes*, filmed at the Soyuzmult Studios in Moscow, and coauthor of the musical *Astra: A Comic Book Opera*, which made its debut in Washington, DC, in 2006. A graphic novel adaptation of *Astra* was published in Japan and the United States.

Robinson served as curator for numerous exhibitions in the US and abroad. They included the first show of American comic art at a major fine art gallery, the Graham Gallery in New York (1972). He served as special consultant for the largest exhibition of the cartoon, at the Kennedy Center in Washington, DC, and for a landmark show at the Whitney Museum in New York. Exhibitions he worked on abroad included some that were the first on American cartoon art in Tokyo, Warsaw, and Moscow, and others in China, Portugal, Slovenia, and the Ukraine. At the invitation of the United Nations, Robinson produced major exhibitions in Rio de Janeiro (Earth Summit, 1992), Vienna (World Conference on Human Rights, 1993, cosponsored by the Austrian government), Cairo (International Conference on Population and Development, 1994), and New York (Sketching Human Rights, 2007). In 2004 he produced the first in-depth exhibition of the genre, *Zap! Pow! Bam! The Superhero: The Golden Age of Comic Books, 1938–1950*, at the Breman Museum in Atlanta. In 2006, Robinson curated the exhibition *Superheroes: Good and Evil in American Comics* at the Jewish Museum in New York.

Robinson led creator-rights cases involving copyright, trademark, censorship, First Amendment, and human rights issues. These cases included representing Joe Shuster and Jerry Siegel, creators of Superman, in their struggle to obtain financial security and restore their creator credits; obtaining the release of jailed and tortured cartoonists in Uruguay and the Soviet Union; writing briefs on behalf of the AAEC and NCS (one related to trademark litigation brought against editorial cartoonists and another presented before a US Senate committee on postal laws); and serving on the joint arts committee that negotiated creator protection in the copyright renewal law.

For eighteen years Robinson was on the faculty of the School of Visual Arts (SVA), the New School, and Parsons School of Design, all in New York City. An exhibition of his color photography from seven countries was held at the SVA Galleries. In 2000 Scriptorium Films produced a ninety-minute television documentary on Robinson's career for Brazilian TV.

More information can be found in N. C. Christopher Couch's biography *Jerry Robinson: Ambassador of Comics* (Abrams, 2010).